I0795048

Waffen-SS Knights and Their Battles

Other Schiffer Books by the Author:

Waffen-SS Knights and their Battles: The Waffen-SS Knight's Cross Holders, Vols. 1-3

Other Schiffer Books on Related Subjects:

Images of the Waffen-SS: A Photo Chronicle of Germany's Elite Troops, 978-0-7643-0078-3

WAFFEN-SS KNIGHTS AND THEIR BATTLES

The Waffen-SS Knight's Cross Holders Volume 4: January–May 1944

Peter Mooney

Schiffer Publishing Ltd®

4880 Lower Valley Road • Atglen, PA 19310

Copyright © 2016 by Peter Mooney

Library of Congress Control Number: 2008928022

All rights reserved. No part of this work may be reproduced or used in any form or by any means—graphic, electronic, or mechanical, including photocopying or information storage and retrieval systems—without written permission from the publisher.

The scanning, uploading, and distribution of this book or any part thereof via the Internet or any other means without the permission of the publisher is illegal and punishable by law. Please purchase only authorized editions and do not participate in or encourage the electronic piracy of copyrighted materials.

"Schiffer," "Schiffer Publishing, Ltd.," and the pen and inkwell logo are registered trademarks of Schiffer Publishing, Ltd.

Type set in Trajan & Times New Roman
ISBN: 978-0-7643-5189-1

Printed in China

Published by Schiffer Publishing, Ltd.
4880 Lower Valley Road
Atglen, PA 19310
Phone: (610) 593-1777; Fax: (610) 593-2002
E-mail: Info@schifferbooks.com
Web: www.schifferbooks.com

For our complete selection of fine books on this and related subjects, please visit our website at www.schifferbooks.com. You may also write for a free catalog.

Schiffer Publishing's titles are available at special discounts for bulk purchases for sales promotions or premiums. Special editions, including personalized covers, corporate imprints, and excerpts, can be created in large quantities for special needs. For more information, contact the publisher.

We are always looking for people to write books on new and related subjects.
If you have an idea for a book, please contact us at proposals@schifferbooks.com.

CONTENTS

MAP LIST

FOREWORD

In memory of the former soldiers of the *Waffen-SS*, who were confronted with a war they did not want and where they were not guilty.

Often they were in hopeless battles. Many of them have fallen. They have all more than done their duty for the Fatherland.

In appreciation for Mr. Peter Mooney's book *Waffen-SS Knights and Their Battles*, written for all people in the whole world.

Karl-Heinz Euling

A signed image of Karl-Heinz Euling taken in a formal setting to show his Knight's Cross. *Herr* Euling unfortunately died on April 14, 2014.

INTRODUCTION

Welcome to the fourth volume of this ongoing project; one that details the chronological bestowal of all Knight's Cross related awards to the soldiers of the *Waffen-SS* during WWII.

The first three volumes covered up to the end of 1943, and detailed 178 separate Knight's Cross related awards (Knight's Cross, Oakleaves, and Swords). This new volume will continue coverage from the start of January until the end of May 1944. This period greatly increased enemy pressure on these soldiers and was one where multiple attempts were made to annihilate large groups in pocket battles. The enemy initiative was on the increase (on various fronts), and the ability of the *Waffen-SS* to seize it back was fast becoming a distant possibility. Survival became the key focus and all efforts were on escaping the enemy trap, or moving forces to rescue soldiers from those traps. There was still another year of the conflict to run, but even at this stage the enemy seemed unstoppable, and that was before the western enemies made their significant game play!

This volume will detail a further fifty-six Knight's Cross related awards and was compiled with the help of some of the soldiers detailed in these pages, including Heinrich Springer, Johannes Goehler, Hans Siegel, Otto Kumm, Albert Frey, Remy Schrijnen, Ernst Barkmann, Karl-Heinz Boska, Karl Brommann, Karl Nicolussi-Leck, Paul Egger, Friederich Blond, Eberhard Heder, Karl-Heinz Euling, Siegfried Brosow, Heinrich Sonne, Harald Nugiseiks, Rudolf von Ribbentrop, Walter Girg, Karl-Heinz Lichte, Alois Schnaubelt, Heinz Jurgens, Oskar Schafer, Josef Rolleke, and Kurt Sametreiter. Unfortunately, since starting this project the majority of these men have died. I am indebted to all of them, alive or dead, and count myself lucky to have met each of them or had correspondence with them. Each contact has provided a greater level of understanding of the conflict and their part in it.

In addition, the following *Waffen-SS* soldiers who served alongside the holders of the Knight's Cross also helped with this compilation: Erwin Bartmann, Robert Soulat, Jan Munk, Werner Volkner, Max Schmidt, Hans Maguscher, Adolf Schaafs, Helmut Hinze, Sepp Bischoff, Paul Rosch, Gerhard Dilling, and Manfred Thorn.

The photographs in this volume have come from a variety of sources, including the Knight's Cross holders and the *kameraden* who served alongside them. Some of these are listed above, but equally, some of them have been handed to me at reunions by kameraden who did not provide their names; a few of these photographs were even posted to me by a kameraden who did not provide any contact details at all! One of the key sources is my own collection, obtained mostly from the veterans themselves. Since writing the last volume, this has been bulked out by my acquisition of the extensive and impressive collection formerly held by my long-time friend, Justin Horgan. Justin is a fellow enthusiast of the history of the *Waffen-SS* and introduced me to my first *Waffen-SS* Knight's Cross holder; we have enjoyed many trips together to these men's houses when they were living. I have made every effort to obtain original photographic sources for this work.

Further help has come from Hazel (and Manfred) Thorn, who made direct contact with Karl-Heinz Euling, which in turn led to me meeting him face to face. I have had contact with Herr Euling over the preceding years, but this has always been in writing. Their assistance has led to Karl-Heinz Euling agreeing to write the foreword to this fourth volume. Karl-Heinz Euling unfortunately died on April 14, 2014, and did not get to see this completed volume; it was an honor to have had his support for this concept while he was alive.

Also my son Karl, who has taken my sketches and turned them into the maps contained within these pages, providing visual understanding of actions and how they relate to one another; his patience is appreciated.

A special mention must go to John P. Moore, who gave his permission to use information contained within his *Führerliste Der Waffen-SS, Parts 1-4*. This excellent publication contains information on around 26,000 *Waffen-SS* officers and the personnel files of the Knight's Cross (and other high award) holders of the *Waffen-SS*. Without his permission this project would not exist. I will take this opportunity to thank Mr. Moore and would advise anyone to invest in his publication, as it provides a superb insight into the lives of the men who served in and shaped the reputation of the *Waffen-SS*. I will also thank Mark Yerger, who has provided research assistance at different stages of this volume. It is assistance like this that takes projects from ideas to reality, which is what you now hold in your hands.

I will finish this introduction by giving special mention to the most important people of all: my son Karl, daughter Alanna, and my wife, Sandra. They provide continued and unyielding support to my hobby. They have joined me on some of my trips to the homes of the *Waffen-SS* Knight's Cross holders and have remained patient and understanding as I have slaved over notes for hours after coming home from long days at work, thereby leaving little opportunity to spend quality time with them. In addition, my daughter Alanna's keen eye for the written word lends itself very well to the proofreading of each volume's manuscript. She has done a superb job since the start of this project, allowing me to go back and correct various typos and grammatical errors amassed when I am in "writing mode." I am grateful to her for the time she devotes to this essential aspect of this book. This work is dedicated to my children and my wife, without whose support the project would not have been completed.

The work on this project began over fifteen years ago. The intervening years have seen the completion of my first book, *Dietrich's Warriors*, and the first three volumes of this project. The work on this overall project continued throughout these fifteen years and I am pleased to see the end result. I hope you, the reader, will find this book interesting, informative, and a worthy continuation of what you read in the first three volumes. I will end by thanking you for your continued interest.

Peter Mooney
Folkestone, Kent

CHAPTER ONE

SS UNITS RETREAT FROM THE "RUSSIAN FRONT" - JANUARY 1944

In the preceding three volumes we have detailed just over four years of front-line combat for the soldiers of the *Waffen-SS* (plus their prewar activities) that took them from Poland to France, southwards to the Balkans, then eastwards into the depths of the Soviet Union. The gates of Moscow, the outskirts of Leningrad, and deep into the Caucausus—almost to the Iranian border—were the farthest advances during those heady days of victory and conquest. The year 1943 saw a series of seesaw actions, mostly in the east, with titanic battles around Kharkov, Kursk, and just west of there, plus the Italians changing sides. The situation at the end of that year was of a defensive posture, as the Soviets made significant gains in the south, re-gaining the initiative they held in the wake of Stalingrad at the start of 1943.

The mainly defensive posture continued in 1944, and January to May would pretty much preclude any offensive plans the Germans may have had in mind; there were instances of having to move formations around the front line or adding more in while having to react to more and more major offensives launched by the Soviets—an enemy appearing to be gaining strength and abilities, despite the losses they had suffered since 1941. The opening of 1944 would also see the first occurrence of German troops forced out of sections of the Soviet Union, a trend that would increase as 1944 unfolded. The days of offense and victory were a distant memory and the focus moved more and more to defense or simple survival.

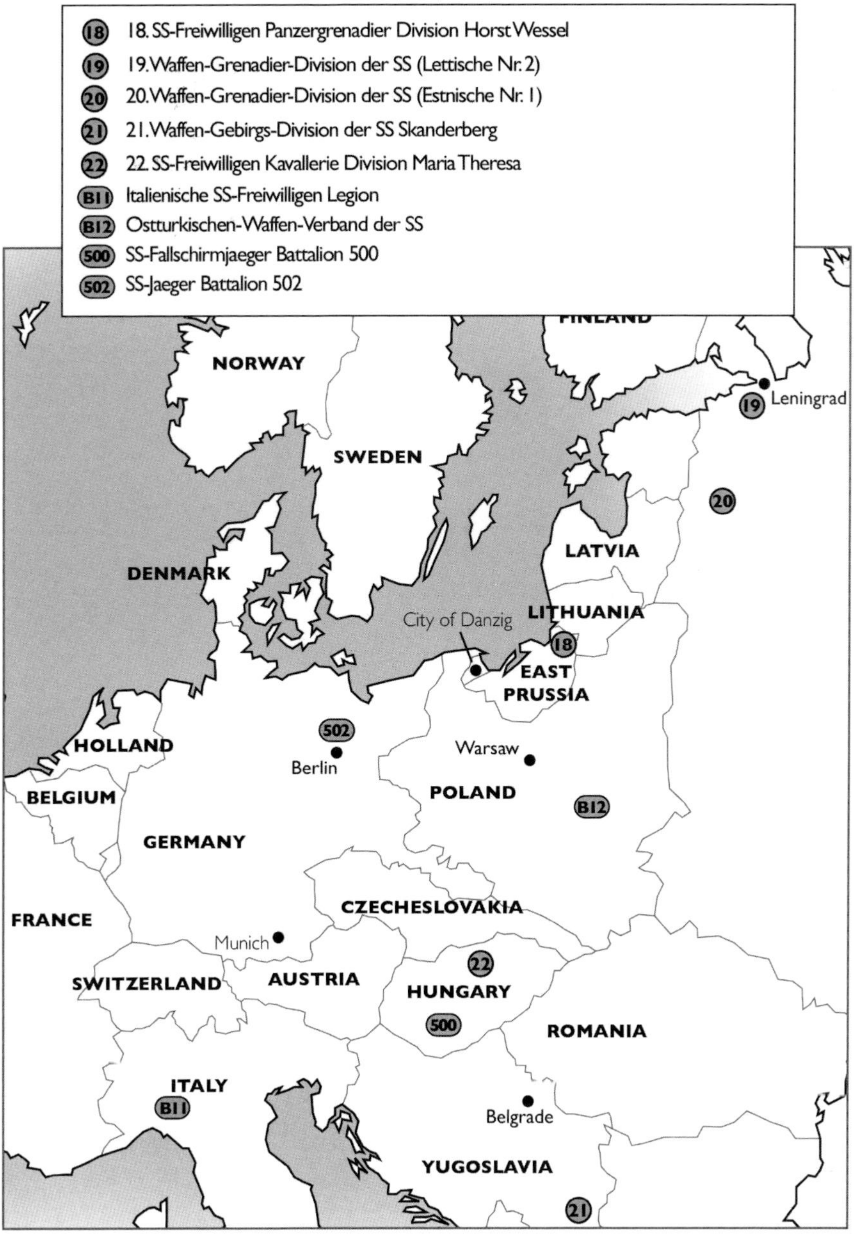

Map 1 – Places of Origin: January to May 1944

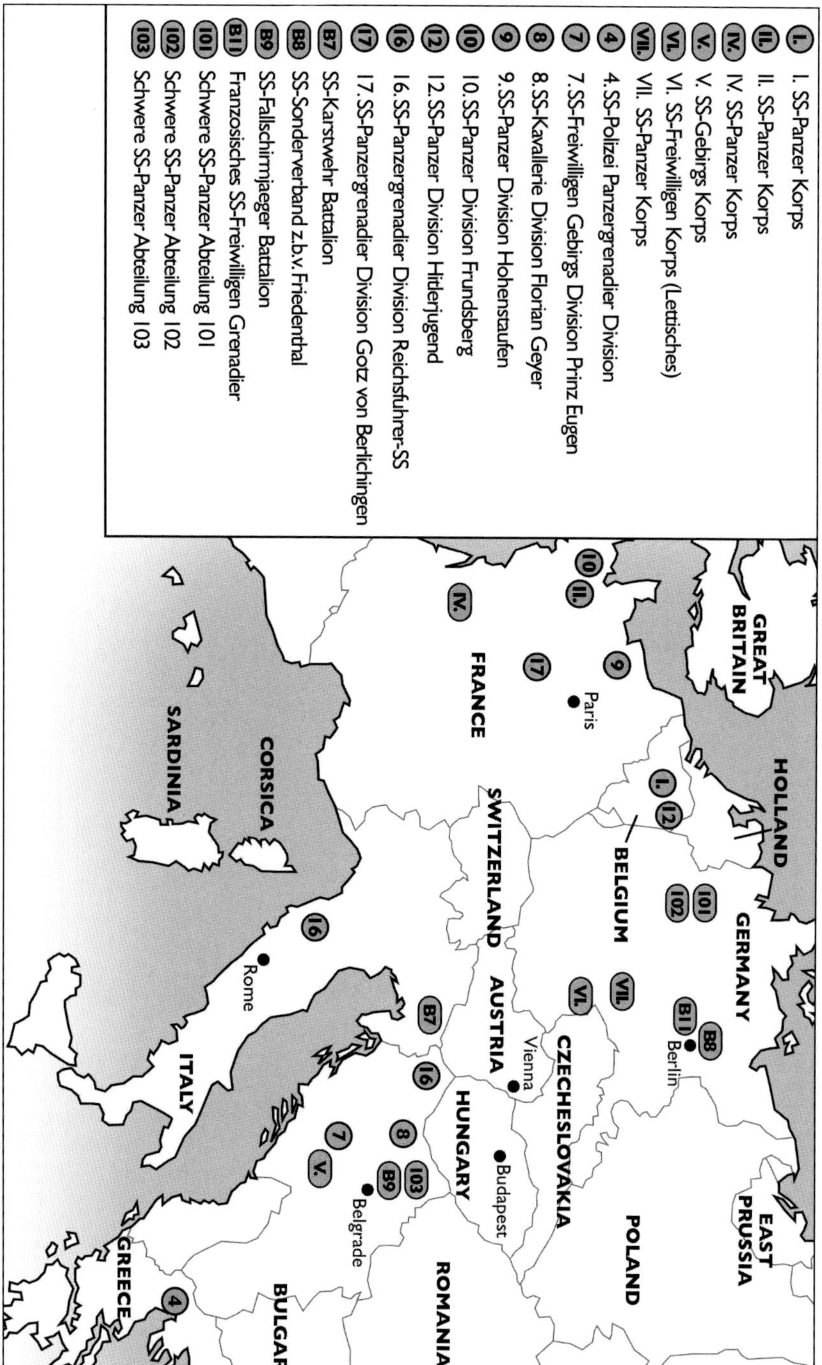

Map 2a – *Waffen-SS* Locations (west), start of January 1944

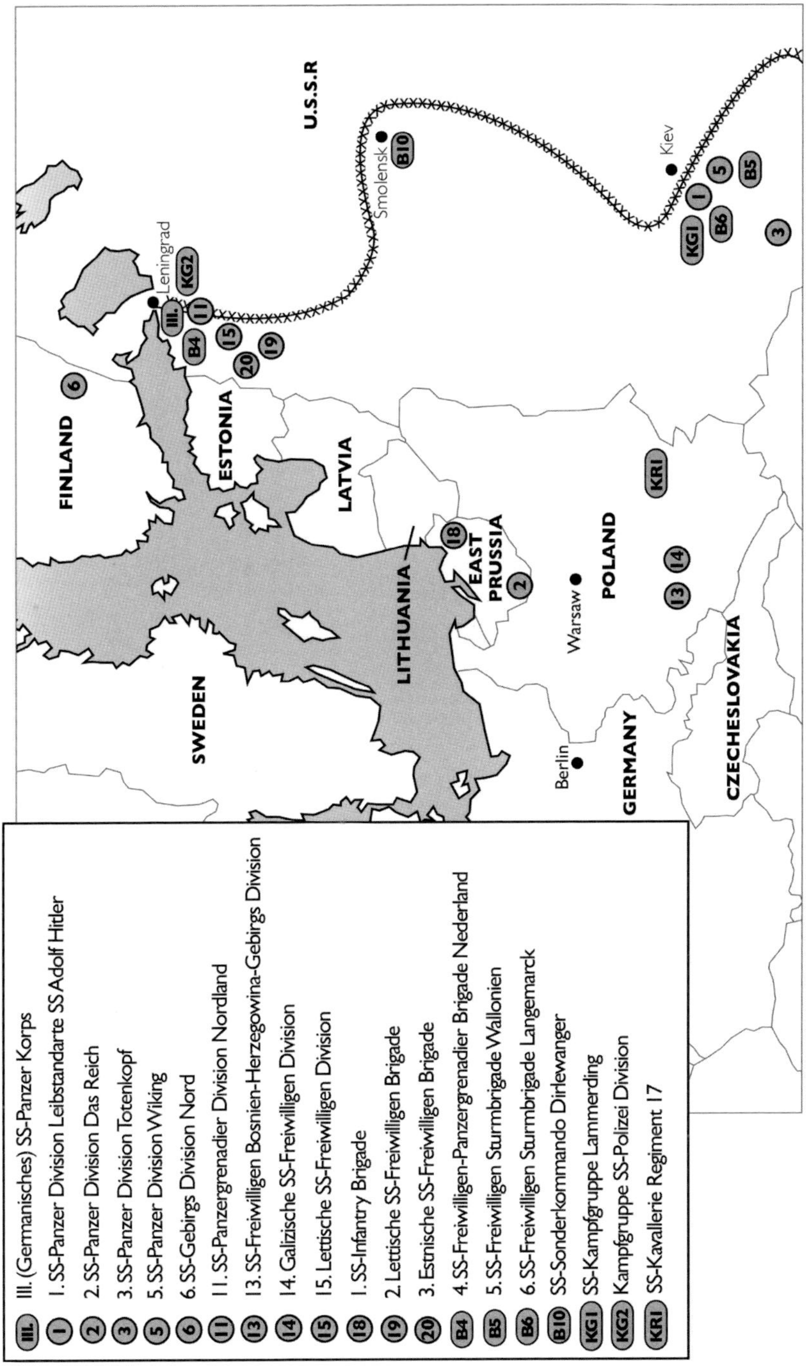

Map 2b – *Waffen-SS* Locations (east), start of January 1944

The start of the Narwa battles—the pocket fighting at Tscherkassy, Kovel, and Kamenets-Podolsky—would all unfold during the time covered by this volume. Those battles would test elements of the *Waffen-SS* almost to their breaking point. They would also provide ample chance to further demonstrate their bravery in battle, and many of them would be recognized accordingly. There would be fifty-six additional awards approved, so let's take a look at why, and what these *Waffen-SS* soldiers had to face in this increasingly difficult and costly conflict.

At the start of 1944, there were forty-one *Waffen-SS* formations (locations in brackets):

Korps:

I. SS-Panzer Korps (Belgium)
II. SS-Panzer Korps (France)
III. (Germanisches) SS-Panzer Korps (Leningrad area, Northern Russia)
IV. SS-Panzer Korps (France)
V. SS-Gebirgs Korps (Yugoslavia)
VI. SS-Freiwilligen Korps (Lettisches) (Germany)
VII. SS-Panzer Korps (Germany)

Divisions:

1. SS-Panzer Division Leibstandarte SS Adolf Hitler (Berditschew / Shitomir, Russia)
2. SS-Panzer Division Das Reich (East Prussia)
3. SS-Panzer Division Totenkopf (Kriwoj Rog, southern Russia)
4. SS-Polizei-Panzergrenadier Division (Greece / Yugoslavia)
5. SS-Panzer Division Wiking (Kanew, southern Russia)
6. SS-Gebirgs Division Nord (Finland)
7. SS-Freiwilligen-Gebirgs Division Prinz Eugen (Yugoslavia)
8. SS-Kavallerie Division Florian Geyer (Yugoslavia)
9. SS-Panzer Division Hohenstaufen (France)
10. SS-Panzer Division Frundsberg (France)
11. SS-Panzergrenadier Division Nordland (Leningrad area, northern Russia)
12. SS-Panzer Division Hitlerjugend (Belgium)
13. SS-Freiwilligen Bosnien-Herzegowina-Gebirgs-Division (Kroatien) (Silesia, Poland)
14. Galizische SS-Freiwilligen Division (Heidelager camp, Poland)
15. Lettische SS-Freiwilligen Division (Novo Sokolniki, northern Russia)
16. SS-Panzergrenadier Division Reichsführer-SS (Laibach, Slovenia, and Livorno, Italy)
17. SS-Panzergrenadier Division Gotz von Berlichingen (France)

Brigades:

1. SS-Infantry Brigade (mot.) (Konigsberg, East Prussia)
2. Lettische SS-Freiwilligen Brigade (Spasskaja Polist, northern Russia)
3. Estnische SS-Freiwilligen Brigade (Idritsa, northern Russia)
4. SS-Freiwilligen-Panzergrenadier Brigade Nederland (Leningrad area, Russia)
5. SS-Freiwilligen Sturmbrigade Wallonien (Irdynn Marsh area, southern Russia)
6. SS-Freiwilligen Sturmbrigade Langemarck (Tschudinow / Shitomir, Russia)

Regiments and Battalions:

SS-Karstwehr Battalion (Isonzo Valley, Italy)
SS-Sonderverband z.b.v. Friedenthal (Berlin, Germany)
SS-Fallschirmjaeger Battalion (Yugoslavia)
SS-Sonderkommando Dirlewanger (Minsk sector, central Russia)
Franzosisches SS-Freiwilligen Grenadier Regiment (Berlin, Germany)
Schwere SS-Panzer Abteilung 101 (Sennelager, Germany)
Schwere SS-Panzer Abteilung 102 (Augustdorf, Germany)
Schwere SS-Panzer Abteilung 103 (Yugoslavia)
SS-Kampfgruppe Lammerding (Uljanowka, Shitomir, southern Russia)
Kampfgruppe SS-Polizei Division (Leningrad area, northern Russia)
SS-Kavallerie Regiment 17 (detached from the 8. SS-Division) (Kovel sector, Russia)

By the end of May 1944, the following nine units would also form part of the *Waffen-SS*' order of battle, although five of them replaced existing units:
18. SS-Freiwilligen Panzergrenadier Division Horst Wessel (replaced the *1. SS-Inf. Brig.)*
19. Waffen-Grenadier-Division der SS (Lettische Nr. 2) (replaced the *2. Lettisches Brig.)*
20. Waffen-Grenadier-Division der SS (Estnische Nr. 1) (replaced the *3. Estnische Brig.)*
21. Waffen-Gebirgs-Division der SS Skanderberg (Albanische Nr. 1)
22. SS-Freiwilligen Kavallerie Division Maria Theresa (incorporated *SS-Kav. Reg. 17)*
Italienische SS-Freiwilligen Legion
Ostturkischen-Waffen-Verband der SS

SS-Jaeger Battalion 502 (replaced the SS-Sonderverband z.b.v. Friedenthal)
SS-Fallschirmjaeger Battalion 500 (replaced the *SS-Fallschirmjaeger Battalion*)

This took the *Waffen-SS*' total formations to forty-four by the end of May 1944. Now let us detail what took place for the soldiers of these *Waffen-SS* formations between the start of January and end of May 1944.

Volume 3 ended with the coverage of a soldier from the *1. SS-Infantry Brigade (mot.)* and the first award for 1944 went to a soldier from the same unit; we will start with him before continuing with the other SS units away from the front line in January 1944, then leading on to those units in action or near the front line.

1. SS-Infantry Brigade (mot.) / 18. SS-Panzergrenadier Division Horst Wessel

You may recall from the end of volume 3 that the *1. SS-Infantry Brigade (mot.)* were sent to East Prussia, near Konigsberg, for rest and reformation. On January 25, 1944, orders were issued to form a new SS Division numbered "18." By the end of that month, it would be officially named the *18. SS-Panzergrenadier Division Horst Wessel*. The *1. SS-Infantry Brigade (mot.)* were to be used as the foundation for this new division and ceased to exist. The recent Knight's Cross awardees would bring their experience to this new division. As these men were enjoying their well-earned rest in East Prussia, the news came through that *SS-Standartenführer* August-Wilhelm Trabandt was to be awarded the Knight's Cross on January 6, making Trabandt the first such award for the men of the *Waffen-SS* in 1944. He was named commander of this new SS division.

I. SS-Panzer Korps

This formation remained in the Belgian area for the majority of the opening months of 1944, moving to France in May and retaining control of the *12. SS-Panzer Division*. They did not engage in any combat so we will return to them in volume 5.

Schwere SS-Panzer Abteilung 101

This heavy tank unit was initially in Sennelager as 1944 began, but by the middle of January they had moved to Mons, in Belgium. It was there they received new tanks and focused on training their men.

12. SS-Panzer Division Hitlerjugend

At the end of the previous volume this division was in the midst of formation and training in Belgium. They were coping with the severe weapons and equipment shortages prevalent at that time for German armed forces. One significant occurrence for the HJ soldiers took place during January 1944, as the Panzer regiment moved to the Hasselt area, close to where the rest of the division was. They conducted an exercise observed by Heinz Guderian and Sepp Dietrich; the result of the exercise was the delivery of more tanks was approved, including Panther tanks. Further exercises by the infantry were also conducted during the month.

II. SS-Panzer Korps

This formation had been in France since the last few weeks of 1943. It assumed overall command and control for the *9.* and *10. SS-Panzer Divisions*, and as such the continued coverage of those two units will incorporate the coverage of this *korps.*

9. SS-Panzer Division Hohenstaufen

Continuing with their training in the Amiens area, they received more and more supplies of equipment in the first few months of 1944.

10. SS-Panzer Division Frundsberg

Just as with *Hohenstaufen, Frundsberg* continued with their training, but in the Normandy area until late March, when things changed dramatically for them. With that in mind, we will return to them in later chapters of this volume.

IV. SS-Panzer Korps

They remained in France, with no significant changes between January and the end of May 1944.

VI. SS-Freiwilligen Korps (Lettisches)

Located in Grafenwohr training camp, Germany, they continued with the final stages of their formation and battle readiness during January 1944.

VII. SS-Panzer Korps

This formation remained in Germany during the opening phase of 1944, with no significant changes during that time.

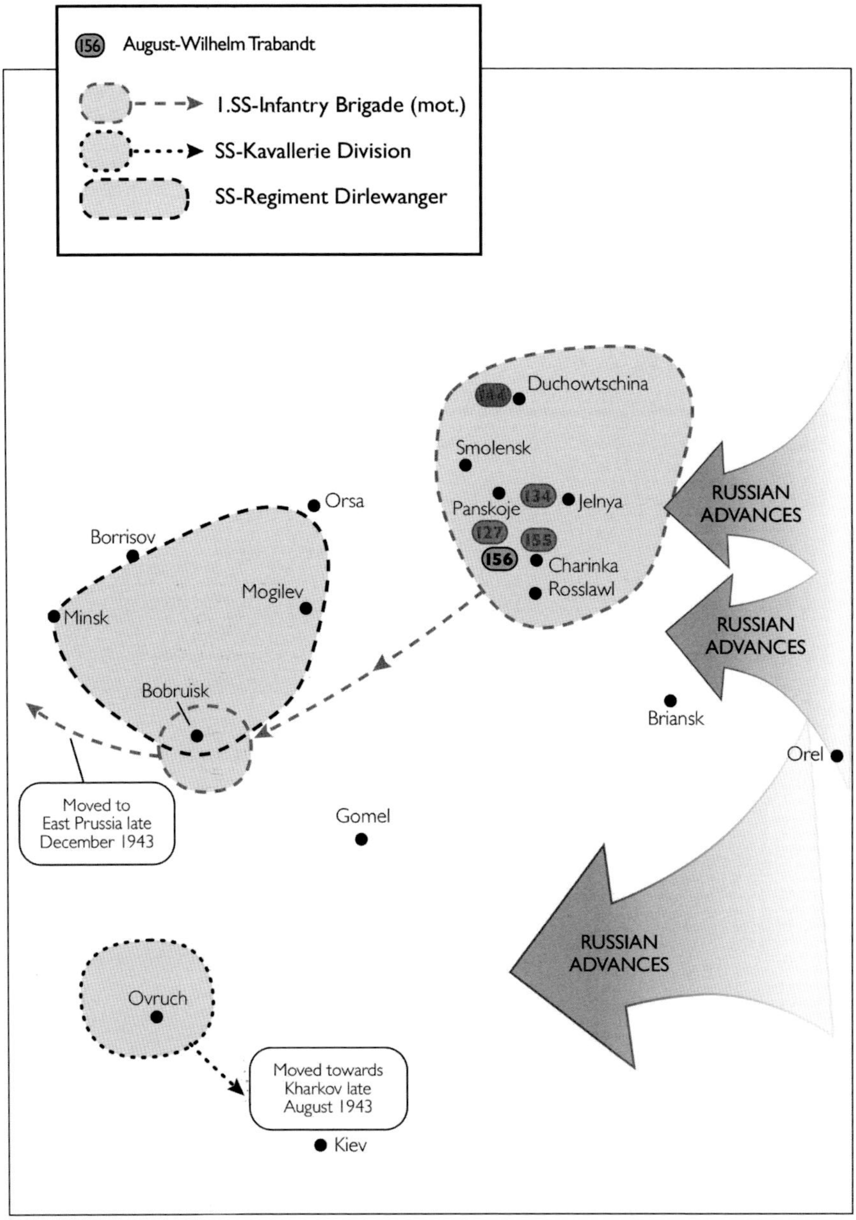

Map 3 – Central Russia: August – December 1943

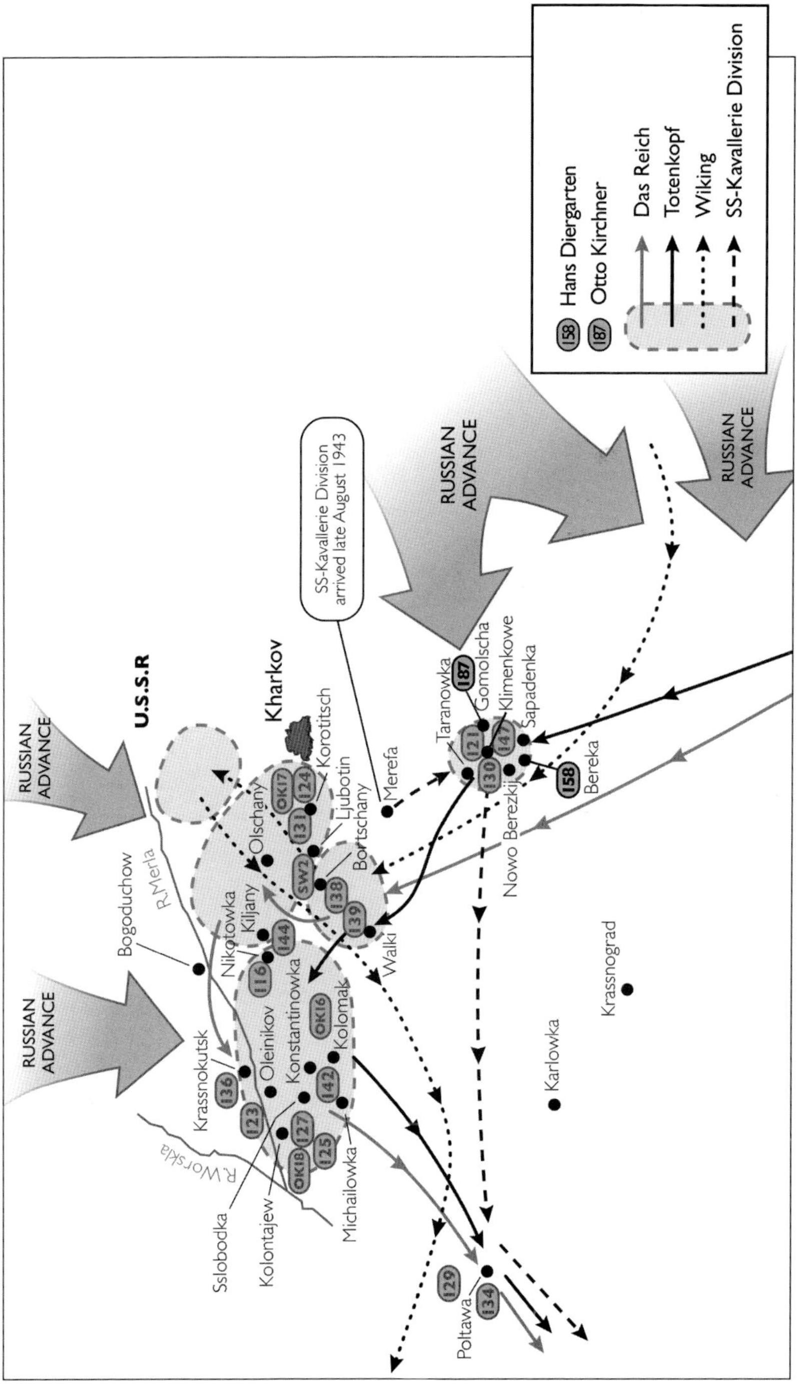

Map 4 – Kharkov Phase II: August – Early September 1943

Coverage of the *IV.* and *VII. SS-Korps* will continue in volume 5.

Schwere SS-Panzer Abteilung 102

They continued with their formation at Augustdorf and received additional men.

Schwere SS-Panzer Abteilung 103

After being in Croatia they were then moved to Zwolle, in Holland, during January 1944. Under the leadership of *SS-Obersturmbannführer* Otto Paetsch, they continued to train under the most difficult circumstances.

2. SS-Panzer Division Das Reich

You may recall the bulk of the *Das Reich Division* was in Stablak, East Prussia, where they were engaged in a large re-fit, while some of their kameraden remained behind in Russia. Their focus on rebuilding would not change their overall situation for the time being, so we will return to them in later chapters.

8. SS-Kavallerie Division Florian Geyer (minus *SS-Regiment 17*)

We left this unit at the end of 1943, as they had relocated to Croatia (*SS-Kavallerie Regiment 17* was in the east). They remained there during January 1944 and were sent new recruits and fresh equipment. On the sixteenth, two soldiers from this division were approved for the Knight's Cross: *SS-Sturmbannführer* Hans Diergarten and *SS-Obersturmbannführer* Joachim Rumohr, who were recognized for various actions from December 1942 through December 1943; both of these men will be detailed in this volume.

SS-Regiment 17 will be covered in the front-line actions detailed below.

13. SS-Freiwilligen Bosnien-Herzegowina-Gebirgs-Division (Kroatien)

We last covered this formation at the end of volume 3, when they were engaged in training and formation in Poland. Heinrich Himmler visited them in November, but he returned in mid-January 1944 for a final time before the division completed its training.

14. Galizische SS-Freiwilligen Division

This division continued gathering strength and improving its training during the opening months of 1944 at the Heidelager camp in Poland, but a large contingent would move to the front line in February; this is detailed in the next chapter.

17. SS-Panzergrenadier Division "Gotz von Berlichingen"

This division's activities between January and the end of May 1944 remained chiefly training and incorporating new men in their Saumur locations. A lack of equipment and vehicles did slow things down, but the soldiers did what they could with what they had.

SS-Sonderverband z.b.v. Friedenthal / SS-Jaeger Battalion 502

In their barracks near Berlin as 1944 opened, they had a pretty uneventful period between January and the end of May, focusing on further training and involvement in small experiments with new weapons being worked on at that time. The only major change came in April 1944, when they were redesignated *SS-Jaeger Battalion 502*. We will continue their coverage in the next volume.

SS-Fallschirmjaeger Battalion

In Maturuschka-Banja, Serbia, at the end of 1943, the emphasis of their training was on successful parachute jumping techniques, which did not change until March; we will return to them later in this book.

Franzosisches SS-Freiwilligen Grenadier Regiment

We briefly touched on this formation in chapter 3 of volume 3 of this project, when they were engaged in training and formation in Sennheim, Alsace; this is how 1944 opened for them, but with some notable changes. Some of these Frenchmen were earmarked for NCO and officer training. The 100 NCO candidates were sent to the SS NCO school in Posen-Treskau, Poland, while the twenty-four officer candidates were sent to Bad Tolz; one of them is very relevant to this project and we will return to him in the final volume. Both of these courses ended in early March 1944.

The first of the new SS formations formed in the period this volume covers:

Ostturkischen-Waffen-Verband der SS

This was one of the new additions added to the order of battle of the *Waffen-SS* during the first stage of 1944. For this unit, their life began on January 4. Its nucleus came from existing Turkestan soldiers fighting within the ranks of the *Heer*. The person Himmler selected to lead this formation was

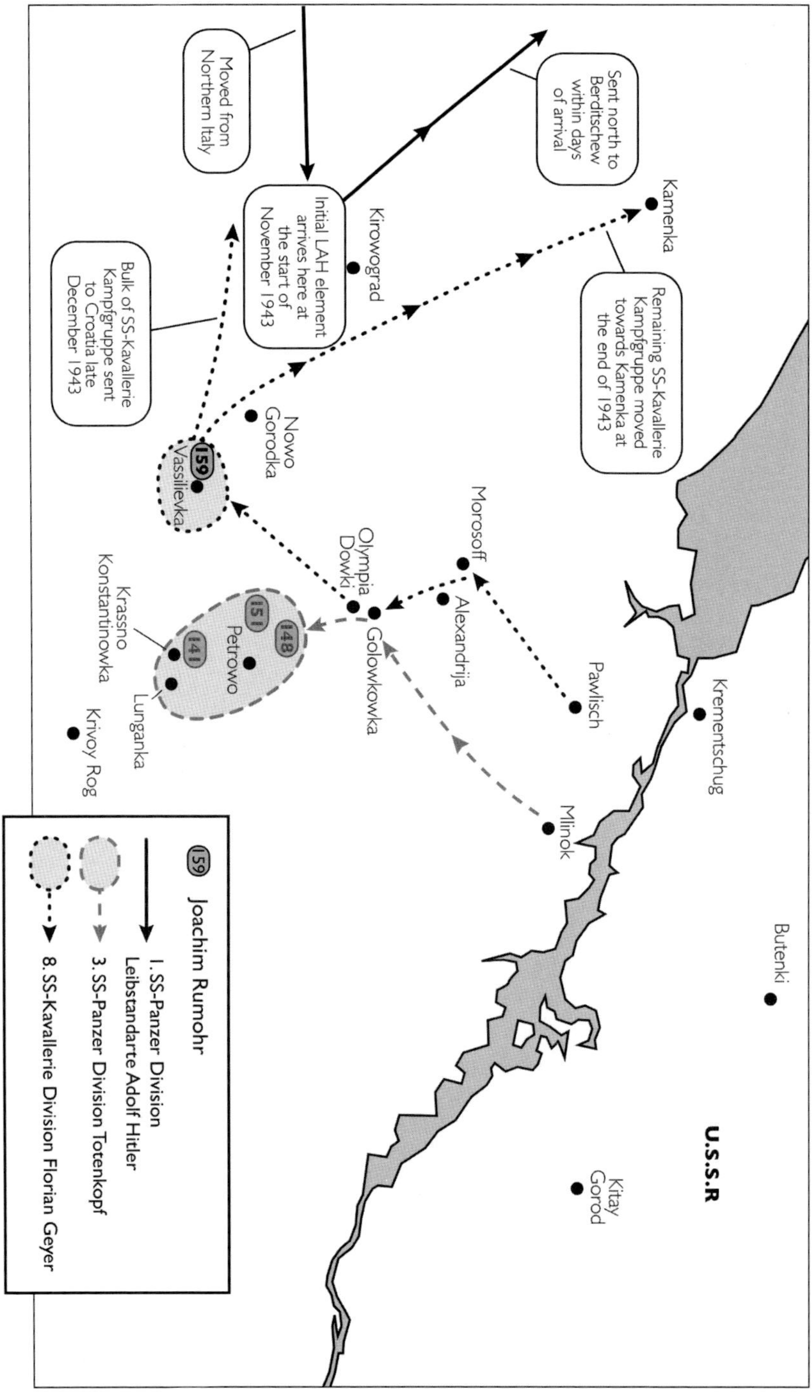

Map 5 – Dnjepr River South: November – December 1943

an existing *Heer* officer named Andreas Meyer-Mader. He was moved to the ranks of the *Waffen-SS* at the start of January 1944 and given the rank *SS-Obersturmbannführer*. Three existing Turkestani battalions were moved en masse to the ranks of the *Waffen-SS* beginning in late December 1943. Their formation location was chosen to be the SS training grounds at Trawniki, slightly south of Lublin, in Poland.

The move of these existing Turkestani *Heer* battalions and the addition of Turkestani men who had been working as POWs in German-controlled areas helped bring their numbers up to 3,000 men by the end of their first month of existence. They werc banded together in the *1st Ostmuselmanische SS-Regiment*. Like the recently created SS divisions formed during 1943, this new unit struggled to find the required equipment level essential for their effectiveness, which overall slowed their formation.

Now to the front line...

Army Group South

That covers all of the *Waffen-SS* units that existed in January 1944 that were not actively engaged against the enemy at that time, totaling twenty-one of the forty-one existing formations. The remaining twenty formations were positioned on the front line and some of them had been continuously engaged against the enemy as 1943 closed and 1944 opened. One of those was the *1. SS-Panzer Division Leibstandarte SS Adolf Hitler*, fighting west of Kiev in Army Group South. The next Knight's Cross approval for 1944 was for a soldier from that formation, so it is a logical place to begin the coverage of the front-line *Waffen-SS* soldiers as January 1944 began.

1. SS-Panzer Division Leibstandarte SS Adolf Hitler

At the end of volume 3, the *LSSAH* was engaged in a difficult struggle with the Soviets to the south of Shitomir. The enemy was exerting pressure all around this area as they focused on removing Germans from the area to the west of the Dnjepr River. As January 1944 began, the men of the *Leibstandarte* were positioned between Berditschew and Shitomir, aiming to retain control of the main road between the two.

The weight of enemy pressure forced the *LSSAH* to move slightly westwards the second day of the month; the Gnilopjat River was the objective. The enemy were already active there and there was no rest for these men. They continued in a southwesterly direction at the end of week one in January. The remaining battle group from the 2. *SS-Panzer Division Das Reich* was fighting in close proximity to the *LSSAH* during these days. Week two bore witness to tank battles with the enemy around Sherebki and Stepok, and at the end of the second week, the first of a series of Knight's Cross awards was approved for soldiers of the *Leibstandarte*. The first award was one of the most famous and frequently detailed Knight's Cross awards of the entire conflict, given to *SS-Untersturmführer* Michael Wittmann on January 14. His actions stretched back to Kursk, but it was the recent heavy fighting in the opening days of 1944 that made up the final part of his recommendation. Two days later, his own gunner, *SS-Rottenführer* Balthasar Woll, was also approved for the same award; these awards will be detailed in this volume.

Joachim Peiper managed a localized offensive push to the north around Krassnopol; the fighting there went on for a few days. The actions came to a halt when the *LSSAH* were ordered to a new location. Their hand-over to the relief units took place between January 19 and 21. They then began their move around seventy-five miles to the southeast, northeast of Winniza. The move took around three days before they were ready to help engage the large enemy forces there in an attempt to blunt their offensive power before the enemy launched their own attack farther westward. It was also on the twenty-fourth that approvals were given for further *Leibstandarte* soldiers to be recognized at the highest levels: the first was *SS-Hauptscharführer* Gerhard Grebarsche, who received the Knight's Cross for his actions around Shitomir in the closing days of December 1943. The second approval that day was for the Oakleaves to Hugo Kraas, recognizing his successful actions stretching all the way back to the opening of the Kursk fighting and right up to December 29, 1943, in the Guiva sector; these awards would soon be joined by others.

Fighting in the new sector began on the twenty-fifth; the first attacks came from partisans. The emphasis was on taking the high ground points in this area while moving farther to the southeast. Over the next few days they pushed on to Lipowez, around twenty miles southeast. They fought the whole way and had to contend with poor road conditions. By the last day of January 1944, they had extended their line a further fifteen miles southeast to Oratoff, then moving to a defensive posture. Back on the twenty-seventh, Panzer Regiment Commander Joachim Peiper was approved for the Oakleaves to his existing Knight's Cross for actions during December 1943 with his newly acquired Panzer regiment. On January 30, a further set of Oakleaves was approved for fellow *LSSAH* soldier Michael Wittmann, who had only been given his Knight's Cross a little over two weeks earlier. In a short time he had taken his credited total of destroyed enemy tanks to 117; not only a testament to his abilities, but also an indication of the size of the enemy forces that engaged the *Leibstandarte* in January 1944. These four awards will be covered in this volume.

SS-Kampfgruppe Lammerding

This battle group, under the command of *SS-Oberführer* Heinz Lammerding, remained behind on the eastern front as their parent division moved to East Prussia to start a rebuilding phase. On January 1, 1944, they were around fifteen miles west of Shitomir, in a small village called Uljanowka.

The arrival of the new year did not blunt the enemy's determination to advance and remove all Germans in their path; *SS-Kampfgruppe Lammerding* was one such unit that received a heavy attack and had to retreat southwest. Another SS unit that was close to the *Das Reich* men was the *6. SS-Freiwilligen Sturmbrigade Langemarck*, which had arrived in this area at the start of 1944. The enemy advanced rapidly and they outflanked the battle group, resulting in retreat to avoid destruction. They moved to the southwest and by January 10, they were around fifty miles south at Nossiwiki, where they had a few days of relative respite before having to engage with the enemy once again.

Fighting resumed on the fourteenth, and Joachim Peiper was attached to the battle group; they pushed eastwards against the Soviets but only managed limited success. Attempts in that direction were halted and emphasis moved to defense for almost a month.

6. SS-Freiwilligen Sturmbrigade Langemarck

At the end of volume 3 this unit had just completed its combat readiness training and was sent east in the closing days of the year. They were placed in the vicinity of the *SS-Kampfgruppe Lammerding* and ordered to support them. Their arrival at the front would place them in the direct path of the advancing Russians.

Towards the end of week one they were in Tschudinov and helped to knock out some enemy tanks. By January 10, 1944, they were in Burkovzy, but had to move back to Sseverinovka over the next two days due to enemy advances. Like *Battle Group Lammerding*, they had a period of relative respite for a few weeks.

Farther to the southeast...

5. SS-Panzer Division Wiking

This division witnessed a relative lull as 1943 came to a close; they retained their positions at Kanew and south of there. Due to enemy advances to the

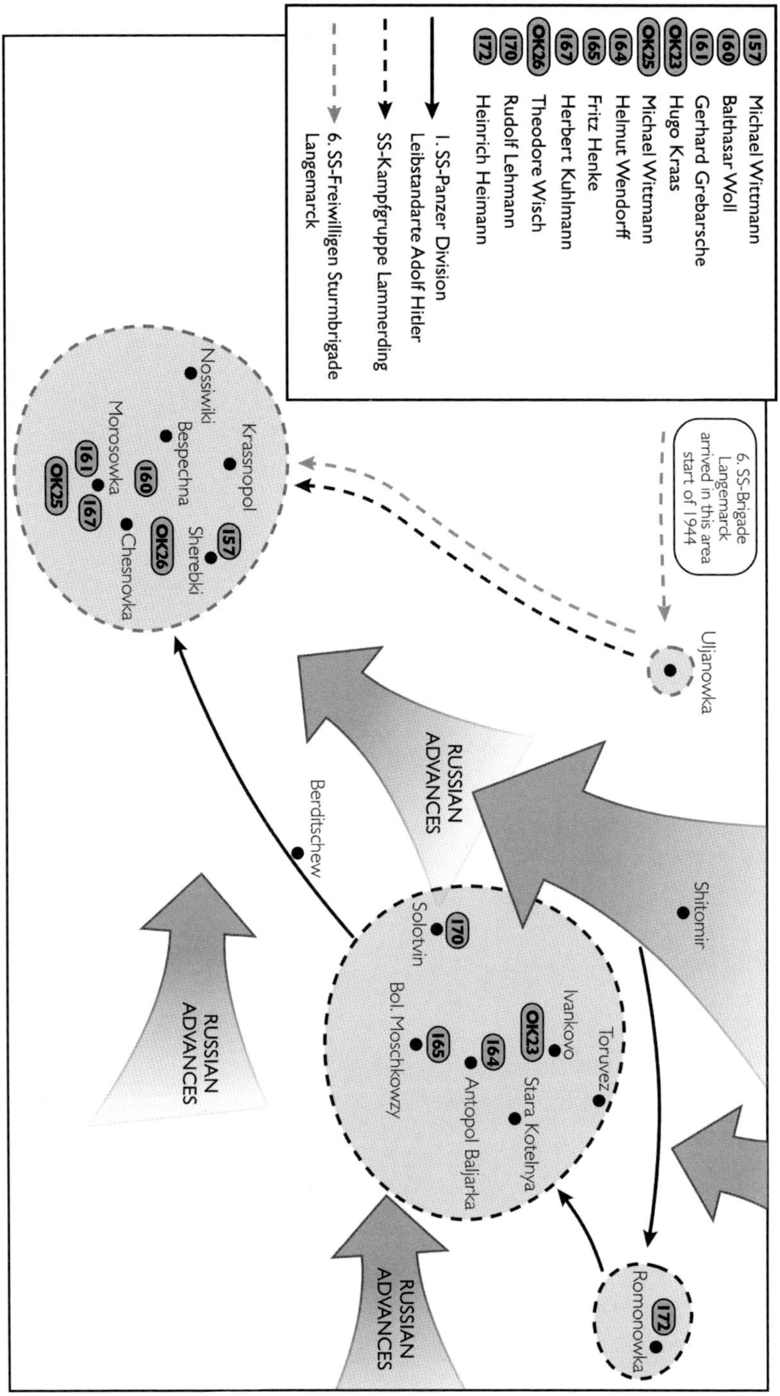

Map 6 – Shitomir - Berditschew: January 1944

north and farther to the south the positions at Kanew represented the only hold the Germans retained on the Dnjepr River, something Hitler was loathe to give up. The decision whether to retain those positions was about to be made for him.

The enemy assault began on January 24 and focused on Kapitanowka—much farther southeast of where *Wiking* was located, as well as farther northwest between the Tinowka and Boljarka—with the clear intent of encircling the men within this large German salient. By January 28, their grip had pretty much tightened and a pocket formed after both elements moved towards one another in a west to east line between these two locations. Referred to as the Cherkassy – Korsun Pocket (Korsun was in the middle of the pocket, but Cherkassy was actually outside the confines of the pocket), this area contained various *Heer* formations, but also *SS-Wiking* (with the *SS-Estonian Battalion "Narwa"* and one *kompanie* of the *SS-Polizei*) and *SS-Wallonie*. The northern sector ran along the Olschanka River and the southern sector was around Olschana. Over the next week, elements of *Wiking* positioned near Olschana fought a desperate defensive battle but eventually had to relinquish, and the survivors moved to join the main divisional elements. One soldier who led elements there was future Knight's Cross awardee Eberhard Heder (who wrote the foreword to volume 2). In relation to this project, his kameraden *SS-Obersturmführer* Willi Hein conducted actions at Olschana that would result in him becoming a holder of the Knight's Cross.

The Soviets proceeded to continuously attack the edges of this pocket with the sole intent of destroying all of the German forces contained within. The Germans intended to relieve the trapped troops, but that would take time and effort and there was no guarantee of success. In the meantime, the men from *Wiking* had to survive as best they could against a vastly superior enemy who was unrelentingly pounding them and inflicting further losses. Of note is that these positions were less than 100 miles northeast of the *Leibstandarte*'s difficult fighting at Uman back in 1941; all the fighting in between had been for nothing!

5. SS-Freiwilligen Sturmbrigade Wallonien

Positioned in the Irdynn Marsh area as 1943 closed, they continued to operate under the overall command of the *5. SS-Panzer Division*. January 1944 would see significant change for them, as the Soviets began the initial stages of the new offensive in this exact area. In mid-January, they were involved in a costly and difficult fight for the Teklino forest. In the final week of that month the enemy launched their main thrust westwards,

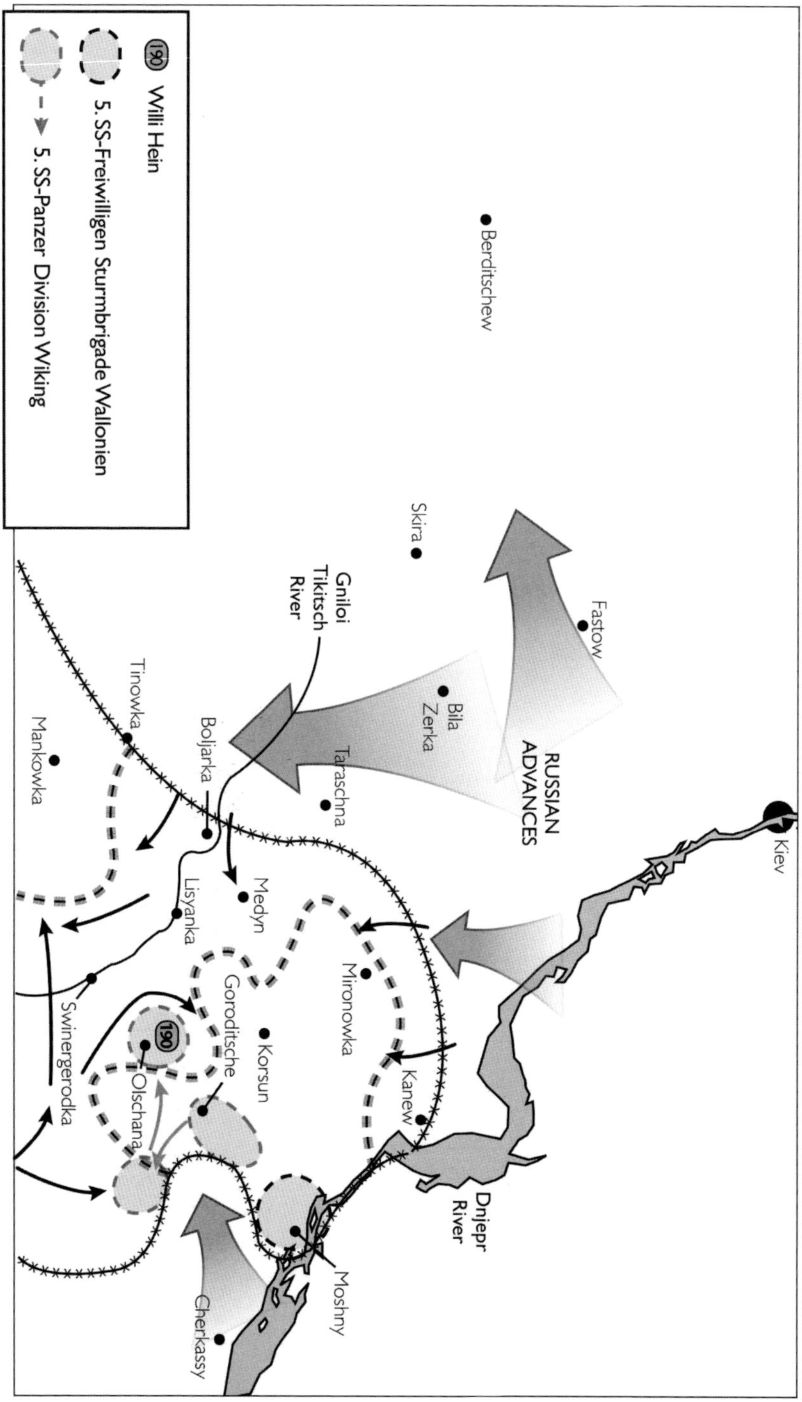

Map 7 – Formation of the Korsun Pocket: January 1944

outflanking the positions of *Wiking* and *Wallonien* and resulting in them becoming part of the trapped soldiers in the Cherkassy – Korsun Pocket closed in the final days of January.

Southwest of there...

3. SS-Panzer Division Totenkopf

They ended 1943 with a stint of relative quiet compared to what they had endured in preceding months, but that changed as 1944 opened. The large-scale Russian advances from the Dnjepr southwest forced the Germans to react and try to halt the enemy.

They started with a move from their sector east of Kriwoi Rog and went farther north to Bobrinez during the second week of January. Through the remainder of the month they fought against enemy incursions and movements across an area eighty miles northwest of Bobrinez; they were playing their part in fighting against a vastly superior and strong opponent in this region. That situation remained throughout February, with the only change being a move farther to the west due to increasing enemy pressure.

In northwest Ukraine. . .

SS-Kavallerie Regiment 17 (8. SS-Kavallerie Division Florian Geyer)

While the bulk of this division was being re-equipped, *SS-Kavallerie Regiment 17* found themselves committed elsewhere. Towards the end of January they were in northwest Ukraine and were part of defensive German forces. Their initial location was Kolki, around forty-five miles east of Kovel, and their first battles with the Soviets began as January 1944 closed. Their proximity to Kovel would bring them within a significant *Waffen-SS* action within a couple months.

In the northern sector of the eastern front:

These seven battle-tested *Waffen-SS* units in the south were enduring the enemy's efforts in the opening month of the new year, but their relatively untested kameraden in the north were about to feel a hammer blow as the Soviets launched a significant operation around the Leningrad sector.

Before detailing that, a quick reminder of the *Waffen-SS* located in the extreme north of the Eastern Front.

6. SS-Gebirgs Division Nord

They remained in their positions on the Finnish front as 1944 opened. The first two months were identical to 1943 for them: little changed and they still had to contend with harassing attacks.

Southwest of Leningrad. . .

III. (Germanisches) SS-Panzer-Korps

The *Korps* staff had moved to the Leningrad area in early December, with their composite formations following soon after. They set up their korps headquarters at Klopizy and assumed responsibility for an area stretching from Lutschki in the west through Petrowskaja in the east. The units that were part of this *SS-Korps* at that time were the *4. SS-Panzergrenadier Brigade "Nederland,"* the *11. SS-Panzergrenadier Division Nordland*, and the *9.* and *10. Luftwaffe Field Divisions* (for coverage of the individual SS formations see following. That coverage will also constitute the unfolding situation for this *SS-Korps*.)

In the first two weeks of 1944, they settled into their new locations, relieving existing units where necessary and awaiting orders—orders that would not be long in coming. The ensuing fighting from January onward would add at least a dozen Knight's Cross related awards for *Steiner's Korps*.

11. SS-Panzergrenadier Division Nordland

This main division centered itself around Kirowa, to the southeast of *Nederland*. One of their *Pioneer* kompanies was ordered to take up a position between Ropscha and Petrowskaj, which was the boundary between the *Luftwaffe Divisions* that were part of *Steiner's Korps*. They were in place by January 12, and this unit and their battalion commander would earn *Nordland* their first of many Knight's Crosses.

The main Russian offensive began on January 14, 1944, and in the early hours of the first day the *Nordland* pioneer positions were hit hard. Despite heavy losses, the battalion commander, *SS-Sturmbannführer* Fritz Bunse, led his surviving men in an organized defense and they began to inflict heavy losses on the Soviets. The SS pioneers were hit by heavy artillery and aerial attacks during the next day, supported by some tanks. Despite losing more irreplaceable men, they halted the tanks and also the follow-up enemy infantry attack. They held on during January 16, and then, on the seventeenth, Bunse mounted a counterattack to remove the threat from the ever-advancing Russians. This was the same day stronger friendly forces

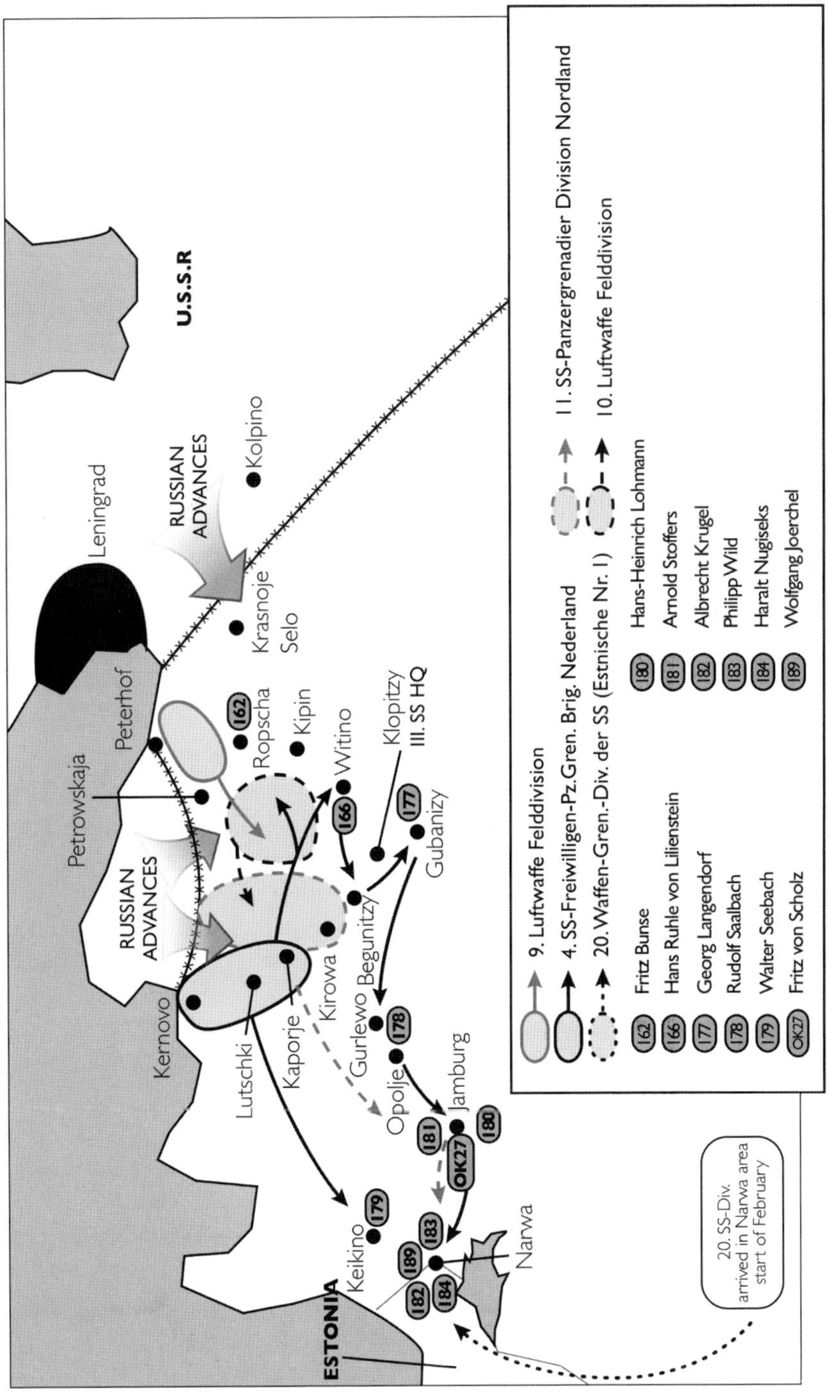

Map 8 – Oranienbaum – Narwa Battles: January – March 1944

arrived and Bunse's handful of survivors (around forty men) were able to take a temporary backseat. The recommendation was written only two days later and was approved rapidly on January 30.

As Bunse and his men were exacting their toll on the Soviets, the Germans moved quickly to counteract the enemy thrust. *SS-Regiments Norge* and *Danmark*, along with *Nordland's Aufklarungs Battalion*, raced into locations around Djatlezy and east towards Ropscha. Elements of *Norge* began their battles with the enemy on the fifteenth and fought the enemy over the next week. *Danmark* was initially held back, but engaged the enemy on the twenty-second—the same day the Soviets made a thrust farther to the south and aimed for Witinino. Elements of *Aufklarungs Battalion* fought here alongside *SS-Brigade Nederland*. The enemy continued to probe the German line and Chulgusi was also attacked; the fighting around that area went on for two more days.

On January 25, *Danmark* troops had to retreat and give up their northernmost positions, allowing the enemy to push westward. The SS soldiers moved from Witino southwest to Gubanizy, where *Aufklarungs* men held a position. The following day bore witness to a heavy tank attack by the Soviets against this location. They were not only held, but defeated by *SS-Hauptsturmführer* Rudolf Saalbach and the men fighting alongside them. Four dozen enemy tanks lay knocked out at the end of the day, resulting in Saalbach earning the Knight's Cross. One of the officers fighting in the same area, *SS-Untersturmführer* Georg Langendorf, would also receive the Knight's Cross for the fighting at Gubanizy. The twenty-sixth was the same day orders were issued to withdraw *Steiner's* korps to the west.

The retreat was in a southwesterly direction and the initial objective was Jamburg—also on the Luga River, but south of Keikino. *Norge* moved via Gurlewo and then Juchkoma, with *Danmark* also moving through Juchkoma but reaching it by a more northerly route. That route took them via Kerstowo and the fighting there earned *SS-Obersturmführer* Walter Seebach the Knight's Cross. Jamburg was reached on January 31, 1944. The enemy pursued them all the way and back on the twenty-eighth, *SS-Hauptsturmführer* Heinz Hamel fought in actions at Gurlewo that resulted in his later award of the Knight's Cross (detailed in a later volume).

4. SS-Freiwilligen-Panzergrenadier Brigade Nederland

They established themselves at the extreme western reaches of the *III. (Germanisches) SS-Panzer* korps area, at Lutschki. Their first engagements with the Soviets began on January 22, as part of the fight for Witinino—at that time the main focus for the enemy thrust into German-held territory.

The first contact with the enemy that day resulted in *Nederland's* first Knight's Cross award to *SS-Hauptsturmführer* Hans Ruhle von Lilienstern, who led a mixed battle group and successfully held the enemy for a vital period.

The engagements against the enemy continued until January 28, when *Nederland* was ordered towards Keikino, on the Luga River, as part of the general retreat of SS troops in that region. Their retreat route took them via Kotly and Krikkowo, with Keikino reached on the thirtieth. The Luga was meant to be a bulwark against the enemy, but the Soviets had other ideas and hit this river line hard.

Farther to the south. . .

3. Estnische SS-Freiwilligen Brigade / 20. Waffen-Grenadier Division der SS (Estnische Nr. 1)

The *Estonian Brigade* soldiers were around Idritsa as 1944 opened and had recently had to contend with heavy fighting in the area. Towards the end of January 1944, trainees at the Debica training grounds had arrived at the front line, raising the number of troops in the *Estonian Brigade* to around 7,000.

On January 24, the *3. Estnische SS-Freiwilligen Brigade* was redesignated the *20. Waffen-Grenadier Division der SS (Estnische Nr. 1)*; the completion of the reformation into a divisional-size unit would be many months away. Their commander, Franz Augsberger, received a promotion to *SS-Oberführer* on January 30. They were about to be sent northward to help the emerging crisis southwest of Leningrad.

East of there. . .

Also in this northern sector of the Russian front were the *Latvian SS* men, who had been placed in the front line as 1943 came to a close, but 1944 would see them engage the enemy and also operate under their own *Korps*.

15. Lettische SS-Freiwilligen Division

Near Novo Sokolniki as 1944 opened, elements of this division took part in the construction of positions near there. That position was named the Lux position, and it was where they fought the Soviets for the first time in the middle of January. The Soviets pushed forward and the Germans had to pull back, bringing the front line to the positions where the Latvians were working. Other elements of the division were subordinated to various German divisions as they sought additional resources to try and halt the general enemy push in January 1944. As January closed, this SS division was sent to Belebelka, south of Staraja-Russa, in the overall region previously occupied by their SS kameraden from *Totenkopf* two years earlier.

To the northeast. . .

2. Latvian SS-Freiwilligen Brigade / 19. Waffen-Grenadier Division der SS (Lettische Nr. 2)

Positioned around Spasskaja Polist, around twenty miles south of Tschudovo, they came under threat due to the enemy advance launched from January 14, 1944. One arm of that advance was to the south of their positions and a battle group from this brigade advanced against the enemy force.

The battle group was led by *SS-Standartenführer* Voldemars Veiss, and they encountered the Soviets at Nekokhovo. From January 17–25, Veiss and his men took control of the location and held it against the enemy. They also defended Dolgovo before having to retreat northwest due to enemy pressure. That battle, which ended on the twenty-fifth for them, resulted in the award of the Knight's Cross to Veiss, the first Latvian-born SS soldier to receive this award.

In the closing days of January, the *Latvian Brigade* had to continue rearward moves in a southwesterly direction. It was also in January that the *2. Latvian SS-Freiwilligen Brigade* was redesignated the *19. Waffen-Grenadier Division der SS (Lettische Nr. 2)*; they would receive a third regiment, but for the time being, they had to continue to defend against an unrelenting enemy thrust in their area of operations.

Closing the northern "ring" around the general Leningrad area. . .

Kampfgruppe SS-Polizei Division

This formation was in the Oranienbaum area at the end of 1943. In the first week of January 1944, the *Kampfgruppe SS-Polizei Division* was relocated from Oranienbaum to the Wolchow area—their old stomping ground—something that was not welcome by the men. During January, they fought mainly east of Ramzy. The main Soviet push in this northern area hit these polizei. Before the end of the month, areas that had been held by the Germans since 1941 were lost back to the Russians; some of these were locations of *Waffen-SS* Knight's Cross successful actions. In the fourth week of January, this battle group was ordered towards Babino to avoid destruction by the

SS Units Retreat From The "Russian Front" - January 1944

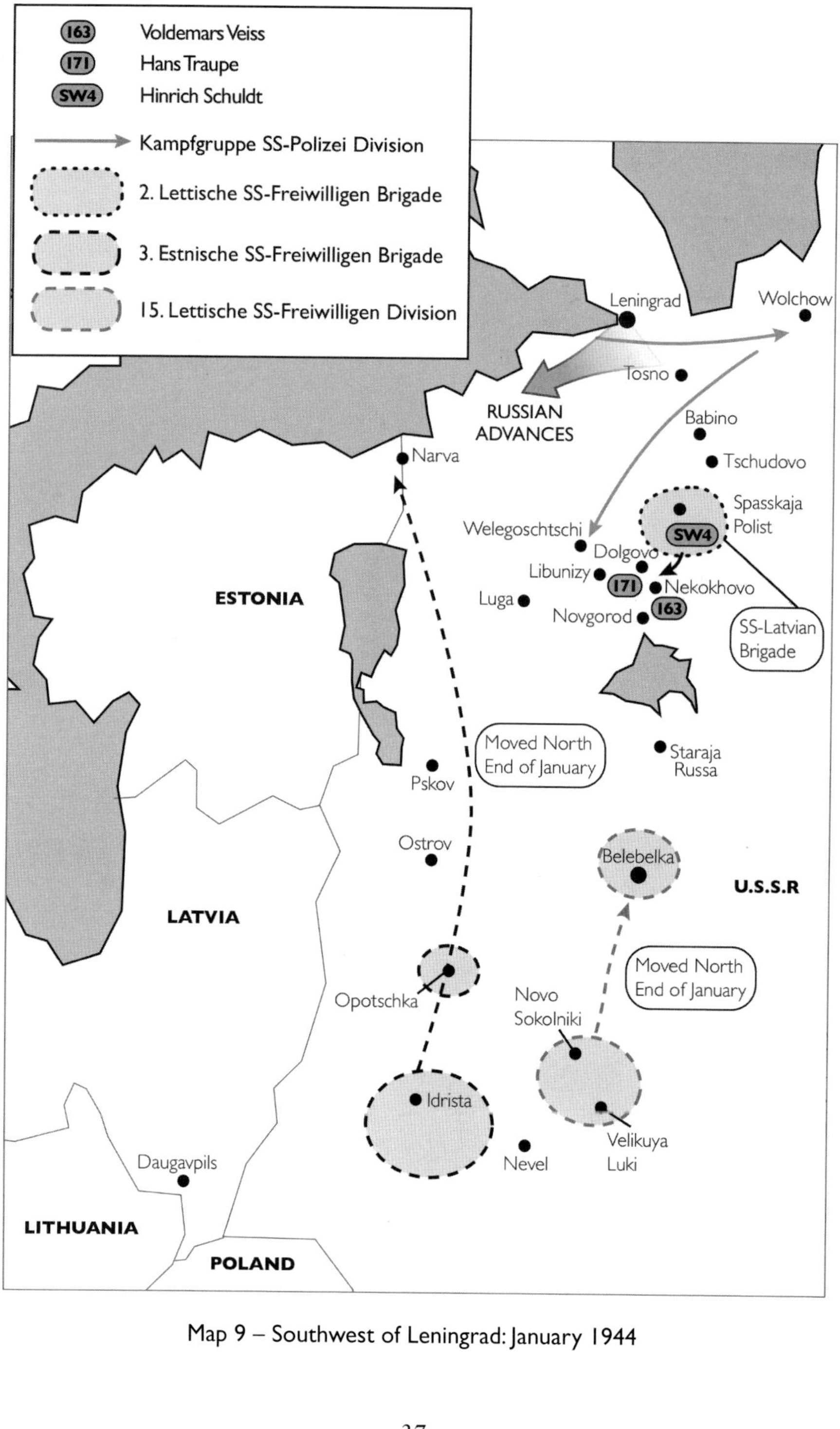

Map 9 – Southwest of Leningrad: January 1944

enemy advance. They then moved on towards Nowgorod, fighting northwest of there. At this time they were referred to as *SS-Kampfgruppe Bock.*

It was during this fighting on January 25 near Libunizy that a Knight's Cross related action was conducted under the command of *SS-Sturmbannführer* Traupe. These polizei continued with their struggle as January closed, even being encircled at one stage. In the final days their location was Welegoschtschi.

Before leaving coverage of the eastern front and the *Waffen-SS* units positioned there, let us briefly remind ourselves of the only remaining *Waffen-SS* formation operating in Army Group Center:

SS-Sonderkommando Dirlewanger

The opening months of 1944 saw no significant changes for this unit in the general Minsk area; they had only harassing enemy fire to contend with, but that changed in March 1944.

We will change regions now as we turn southwards and cover the various *Waffen-SS* units in Italy and the Balkans as 1944 opened.

16. SS-Panzergrenadier Division Reichsführer-SS

We left this newly raised division during November 1943, as they were in the midst of early formation. They were in two separate areas: the new recruit element was in Laibach (Ljubljana), Slovenia, while the former *Sturmbrigade* elements were in Livorno, Italy. It was the latter unit that was about to engage in action once more.

In late January 1944, the western Allies made their fourth landing attempt on European soil (Dieppe 1942, Sicily 1943, and Salerno 1943) on the beaches at Nettuno, very close to Anzio. A hastily gathered battle group was sent southwards—initially at Cisterna—under the command of *SS-Sturmbannführer* Knochlein.

SS-Karstwehr Battalion

We last featured this formation in the early part of volume 3, after they had taken part in their first actions around the Isonzo valley area in September 1943, an area they remained in for the rest of the year. In mid-January 1944, they were part of anti-partisan operations around Gorizia.

To the east in Yugoslavia. . .

V. SS-Gebirgs Korps

In Bosnia, they oversaw the use of mainly SS mountain troops in this region—including the *Prinz Eugen Division*—as 1944 opened, alongside Wehrmacht units.

7. SS-Freiwilligen-Gebirgs Division Prinz Eugen

The men of this formation were allowed a brief respite during the last few days of 1943, before they had to undertake a fresh operation against large bands of partisans. Operating in central Bosnia northwest of Sarajevo, this new fight began on January 4, 1944. They advanced westwards to play their part in clearing western Bosnia of the Tito menace. Advancing towards Travnik, they immediately ran into difficulties, and losses were suffered by the weakened units. The operation continued for around ten days before coming to a halt when Travnik was reached; a distance of around fifty miles from their starting point.

Following this operation, *Prinz Eugen* was relocated to Mostar. They also had a change of commander when *SS-Brigadeführer* von Oberkamp was replaced with existing Knight's Cross with Oakleaves holder *SS-Oberführer* Otto Kumm. Kumm had recently been promoted and moved from his existing post as Phleps' first general staff officer of the *V. SS-Gebirgs* korps to this new position towards the end of January 1944.

South of there. . .

4. SS-Polizei-Panzergrenadier Division

The main bulk of the division in Greece had pretty much an uneventful time in the opening months of 1944. They did conduct extensive patrols against partisan activity, but no successes were listed.

Now let us cover the first ten Knight's Cross related awards that were approved up to the end of January 1944.

Name: August-Wilhlem Trabandt
Award: Knight's Cross
SS Number: 218 852
Date of birth: 21.07.1891

Born in Berlin, he was a pre-WWI member of the armed forces and served with the *Jaeger Battalion* from 1913. By the end of that conflict he held the rank of *Leutnant* and also had been awarded the Second and First Classes of the Iron Cross, as well as the Black Wound Badge. He had also been noted as someone who was very brave in combat.

After gaining experience in this first global conflict, he lent this experience to the border police on the Polish border and the Baltic states and was also a member of the *Freikorps* during 1918 and 1919. In late 1920, he once again joined the army and remained there until October 1933. In May 1924 he moved to *Oberleutnant* and then *Hauptmann* in February 1929. Straight after his time with the army he moved to a stint with the *SA* that ended in April 1936, obtaining the rank *SA-Standartenführer*.

Trabandt then moved to the *SS* in early May 1936, retaining his captain rank (*SS-Hauptsturmführer*). He was placed with the *Leibstandarte*, but spent a training phase with *SS-Regiment Deutschland* before returning to the *Leibstandarte* and assuming command of their *III Battalion*. In November he was promoted to *SS-Sturmbannführer*. Further promotion to *SS-Obersturmbannführer* came in April 1938. Prior to WWII he also took part in the Austrian and Sudetenland campaigns, earning medals for both.

As this second global conflict began, Trabandt led his *III Battalion* during the fighting in Poland. He earned the Bar to the Second Class Iron Cross on September 18 and then the bar to the First Class Iron Cross on September 25, 1939.

He then went west in 1940, and soon after was promoted to *SS-Standartenführer* on May 11.

He had some highs and lows in 1940: first, he designed the key symbol used by the *Leibstandarte* for the remainder of their existence (see volume 1 for more detail). Second, an incident took place during this campaign that would result in severe implications for Trabandt. Some reports indicate he had a bet with Max Wunsche with bottles of French wine as the wager. He took ill towards the end of the fighting and a quantity of wine he had sent towards Germany was impounded at the border. An investigation began under the direct control of Heinrich Himmler. He was implicated in this theft and the outcome was his removal from command. Investigations continued and in May 1942, he was removed as a member of the *SS*. His former commander, Sepp Dietrich, stepped in and wrote an appeal to have Trabandt reinstated; it appeared to help, as Trabandt was allowed to assume command once more, this time with one of the anti-partisan *Schuma* units operating on the Russian front; he was moved back to the rank of *SS-Hauptsturmführer* during that phase. In the early part of 1943, he was with the *8. Infantry Regiment* within the *1. SS-Infantry Brigade (mot.)*. By August he was regarded as "rehabilitated" by the *Reichsführer-SS*. He had been moved up to *SS-Sturmbannführer* during that time. His fortunes then started to move in the right direction once more.

In late September 1943, he was in temporary command of the whole brigade and they became embroiled in heavy fighting with front-line Russian soldiers (covered in volume 3); a number of his men were awarded the Knight's Cross for their actions during that fighting—some in 1943 and

August-Wilhelm Trabandt after the award of his Knight's Cross—the first such *Waffen-SS* award for 1944. Some of his other awards are clearly visible.

some more to follow in this volume. As the fighting ensued he received two rapid "re-promotions" and found himself back at the rank of *SS-Standartenführer* from early November 1943. By then, he had also been awarded the Silver Wound Badge on September 21, plus the German Cross in Gold on October 22.

Brigade Adjutant *SS-Hauptsturmführer* Ekmayr penned a recommendation for the award of the Knight's Cross to the Iron Cross for *SS-Standartenführer* Trabandt:

> On September 21, 1943, at 21:00 hours, the brigade was given the task—from the area northeast of Smolensk, over Smolensk towards the southeast—to reach Dolgomostje in motorized march without one regiment and to establish contact there with the *35. Infantry Division*.
>
> There the brigade remained with one regiment as Army reserve.
>
> On September 22, 1943, 06:30 hours, *SS-Standartenführer* Trabandt was advised of the situation by the Ia at the command post of the *35. Infantry Division* in Sswiridinowo. The enemy had crossed the railway line on both sides of Cholm towards the west, encircled *Grenadier Regiment 11* in Cholm, seized Lichatachewo and Rossnowo, and attacked further to the west with the goal of reaching the road Rosslawl-Smolensk. At the same time strong enemy forces tried to push forward from Cholm on both sides of the railway line towards the north.
>
> An unbroken German line south of Arefino was no longer in existence. At first the brigade did not receive any further orders and remained in Army reserve.
>
> After the regiment arrived, recognizing the dangerous situation *SS-Standartenführer* Trabandt, without orders, decided to advance at 09:00 hours from Panskoje towards the south, immediately pushing forward on Cholm on both sides of the railway line to relieve *Grenadier Regiment 11*, to destroy the enemy elements that had penetrated west of the railway line, and to deploy his troops for defense along the railway line by Cholm facing east. After the regiment started the attack it received an order from the division in similar terms.
>
> During the attack, which the *SS-Standartenführer* led, *Grenadier Regiment 11* managed to make its way and join with the attacking brigade before the attack goal. The enemy assault in the direction of the road was stopped by the quickly-built blocking position that ran in the line of Hill 225.7 (about four kilometers northwest of

Cholm) – Hill 239.5 – Panskoje. Numerous attacks carried out with superior forces—partially with tanks—were beaten off with bloody losses for the opponent and the enemy penetration attempt in the direction of the road was thwarted. This success must be fully appraised, because had the enemy reached the road Rosslawl – Smolensk, our forces fighting south of the Rossash would have been cut off from rear communication and the planned retreat in the direction of Smolensk hindered.

On September 24, 1943, the brigade was given the order to disengage the enemy and prepare itself for defense on the general line Sumarokowo – Poststrasse – Talashkino – Swch. Chlenowo, with the front towards the southeast.

Meanwhile, coming from the east, the enemy had occupied the line to be reached with a front towards the south. Trabandt, again at his own decision, ordered to attack and throw the enemy back towards the east to prepare for the defense. The enemy was thrown back towards the east with heavy losses in dead and wounded, and large numbers of prisoners, weapons, equipment, and ammunition were captured. With it the planned withdrawal in the area south of Smolensk was enabled.

The commander of the *35. Infantry Division* wrote on October 9, 1943, to the commander of *1. SS-Infantry Brigade*, recognizing that the brigade had a decisive participation in the defensive successes. This led to the honorable mention of the *35. Infantry Division* in the Wehrmacht report.

The order of the day of the *XXXIX. Panzer* korps for October 23, 1943, reads:

Especially southeast of Smolensk the brigade in the heaviest fight has hindered the penetration of vastly superior forces on Smolensk, enabling with it the undisturbed evacuation of the city.

In the ensuing development of the fight on the highway west of Smolensk the brigade stood under the leadership of *SS-Standartenführer* Trabandt in continuous heavy fighting, always at the focal points of the defensive battles.

Honorable mentions of the brigade in the Wehrmacht report took place on October 15 and November 23, 1943.

The feats and exploits of the brigade under the leadership of *SS-Standartenführer* Trabandt are described in the attached army, korps, and divisional orders covering the September 1 to December 3, 1943.

This multi-level recommendation was approved January 6, 1944.

Trabandt remained in command of the brigade up to when it was incorporated into the newly created *18th SS-Freiwilligen Panzergrenadier Division "Horst Wessel"* in January 1944. Promotion to *SS-Oberführer* came at the start of July; then, in early December, he moved to the *IV. SS-Panzer Korps*. His next posting was the SS training school in Kienschlag from February 1945, the same month he was awarded the Honor Roll Clasp. The men from this school were formed into the *SS-Brigade "Bohmen und Mahren"* during April 1945. It was also during April that he received his final promotion to *SS-Brigadeführer und Generalmajor der Waffen-SS*. His new brigade fought in the eastern area of Austria, close to the Hungarian border, but were pushed westward in the closing weeks of the war. They eventually surrendered to the Americans in May near Linz.

Considering his long military career (including the inter-war paramilitary groups), obvious bravery—which was recognized multiple times and in two world-wide conflicts—and his seemingly criminal activities concerning the theft of the French alcohol, he ended the conflict on a high and his transgressions from 1940 appear to have been well and truly overlooked in the closing months of the war.

His postwar experiences would not be so good: he was captured by the Soviets and was one of the men not released until the mid-1950s. He died on May 19, 1968.

Name: Michael Wittmann
Date of birth: 22.04.1914
SS Number: 311 623
Award: Knight's Cross

Born in Vogelthal, his service for his country began in February 1934, with the *R.A.D.* In October, he moved to the *Heer*'s *Infantry Regiment 19*, staying there until the end of September 1936; he obtained the rank of *Gefreiter* with the army. He then moved to the *SS* at the start of April 1937, and was placed with the *Leibstandarte*. His initial rank was *SS-Mann*, but by mid-November that same year he had moved to *SS-Sturmmann*. He took part in the Austrian and Sudetenland campaigns in 1938 and gained his first medals. In April 1939, he was promoted to *SS-Unterscharführer*. During that time he served in various armored scout cars and by the time of the looming Polish issues he was in one of the eight-wheeled versions.

He fought in Poland in the same role, but then in February 1940, he moved to the newly created *Leibstandarte* assault gun unit; this unit was in their formation training as their kameraden advanced westwards so he did not participate. Wittmann's next action was in Greece as part of this small six-vehicle unit. The advance into the Soviet Union followed soon after, and it was not long before Wittmann received further awards: the first was the Second Class Iron Cross on July 12, 1941, which may have been for actions during the Balkans campaign. Some sources also list him as being presented with the Bulgarian Bravery Medal 4th Class, 2nd Grade. The Black Wound Badge came the following month on August 20. On September 8 he added the First Class Iron Cross. He was promoted to *SS-Oberscharführer* on November 9; following the battle for Rostov, the Tank Assault Badge was awarded on November 21.

His qualities had been recognized with the list of awards he accumulated in the second half of 1941. His superiors took that a stage further and sent him for officer training at Bad Tolz between June and September 1942. While there he would have been given the Russian Front Medal. He left Bad Tolz and briefly joined the *SS Heavy Tank Training and Replacement Battalion*. His promotion to *SS-Untersturmführer* was approved on December 21 and three days later, on Christmas Eve, he was placed with the *Leibstandarte's* Tiger tank *kompanie* at Fallingbostel. Wittmann was not assigned to a Tiger tank at that point, but instead commanded the Light Platoon equipped with the Panzer III, which had a supplementary role to play alongside their larger stable mates. Wittmann's arrival coincided with the arrival of the Tiger and Panzer IIIs, which were collected from the factories by some of the crews and taken back to the training ground at the start of January. Once again, Michael Wittmann found himself in a fledgling armored unit that would acquire a superb fighting reputation as the war progressed, but for now training was the focus.

Towards the end of February 1943, this kompanie was sent to the Kharkov area to help with the rapidly developing situation there. Following this very difficult but successful campaign that led to the capture of Bjelgorod to the north, Michael Wittmann was placed in command of the *III Platoon*; this was when he got into a Tiger tank for the first time. The next battle would be the Kursk offensive, but just prior to the start of that, the kompanie was renumbered the *13. (Heavy) Kompanie*. Wittmann commanded tank number 1331.

It was in this role that Wittmann really began to stack up an impressive list of destroyed enemy tanks and anti-tank guns. During the short Kursk campaign he is listed as knocking out thirty enemy tanks and more than

Michael Wittmann with his newly awarded Knight's Cross, an award soon to be joined by the next level of recognition.

two-dozen anti-tank guns. Of note is during the testing battles of 1943, Wittmanns's rank or list of awards remained unchanged. Following Kursk, a quieter time in Italy followed before a return to Russia towards the end of 1943. Prior to leaving Italy, Wittmann assumed command of *II Platoon* and tank S21. He continued to add kills to his tally and by the first few days of January 1944, he was credited with fifty-six destroyed enemy tanks. This was about to change considerably.

The winter fighting for the *Leibstandarte* in late 1943 and the opening days of 1944 presented many challenges, and Wittmann was one of the men who stood up to those challenges. He conducted actions beginning on January 8 that resulted in his recommendation for the Knight's Cross. The initial telex recommendation (signed by divisional commander Wisch on January 10) stated:

> *SS-Hstuf.* Pfeiffer, Führer headquarters, with request for delivery to *SS-Obergruppenführer* Dietrich, subject:
>
> Awarding of the Knight's Cross of the Iron Cross to *SS-Ustuf.* Wittmann, Michael, Platoon Commander *13. (S) SS-Panz.Rgt.1 Lssah* on 8 and 9/1/1944 for outstanding bravery during penetration by Russian Tank Bridgade near Sherepki (see daily report). 56 tanks destroyed himself as platoon commander from July 1943 to 7/1/44, several KVI, KVII, General Sherman, the rest T 34.
>
> On 8/1/44, following penetration by Russian Tank Brigade, stopped attack with his platoon and himself destroyed 3 T 34 and 1 Assault Gun. Another 6 T 34s during another armored penetration; thus, 10 by him alone. Now 66 tanks destroyed. Personal info *SS-Ustuf.* Wittmann, Michael, position: SS Officer, unmarried. Born 22/4/14 in Vogelthal, Upper Pfalz. Father: Johann Wittmann, Ingolstadt, Danube, Baselstr. 34 Decorations: EK 1, EK 11, Wound Badge Black, Tank Battle Bagde Silver
>
> Signed Wisch, *SS Oberführer* and Division Commander of the 1st SS-Panz.Div.*Lssah*.

That initial telex was then rewritten in Berlin and put forward for consideration and is presented for comparison:

> *1st SS-Pz.Div.Lssah* Div.C.P. 10/1/1944
>
> *SS-Untersturmführer* Wittmann, platoon commander *13.(s)/ SS-Pz Rgt.1 Lssah*, has himself destroyed 56 tanks in the period July 1943 to 7/1/1944, including several KV 1 , KV 11, and General

"Sherman"; the rest were T 34s. During a penetration near Sherepki by a Russian Tank Brigade on 8/1/1944, he and his platoon succeeded in stopping the attack and he himself knocked out 3 T 34s and 1 assault gun.

On 9/1/1944, he destroyed another 6 T 34s during a penetration by enemy tanks and raised his total tanks destroyed to 66. He once again demonstrated exceptional bravery in meeting and smashing the Russian tank attack.

Signed Wisch, *SS-Oberführer* and Div.C.O.

This proposal was quickly approved on January 14, 1944, but would be very soon joined by another.

Name: Hans Diergarten
Date of birth: 05.04.1913
SS Number: 421 976
Award: Knight's Cross

Born in Schalksmuhle, Westfallen, he initially spent time with the *SA* from July 1933 to October 1935. He then entered army service from November 1935. He served with a machine-gun kompanie and less than a year later moved to the *Schutzpolizei*. Prewar he attended officer school with them and in March 1938 became a *Leutnant*. He was then promoted to *Oberleutnant* in September 1939.

He was moved to the newly created *SS-Polizei Division* in October. In early January 1940, he officially joined the *SS* and held dual police and *SS* rank (*SS-Obersturmführer*). He was awarded the Second Class Iron Cross on June 25, 1940, while fighting in the west. The award of the First Class Iron Cross came on September 25, 1941. A move to *SS-Hauptsturmführer* was made in early January 1942. Starting in July, he spent a two-month stint with the *XXXVIII Army* korps (for staff training), immediately followed by attendance at a staff officer's training course that lasted until November. He then moved to the replacement battalion for *SS-Polizei Regiment 1*; this was the same month the award of the Russian Front Medal was made. December was a busy month for Diergarten: he was placed with *SS-Kampfgruppe Fegelein* as their first staff officer. While there he received the Infantry Assault Badge and a promotion to *SS-Sturmbannführer*. The German Cross in Gold was awarded in mid-January 1943, but that document is not contained in his file, so there are no details of the actions that warranted this significant level of recognition.

He became the first staff officer of the *SS-Kavallerie Division* in March 1943. Other posts he held while with the *kavallerie* include ordnance officer, regimental staff officer, kompanie commander, and regimental adjutant. Additional awards he held were the Close Combat Clasp in Bronze and Black Wound Badge, but the award dates for these are not known.

In September 1943, he conducted actions that would result in his divisional commander, Streckenbach, recommending him for the Knight's Cross. That document was put together at the start of December and contained the following details:

> *SS-Sturmbannführer* Diergarten has already been brought to the attention of the *Reichsführer-SS* as someone being worthy of the award of the Knight's Cross due to various cold-blooded acts as a military commander, as well as outstanding decisions made as battle group commander that led to success in the most difficult situations. This was done after the proposal for the German Cross in Gold on 23.12.1942 and given on 14 January 1943. They covered the breakthrough of the 58th Russian Infantry Corps, together with a tank corps and other armored units. He thus prevented and delayed the intended breakthrough in Kharkov.
>
> The Russians had attacked Michailowka again and again, at least ten times over against the decimated battle group on 28, 29, and 30 December 1942. Repeatedly, Diergarten was at the head of his battle group as they met these attacks and halted them with lightning speed reactions and excellent leadership. Against the attacks on Molot on 28.12.1942, 29.12.1942 at Mitrowka, and on 30.12.1942 at Passjukowa, solely using his own initiative he led counterattacks that destroyed the tank corps and the leadership decisions he made were important for the holding of these locations.
>
> On September 9, 1943, the Russians attacked with heavy tank and infantry forces in the area of the main battle line. Reiter Regiment 2 was south of the "Well- forest" (Bereka positions). Diergarten had no link to his right-hand neighbor and he had reports there was a deep breakthrough attack that could only be stopped with lightning-quick reaction to it. He also could see the obvious intent of the enemy, with the emphasis of their strength, was to roll the front backwards on the left (Isjum).
>
> Because the divisional commander was on the left wing of the regiment and Diregarten could not immediately reach him, he decided to intervene. He immediately drove the 1.5 km from the

SS-Obersturmbannfuhrer Hans Diergarten looking pleased after being awarded the Knight's Cross that added to his existing impressive list of medals.

divisional field position to where the incursion was; parts of field positions were unmanned due to the confusion that reigned. He seized the initiative and placed two 7.5 heavy PaK guns there. Then, at the head of his men with a "Hurrah," he engaged the huge enemy, who were superior in number, several times over; the enemy collapsed upon this. That cleared the disorganized situation and he heroically pushed his lead fighting elements forwards. That independent decision, apparent from captured men, foiled the intended breakthrough and rolling up of the front to the south. The imminent danger that existed to the Donets Front was halted through the independent decision by Diergarten, who was responsible for this.

An additional short document lists the successes of this action by Diergarten as:

38 Prisoners
10 Heavy machine guns
15 Light machine guns
5 Anti-tank rifles
4 Mortars
33 Rifles
2 Rapid-fire pistols
15 Machine pistols

This recommendation was approved on January 16, 1944, and soon after, on January 30, Diergarten was promoted to *SS-Obersturmbannführer*. Remaining with the SS Cavalry, his life came to an end on August 24, 1944, after the reconnaissance plane he was flying in was shot down near Petrikan, in Poland. This crash happened five days earlier and Diergarten was evacuated to a hospital in Litzmannstadt, where he succumbed to his wounds.

Name: Joachim Rumohr
Date of birth: 06.08.1910
SS Number: 7 450
Award: Knight's Cross

Born in Hamburg, he spent time as a member of the *SA* between April 1930 and January 1931. From February, he moved to the *SS* and was a member of the *4. SS-Standarte*. His first officer promotion was made on November 9, 1933, when he was moved to *SS-Sturmführer*, accompanied by the command of the *3. Sturm*. Remaining there until early March 1935, he then moved to the *SS-Verfugungstruppe* and a position with the forerunner to *SS-Regiment Germania*. Placed with the *13. Kompanie*, a further promotion to *SS-Obersturmführer* followed in November. His next changes came in 1938; the first of those was a move to the *12.* kompanie in May, the second being a promotion to *SS-Hauptsturmführer* in early November. It was in this position that he entered the war.

Rumohr displayed his bravery from the outset and earned the Second Class Iron Cross on November 14, 1939, for actions in Poland. The advance westwards in 1940 would see him add the First Class Iron Cross on August 28. A month earlier, he was posted to the artillery regiment of the *SS-VT*. When this unit became part of *SS-Division Reich* in the latter stages of 1940, he was given command of *II Battalion*. Leading this battalion during the Balkans campaign, he was promoted to *SS-Sturmbannführer* on June 21, 1941, just in time for Operation Barbarossa. During the early stages of the advance into the Soviet Union (mid-September) he suffered a heavy wound that removed him from the front line.

Rumohr was not considered fit for duty until June 1942, when he was given command of the artillery regiment within the newly raised *SS-Kavallerie Division* (expanded from the previous *SS-Kavallerie Brigade*). His run of luck with wounds continued with a further wound inflicted in July, earning him the Silver Wound Badge. Serious illness removed him from the front line once again in September. While in hospital, a further promotion to *SS-Obersturmbannführer* was made on November 9; he returned to his previous role in mid-December.

Rumohr was awarded the German Cross in Gold on February 23, 1943. His brushes with death occurred for a third time, with another serious wound exactly one month later. Back at the front in June, he then assumed the role of first staff officer the following month for five weeks before returning to his previous role. Just over six months later, he received his first recommendation for the award of the Knight's Cross, this one written by his Divisional Commander Hermann Fegelein; the proposal was not approved. Fegelein was badly wounded at the end of November and left the front line. Bruno Streckenbach took over divisional command and took the decision to recommend Rumohr for the award of the Knight's Cross, writing his own document in the closing days of December 1943. That document contains:

> After parts of the division drew up and reached the battle area the personality of *SS-Obersturmbannführer* Rumohr became even more noticeable; the following events are for consideration.

Joachim Rumohr with his Knight's Cross awarded as an *SS-Obersturmbannfuhrer*. He is carrying his later rank of *SS-Standartenfuhrer*.

11. October 1943, Hof. Sapolitschi: after attacking with the support of tank forces the Russians penetrated the main fighting line. Our infantry units were defeated. Hidden in the large cornfields, the Russian infantry emerged in the artillery positions. A battery chief organized the first resistance, then Rumohr quickly gathered an infantry battle group from his own detachments and the attached army troops and personally led it to counterattack. He forced the enemy back behind an important route and during the night defended the reached line until the artillerymen were relieved by corps reserves the next morning.

17. October 1943, Klin: the remnants of the *SS-Kavallerie Division* were deployed north of Klin to prevent an advance from the route towards Piatichatky by the enemy that had broken through in Lichowka. By mistake the order given that day for retreat was not passed on to the *SS-Kavellerie Division*, so it found itself still in the middle of the enemy long after neighboring divisions *Grossdeutschland* and the *9. Panzer Division* had carried out withdrawal movements. The division was becoming quickly encircled. Here again Rumohr assembled parts of his artillerymen for an infantry action and assumed personal leadership. He shielded the *SS-Kavallerie Division* against the enemy pressing from the west side. With these actions severe losses to the fully exhausted infantry elements were avoided.

20 / 21. October 1943, Saxagan: The *SS-Kavallerie Division* was assigned the task of defending Saxagan until the deployment of army reserves intended for a counterattack was completed. The infantry forces and the heavy infantry weapons put at his disposal were extraordinarily weak in numbers for the assignment. Rumohr commanded the five detachments arranged for this task. Through the skillful guidance of coordinated fire that was evidence of his high artillery knowledge, the enemy attack groups were decisively broken to pieces in their assembly positions, or so decimated during the attack that, despite the weakness of the infantry, Rumhor was able to hold Saxagan for forty-eight hours. They repelled more than ten large attacks in this period. The commanding general of *LII* korps expressed through his korps artillery commander—besides a general recognition to all the *SS-Kavallerie Division*—his personal acknowledgement to Rumhor for his excellent artillery performance.

> 9. – 12. November 1943, north sector of Sofijewka: Here also the main burden of defense was borne by the artillery coordinated under the leadership of Rumohr. Through the independent guidance of artillery fire he repeatedly mastered the most difficult situations, as in the enemy tank breakthrough towards Melodorowka, or during the infantry attacks in the area southeast of Schirokkin. In both instances, after rolling up the infantry units wide breaches were opened through which the enemy launched piercing assaults. Thanks to a clear impression of the situation and independent fire concentration with compact, quick, and good effect, here he also took a decisive part in the battle. His deeds were repeatedly praised by the commander of the *9. Panzer Division*, *Obst* Dr. Johannes Schulz.
>
> Also, the supreme commander of the *1. Panzer Armee*, *General der Panzertruppen* Hans Hube, has expressed his special recognition to Rumohr and the artillery led by him.

This second submission for the award of the Knight's Cross for Joachim Rumohr was approved on January 16, 1944; this made him the second *Florian Geyer* soldier to be approved for this medal that day. Rumohr would later add to his connection with this medal and its grades.

Name: Balthasar Woll
Date of birth: 01.09.1922
SS Number: not listed
Award: Knight's Cross

Born in Wemmetsweiler, in the Saar region, he was a member of the Hitler Youth from his eleventh birthday to mid-September 1939. Following this, he started an apprenticeship as an electrician. In mid-August 1941, he entered the *Waffen-SS*. He was initially placed with the *3.* kompanie in the *Totenkopf Division*. He was wounded badly in 1942, during the Demjansk Pocket battles, and was sent back to Germany. While in hospital he was awarded the Second Class Iron Cross on July 23 and the Black Wound Badge on July 26, 1942; his rank at that time was *SS-Oberschutze*.

After his recovery he was placed with the newly created *Tiger* kompanie of the *Leibstandarte*. He fought with this kompanie in Kharkov and by the time of Kursk, *SS-Sturmmann* Woll was Michael Wittmann's gunner. The successes listed in the preceding Wittmann recommendation can mostly be attributed to the assistance of Bobby Woll. He was awarded the First Class

Iron Cross on October 14 and was then promoted to *SS-Rottenführer* on November 9, 1943. The Tank Assault Badge followed on New Year's Day 1944, while he was embroiled in the heavy defensive fighting in southern Russia.

Leibstandarte Divisonal Commander "Teddi" Wisch took the unprecedented decision to recommend this tank gunner for the Knight's Cross due to his huge success as part of Wittmann's crew. The initial telex recommendation was put forward on January 13, 1944, reading as follows:

> To Führer Headquarters, attn. *SS-Hstuf.* Pfeiffer.
>
> Subject: Knight's Cross recommendation *SS-Rttf.* Woll, Balthasar. Gunner in *13.(S) SS-Panz.Rgt.1 Lssah.*
>
> Personal information: Surname: Woll.
>
> First name: Balthasar. Born 1/9/1922 in Wemmetzweiler, Ottweiler District. Married Status: Single. Profession: Electrician.
>
> Parent's Address: Johann Woll, Worker Wemmetzweiler, Ottweiler Dist., Strasze D. 13. January 1943.
>
> Justification: Exceptional conduct in earlier fighting at Kharkov – action March 1943. Summer action Belgorod 1943 and present winter battles. 61 tanks destroyed as of 11/1/44, including numerous assault guns.
>
> During elimination of armored penetration on 12/ and 13/1/44 in Mal.Bespechna-Chesnovka area, 16 T-34s and 3 assault guns were knocked out by tank with *SS-Rttf* Woll as gunner, thus raising total of tanks destroyed to 80.
>
> Wisch, *SS-Oberführer* and *Div.C.O.SS-1 SS-Pz.Div.Lssah*

Like Wittmann's, this telex was transferred to an official recommendation in Berlin:

> *1st SS-Pz.Div.Lssah* Div.C.P 13/1/1944
>
> *SS-Rottenführer* Woll, gunner in the *13.(S)/SS-Pz.Rgt. 1 Lssah*, performed exceptionally well in earlier fighting in the Kharkov action of March 1943, summer action at Belgorod. During the elimination of several armored penetrations on 12/ and 13/1/1944

Balthasar (Bobby) Woll, Michael Wittmann's Tiger tank gunner, in a formal photo to show his Knight's Cross worn alongside his low rank of *SS-Rottenfuhrer*.

in Mal.Bespechna-Chesnovka area, 16 T-34s and 3 assault guns were destroyed alone by the tank in which *SS-Rttf.* Woll was serving as gunner. He thus raised his total of enemy tanks destroyed to 80.
Signed Wisch, *SS-Oberführer* and Div.C.O.

This recommendation for a gunner, rather than a tank commander, was approved on January 16, 1944, two days after his commander's approval. The action was considered exceptional, and the Führer agreed. Woll is the only known SS tank gunner to be approved for this high award. The presentation to both men the same day was well photographed by war correspondents and is no doubt well known to most readers.

In March 1944, he attended the wedding of Michael Wittmann and Hildegard Burmesiter, where he was Wittmann's best man. By the time of the Normandy battles, Woll had been given command of his own Tiger I. He was wounded during that campaign and his injuries removed him from the front line until March 1945. While recuperating he was promoted to *SS-Oberscharführer* in October 1944. He took part in the final fighting on the western front and survived the war, dying on March 18, 1996. According to kameraden who served with Woll, he apparently wrote his memoirs postwar, but decided to destroy them. I am sure we all would have liked to read that account of WWII!

Name: Gerhard Grebarsche
Date of birth: 15.02.1913
SS Number: 265 770
Award: Knight's Cross

Born in Grunweiler, near Rawitsch. After completing his schooling, he spent over three years as an apprentice builder. In early November 1932, at the age of nineteen, he joined the early version of the *RAD* and remained there until the end of July 1934, reaching the role of foreman. He immediately joined the *Leibstandarte*, remaining there in the prewar years. On April 20, 1938, he was promoted to *SS-Unterscharführer*. He is not listed as taking part in the Austrian or Sudetenland campaigns, nor did he hold medals for those campaigns.

His first campaign was in Poland 1939, and was followed by fighting in the west in 1940. He was awarded the Second Class Iron Cross and the Infantry Assault Badge on October 2, 1940. He fought in the Balkans campaign in 1941, during which, on April 20, he received a promotion to

SS-Oberscharführer. Movement into Russia followed soon after, where his first wound (in fighting near Shitomir) earned him the Black Wound Badge at the start of September. This may have resulted in a return to Germany, as in 1942, he was fighting with *V Battalion* in Leningrad; this battalion was commanded by Hugo Kraas. In April 1942, he moved to *SS-Hauptscharführer*, with the Russian Front Medal coming in late August.

Returning to Russia in early 1943, he earned the First Class Iron Cross on March 20, 1943, for fighting around Kharkov. In late July, he was put forward for the award of the German Cross in Gold by his battalion commander; this recommendation mostly covered Grebarsche's actions in Kursk and was approved by "Teddi" Wisch and Sepp Dietrich. Despite this, the recommendation was rejected on October 10, 1943. This recommendation mentions frequent close combat actions in Grebarsche and one of the documents mentions the award of the Bronze Close Combat Clasp, although the exact award date is not listed. During 1943, he was with *3.* kompanie of the *2nd Panzergrenadier Regiment*; his battalion commander was once again Hugo Kraas.

He was back in southern Russia in November 1943, fighting once more near Shitomir; his bravery during these testing days resulted in "Teddi" Wisch recommending him for the Knight's Cross. The document was written on January 11, 1944, and contained the following details:

> The *SS-Hauptscharführer* Grebarsche has participated in the campaigns in Poland, the West, and the East.
>
> As a group leader, he was recognized for his bravery in the western campaign with the award of the Iron Cross Second Class and the Infantry Assault Badge in Bronze. In other winter fighting of the "*LSSAH*" in Leningrad—also the winter battle in 1943 in Kharkov, as a group leader—after the loss of his kompanie commanders, he was temporarily the kompanie leader and *SS-Hauptscharführer* Grebarsche stood out particularly. For his achievements in the area of Kharkov he was awarded the Iron Cross First Class on 20.03.1943.
>
> At the start of fighting against the enemy ring north of Belgorod in July 1943, *SS-Hauptscharführer* Grebarsche displayed the highest bravery in severe crisis. During the hard fighting against enemy field positions by Bykowka, several anti-tank positions were destroyed and on his own initiative, he formed a bridgehead with his few men over the Worskla River.

Gerhard Grebarsche shown with his later officer rank.
His Knight's Cross was awarded when he was an *SS-Hauptscharfuhrer*.

In the immediate fight south and southeastwards of Shitomir, *SS-Hauptscharführer* Grebarsche showed outstanding bravery and prudent leadership, especially during the night of 18. / 19.11.1943 at Morosowka (southern Brussiloff), and also the attack on Jastrebenka on 19.11.1943.

The *I. / SS- Panz.Gren.Rgt . 2 / "LSSAH"* launched an attack towards Ssolowjewka on 18.11.1943, supported by a panzer battalion, from their defensive area at Brussiloff. After an extremely fierce fight, at 11:30 hours on 18.11.1943, they had taken possession of Morosowka and thus a favorable position for attacking other objectives.

The enemy placed our positions under attack all day using all of their weapons, tanks, and infantry, and won some of these positions. The battalion fought during these various crises with strong will. During the night of 18. to 19.11.1943, 00:30 hours, the enemy attacked again with about two battalions, supported by 10-15 tanks. They came forth from the northeast of Morosowka. The *grenadier* kompanies were used in the front line during this strong enemy swarm. In the northern part of the village, invading enemy forces had the intention of widening this push to the south and cutting the only supply route for this forward *kampfgruppe* of the division "*LSSAH*" along the road from Kiev - Shitomir.

In this difficult situation, *SS-Hauptscharführer* Grebarsche, immediately recognizing the danger, made the decision to use a reserve platoon in the center. He attacked with his few men against this enemy stream of advancing Soviets coming from the north. As the lead fighter at the head of his men, he raced back and forth between them and, during a favorable lull, a new main battle line was gained. They were withdrawn at dawn under tank support against the threat of further attacks. The enemy lost 120 dead, 14 MG, and numerous handguns and firearms during this unexpected attack by Grebarsche.

Through this independent decision of *SS-Hauptscharführer* Grebarsche, the combined intention of the enemy to not only cut the supply route for Kotscherowo (runway Kiev - Zhitomir) but also defeat *Kampfgruppe Frey* in hard fighting was frustrated.

Also on 20.11.1943, the battalion launched strong mutual flank fire for their assault on Jastrebenka, intending to cut the road eastwards from Brussiloff, and *SS-Hauptscharführer* Grebarsche once again came to the fore. The attack, while delivered with the support of tanks, was mostly caught up with the hard defense against

> the enemy in the south of Jastrebenka. The outskirts of this place had Pakfronts there and the assaulting tanks were busy engaging them. Taking advantage of nightfall, *SS-Hauptscharführer* Grebarsche worked forward with his few men under difficult circumstances up to the enemy Pak positions. Here he destroyed several Pak and in the melee, the armored Battalion penetrated into the south part at the same time.
>
> *SS-Hauptscharführer* Grebarsche thus removed the requirement for the successful attack on the location and, connected to this, he removed the ability for the enemy to resupply there using this major road.
>
> *SS-Hauptscharführer* Grebarsche has, in all of his battles, been the last leader in the kompanie and is well proven to the highest degree. He has always proven how courageous and resolute he is.
>
> I think *SS-Hauptscharführer* Grebarsche, because of the bravery shown above and because of his almost daily proven boldness, his personal courage and strength, and above all his absolute crisis in defensive fighting is worthy of the high award of the Knight's Cross of the Iron Cross and please ask that we give this to him.

The *2nd Regiment* was running with a fighting strength of 281 men at this time, or to put that into context, less than half the normal strength of a battalion! This may help give the reader perspective on what Grebarsche and his men had to contend with.

The approval for this recommendation was given on January 24, 1944. This highest award was also accompanied by a promotion to *SS-Untersturmführer* backdated to November 9, 1943.

On April 20, 1944, Grebarsche was promoted to *SS-Obersturmführer*. He was wounded once more at some point later in 1944 (or this could have been during the heavy fighting in the first part of 1944). He was placed with SS Training and Replacement Battalion 1 based in Spreehagen and was in charge of one of the kompanies there. Between mid-August and late October 1944, he was in the training schools at Kienschlag, Putlos, and then Krampnitz.

He returned to the front line and, by the end of the war, was found in Austria with his *Leibstandarte* kameraden, where he surrendered in early May. He survived the war and died on February 11, 1992, in Zeuthen, Berlin.

Name: Hugo Kraas
Date of birth: 25.01.1911
SS Number: 289 633
Award: Oakleaves to the Knight's Cross

This *Waffen-SS* soldier was last featured in volume two, when we detailed his award of the Knight's Cross on March 28, 1943, for his various actions in February and March 1943, during the defensive and offensive actions around Kharkov.

He was promoted to *SS-Obersturmbannführer* on June 21, 1943, then in mid-October, he was awarded the Close Combat Clasp in Silver. Divisional Commander "Teddi" Wisch wrote a recommendation on January 3, 1944, for the award of the Oakleaves to his existing Knight's Cross. This comprehensive document read:

> I. On 05.07.1943, during operation "Zitadelle," *SS-Panzer-Grenadier Regiment 2* had the task of breaking open bunkers in the Russian positions south of Bykovka and to take Hill 234.8, north of Bykovka. The bunkers were tenaciously defended and well built up, enjoying an approach saturated with mines.
>
> During the night of 4. to 5.7.43 the unit attacked, after which the regiment's command posts were pushed forward to the former Russian outposts on Hill 228.8. After the new command post was situated, the regiment prepared to attack the forward lines at 04:00 hours in the strength of two battalions. The enemy's defensive fire was extremely strong. The grenadiers fought against the tenaciously defending Russians, and in spite of the enemy's performance were able to slowly gain more ground meter-by-meter. The enemy's resistance could only be broken with attack groups that annihilated his machine guns, heavy grenade launchers, and anti-tank gun positions in the tank ditches.
>
> During the extremely difficult battle there were heavy casualties. During the reorganization of the units there was a pause in the battle, enabling the Russians to strengthen their resistance. This crisis was resolved by the decisive personal action of Regimental Commander *SS-Obersturmbannführer* Kraas. Kraas, in the furthermost lines in the tank ditches, organized all remaining forces so the attack could be continued, and, since the combat engineers that had been subordinated to his battle group were all casualties, personally blew the tank and assault gun crossing over the tank ditches. Kraas,

himself a member of one of the attack groups equipped mostly only with shovels and hand grenades, then attacked the tanks on Hill 220.5 with his attack groups and broke them in the shortest time. Only by his heroic and personal example could the advance of the attack be continued.

After Hill 220.5 was taken, *SS-Obersturmbannführer* Kraas immediately ordered the continuance of the attack onto Bykovka and Hill 234.8 to the north of there. Rallied on by the exemplary bravery of their commander, the grenadiers reached their day's goal despite dogged defense by the Russians. *SS-Obersturmbannführer* Kraas was the driving force during these attacks. Continuously rushing to the hot spots of the battle with a handful of men he had gathered together he rallied his grenadiers to continue on and together with them managed to take Bykovka and Hill 234.8 at about 16:00 hours.

The exemplary bravery of *SS-Obersturmbannführer* Kraas and his decisive action is to be acknowledged, as the grenadiers accomplished the very important attack goals of the first day of the battle. These goals were necessary for the continuance of the attack along the entire southern front of the division.

II. On 27.12.1943, *SS-Panzer-Grenadier-Regiment 2*, under the leadership of *SS-Obersturmbannführer* Kraas, was positioned on the left open flank of the division in defense of the wide front from north to east. The Russians were deployed and ready for action with their strong tank and infantry forces near the eastern edge of Starosselje, to the eastern edge of Kotelnja, and up to the north of the railway. After the Russians advanced from north to east and back with tanks and lively reconnaissance forces, they attacked at about 13:00 hours in regimental strength, supported by thirteen T-34s used as assault guns. The attack became mired in the defensive fire of the grenadiers of *SS-Panzer-Grenadier-Regiment 2* and three T-34s were knocked out. Because of this strong defense, the enemy prepared their infantry and tank forces to advance on 27.12.1943. These forces, which were positioned before the section of the left open flank of *SS-Panzer-Grenadier-Regiment 2*, had the strength of about a *korps*. They were obviously positioned there to advance in a general southwesterly direction to break through the defensive front of *SS-Panzer-Grenadier-Regiment 2*, after which they would reach and secure the highway between Shitomir and Berditschev, and would then be able to surround Berditschev itself and attack the city.

This large attack began on 28.12.1943, at 02:30 hours, with an advance of 15 T-34s carrying infantry. The tanks advanced into the open left flank of the regiment from Toruvez. With a counter-advance by the Panzer group that was subordinated to the regiment the attack was beaten back. A further attack of 35 tanks carrying infantry came about an hour later and penetrated the left flank of the regiment and the regimental headquarters in Volossovo. The Panzer group of the regiment and its anti-tank weapons annihilated 19 T-34s together with the tank close combat troops. Many enemy casualties were counted. Regimental Commander *SS-Obersturmbannführer* Kraas, with the men of his regimental staff, personally led a counterattack against the right flank of the attacking enemy infantry. During this attack his men were able to annihilate the majority of the enemy infantry.

After this unsuccessful attack that claimed many Russian casualties, the enemy tanks pulled back to the railway to regroup. Their new plan was to attack at 12:30 hours in a strength of two regiments with 40 tanks and in a strength of two regiments and 20 tanks from the north and east out of the area between the villages Schubarovka, Toruvez, and Jusofovka to Staraja-Kotelnja. Even though the division and korps both foresaw a retreat of the regiment to the southern bank of the Guiva section, *SS-Obersturmbannführer* Kraas was able to hold up the enemy by building a new main fighting line directly south of the street intended to be used by the attacking Russian forces.

Through this decision, his personal action at the build-up of the main fighting line, and his decisive engagement at the defense of this attack, *SS-Obersturmbannführer* Kraas avoided the encirclement of his regiment and the heavy weapons under his command.

Meanwhile, the Russians achieved a breakthrough on the left flank of the regiment. *SS-Obersturmbannfuhrer* Kraas led the men of his regimental staff and some tanks in a counterattack; seven enemy tanks were knocked out. After successfully defending against an infantry attack, the Russians pulled back with the mass of their tanks to the northwest.

In the meantime, a divisional order arrived to retreat to the new security line south of the Guiva section. The carrying out of this order became difficult because the bridge foreseen to be used by the regiment for the crossing of heavy weapons had been destroyed.

Hugo Kraas in a formal pose to reflect the award of the Oakleaves to his existing Knight's Cross—the first set awarded in 1944.

Despite constantly increasing enemy pressure and strong fire of enemy tanks and rockets from the east and north of the crossing, *SS-Obersturmbannführer* Kraas successfully brought over all heavy weapons in the company of Panther tanks (which were driving parallel to the Russian lines) to a crossing farther to the west. It is without question the decisive and meaningful leadership of *SS-Obersturmbannführer* Kraas, who himself was the last to remain on the bridge, must be thanked for the fighting portions of the staff and vehicles of heavy weapons did not fall into enemy hands, or, better said, were not surrounded by them.

During the evening of 29.12.1943, the enemy occupied the new main fighting line with tanks and infantry and won a strong bridgehead position over the Guiva section. From this strong bridgehead the Russians attacked positions of *SS-Panzer-Grenadier-Regiment 2* with strong infantry forces and 20 tanks on numerous occasions during the late morning hours.

Fully utilizing a ditch northwest of Voroschino, the opponent attacked the village directly with tanks, during which the first portions of the enemy infantry managed to push their way into the northern sector of the village. This caused a battle crisis, as portions of I Battalion pulled back to the village following the death of its battalion commander and almost all of its NCOs, during which the enemy went directly to the west and around Voroschino, then around our positions and advanced to the south. In this critical situation, *SS-Obersturmbannführer* Kraas pulled together all available forces: messengers, signals men, radiomen, drivers, medics, etc. Himself armed with a machine pistol and later a machine gun, he accompanied them, and along the row of houses to the north and northwest he threw back the enemy units that had broken through and built a new main fighting line directly on the edge of the village. All further enemy attacks were beaten off, and, with that, an orderly withdrawal was secured for the entire regiment before the coming sunset.

By holding this village and inflicting an extraordinary amount of casualties upon the opponent during the defensive fighting of the previous day, *SS-Panzer-Grenadier-Regiment 2* depleted the spearhead of the Russian tank army heading to the southwest of the majority of its attack forces. They also enabled the withdrawal of all portions of the division to the new main fighting line northeast of Berditschev and enhanced their ability to establish positions there.

> Under the leadership of *SS-Obersturmbannführer* Kraas *SS-Panzer-Grenadier-Regiment 2* either captured or destroyed the following:
>
> | | |
> |---|---|
> | 91 | Enemy tanks, almost all of which were T-34s, of which 29 were taken in close combat |
> | 63 | Anti-tank guns |
> | 15 | Cannons |
> | 36 | Trucks |
> | 49 | Hand-held anti-tank weapons |
> | 118 | Machine guns |
> | 31 | Grenade launchers |
> | 3 | Airplanes |
> | 6 | Field Kitchens |
> | 8 | Limbers (horse-drawn artillery ammunition wagons) |
> | 29 | Horse and carriage teams |
> | 3,200 | Enemy killed |
> | 900 | Prisoners |
>
> *SS-Obersturmbannführer* Kraas proved himself as a fighter, tutor, and leader at all times and in the highest manner. His personal courage, decisiveness, and composure are exceptional and remain a shining example for his men.
>
> I hold *SS-Obersturmbannführer* Kraas as worthy of the award of the Oakleaves to the Knight's Cross of the Iron Cross because of his excellent leadership and his spirit of adventure, as well as his exemplary personal bravery and ability to remain unshakable.

In addition to this, there was a one-word addition from Dietrich which simply said, "Agreed."

This recommendation was approved on January 24, 1944. Kraas was promoted less than a week later to *SS-Standartenführer* on January 30, 1944. However, there is a document in his file dated November 28, 1943, which states he was promoted on that date. From mid-January, he is listed as being with the SS main office, followed by a stint with the *I. SS-Panzer Korps*. He took part in a divisional commander's course in September and October, then assumed command of the *12. SS-Panzer Division "Hitler Jugend"* on November 19, 1944. He led this division through the Ardennes campaign at the close of 1944; a promotion to *SS-Oberführer* followed at the end of January 1945. He then went with his men into Hungary and Austria in 1945. A final promotion to *SS-Brigadeführer* came on April 20, 1945. He led his soldiers to the Enns River on May 8 and surrendered to American forces there. He was kept as a prisoner of war until 1948. After his release, he kept in touch with his former kameraden via the HIAG organization. He was one of the men in the front row at Sepp Dietrich's funeral in 1966. Kraas himself died on February 20, 1980.

The next award would continue with recognition for the *Leibstandarte*. This soldier is one who had an almost two-year length of service under the overall command of Hugo Kraas and would be approved for his award the same day as Kraas.

Name: Joachim Peiper
Date of birth: 30.01.1915
SS Number: 132 496
Award: Knight's Cross with Oakleaves

Joachim Peiper is another of the *Waffen-SS* soldiers who was previously featured in volume 2—in chapter 2, when he was awarded the Knight's Cross on March 9, 1943, for his forming of the bridgehead near *Federowka-Hf. Bridock*. Let us now detail his further activities since that date.

On May 6, 1943, Peiper could add the German Cross in Gold to his growing list of awards, which was approved following actions in early February. During the Kursk offensive he knocked out an enemy tank and was awarded the Tank Destruction Badge on July 21. The Close Combat Clasp in Silver followed on October 20 and then in November, Peiper's career would take a direction that most people know him for: command of the *Leibstandarte's* Panzer regiment. The existing commander, Georg Schonberger, was killed on November 20 and Peiper was chosen as his replacement. The remaining days of 1943 were among the hardest endured by the men of the *Leibstandarte*. It was also these remaining days of 1943 that would form the basis of Peiper's Oakleaves recommendation put together by "Teddi" Wisch on December 27; the lengthy document read:

> On 4.12.1943, the division was given the mission to launch an attack from the area northwest of Tschernjachoff and over the line Mokrentschina – Pekartschina into the flank of the enemy forces facing the *XIII. Army* korps and smash these forces. Then, along with the other divisions of the *XXXXVIII. Panzerkorps*, it was to

make it possible for the *XIII. Army* korps to wheel against the Teterew in combination, then proceed with that korps and establish contact with the *LIX. Army Korps*.

Kampfgruppe Peiper (*SS-Panz.Rgt. 1* reinforced *SS-Pz. Aufkl. Abt. 1*, *III. (armored)/SS-Panz.Gren.Rgt. 2*, *2./SS-Pz.Pi. Btl. 1*, and *5./SS-Flak-Abt. 1*) was given the mission, starting at 15:00 hours on 5.12.1943, of bypassing enemy occupied Tschernjachoff on the west by night, gaining ground north of Tschernjachoff on a broad front through Andrejew and the high ground on both sides of Styrty and later, without regard to flanking threats, moving towards Radomyschl.

After the forward elements of the *kampfgruppe* had taken Sseljantschina at 20:00 hours on 5.12.1943, reconnaissance by the *III. (armored) / SS-Panz.Gren.Rgt. 2* discovered the enemy had taken up positions in depth west of Pekarschtschina and had set up for an all-round perimeter defense in the village itself. As the village could not be bypassed because of unfavorable terrain conditions and the bridges in the village had to fall into our hands undamaged, *SS-Sturmbannführer* Peiper took over personal command of the armored battalion. He had commanded that shortly before and carried out a night attack on the village with incredible courage, relentlessly destroying the enemy forces in their positions in and in front of the village using flame throwers and other weapons from the armored personnel carriers.

With a subsequent reconnaissance against Andrejew during which *SS-Sturmbannführer* Peiper personally led the way, he obtained important documents for the day's attack by his armored group.

With this, he was able to move forward due to nighttime reconnaissance and in a morning attack took Andrejew at 06:00 hours—after close combat with a Pakfront—and blocked the main road between Tschernjachoff – Korosten. The *kampfgruppe* advanced eastward from Andrejew with a *batterie* and won several more anti-tank positions. By 10:00 hours, the high ground on both sides of Styrty had been taken and, with this, the first day's attack goals had been reached.

In an unrelenting march the kampfgruppe moved further east, destroying enemy batteries and Pakfronts; by this advance they reached the positions of the *121. Schtz. Div.* in Klisselowka, the *322. Schtz. Div.* in Seliyzschy, the *148. Schtz. Div.* in Kamenny

A happy-looking Joachim Peiper with the Oakleaves on top of his Knight's Cross.

Brid, and the *336. Schtz. Div.* in Kaitanowka, where they had to stop and resupply.

The kampfgruppe captured or destroyed on this day:

22 Guns,
76 Anti-tank guns 7.62cm,
38 Anti-tank rifles,
49 Machine-guns,
40 Vehicles
71 Horse-drawn vehicles and
1450 Dead.

Through this advance, which took the armored group through extraordinarily difficult ground and 30 km into the rear of the enemy, the entire Russian front was captured on a broad front and allowed the divisions of the *XIII. Army* korps to proceed.

Since the enemy had temporarily interrupted the supply route during the course of 6.12.1943, the *Panzergruppe* wasn't able to continue its advance west to Tschaikowka until sometime in the afternoon of 7.12.1943.

The Russians had rapidly brought in anti-tank guns and fortified the terrain to an extraordinary degree in this location. To avoid losses, *SS-Sturmbannführer* Peiper decided not to move out until darkness, when he would bypass Tschaikowka to the north and then advance east.

Around 19:00 hours, the *Panzergruppe* was already in the enemy's rear, had eliminated the resistance of a few anti-tank guns, and had advanced about 10 km to the east. The kampfgruppe then wheeled to the north on orders from division, took Chodory, then pushed on to the north into heavily fortified Sabolot. After intense house-to-house fighting, *SS-Sturmbannführer* Peiper was able to report by 10:00 hours in the morning that the village was firmly in our hands.

During this night attack *Kampfgruppe Peiper* captured or destroyed:

1 T-34 Tank
8 Guns
1 Anti-tank gun 4.5cm
61 Anti-tank guns 7.62cm
21 Anti-tank rifles

55 Machine-guns
5 Trucks
930 Enemy dead and
3 Prisoners

As a result of this night attack—once again operating deep behind enemy lines—*SS-Sturmbannführer* Peiper had smashed a breach through the enemy's defensive system of deeply echeloned strongpoints and prevented it from establishing an operational bridgehead across the Teterew.

During this period of combat *SS-Sturmbannführer* Peiper demonstrated extraordinary personal bravery and outstanding tactical leadership of his strong unit. His personal dash, his battle plan, and the decisive execution of that plan, as well as his lightning-fast recognition and exploitation of favorable opportunities, contributed to this major victory for his *Panzergruppe* and by extension for the division.

In addition, during the brief period from 21.11. to 24.12.1943, *SS-Panzer-Regiment 1,* under the command of *SS-Sturmbannführer* Peiper, captured or destroyed a total of:

100 T-34 Tanks
11 Guns
124 Anti-tank guns 7.62cm
24 Anti-tank rifles
16 Trucks
14 Prime-movers
7 Anti-aircraft guns and
2 Aircraft (Li 2).

I consider *SS-Sturmbannführer* Peiper—for the extraordinary personal bravery which he has continuously shown and for the outstanding leadership he has given his regiment—worthy of the award of the Oakleaves to the Knight's Cross of the Iron Cross and request that this high decoration be granted to him.

As this recommendation was being considered, Peiper himself left the front line due to illness on January 20, 1944. The approval for adding the Oakleaves to his existing Knight's Cross came one week later and Peiper was sent to receive the award personally from the Führer. He then received a promotion to *SS-Obersturmbannführer* on January 30. We will leave the coverage of Joachim Peiper at this point, but return to his history in the final volume, as he was not done with the various grades of this medal just yet.

Name: Fritz Bunse
Date of birth: 04.07.1911
SS Number: 30 303
Award: Knight's Cross

Born in Hagen, Westfalia, he entered the *SS* at the start of November 1931. He was one of the initial 117 men that formed the basis of what became the *Leibstandarte Adolf Hitler* in March 1933. At the start of April 1936, he was holding the rank *SS-Oberscharführer* and was sent to the SS officer's school at Braunschweig, staying there until early 1937. He was promoted to *SS-Untersturmführer* on April 20, 1937. During the remainder of 1937 and into 1938, he attended various pioneer training courses, with a promotion to *SS-Obersturmführer* coming at the start of September 1938. Remaining with the *LSSAH*, he took part in the Sudetenland campaign prewar.

He remained with the *LSSAH* during the Polish and Western campaigns and was awarded the Second Class Iron Cross on June 3, 1940. At the start of August, he moved to *16.* kompanie within the *SS-Germania Regiment*, which became part of the *SS-Division Wiking*. A promotion to *SS-Hauptsturmführer* came at the end of January 1941. He went east into Russia in mid-1941 and soon earned the First Class Iron Cross on August 12. The Infantry Assault Badge was awarded on February 18, 1942. At the start of May, he was with the Pioneer Replacement Battalion, then the pioneer schools at Beneschau and Hradischko until the end of June 1943. While there, the award of the Russian Front medal came on September 9, 1942, then the War Merit Cross 2nd Class with Swords on April 20, 1943. It was also in June 1943 that he received a promotion to *SS-Sturmbannführer*. When he returned to the front line, he was sent to the *III. (Germanisches) SS-Panzer* korps as SS-Pioneer Battalion 11 Commander. He had also been awarded the Black Wound Badge, but no exact award date is listed.

On January 19, 1944, *11. SS-Freiwilligen Panzergrenadier Division Nordland* Divisional Commander Fritz von Scholz wrote the following recommendation for the Knight's Cross to the Iron Cross (endorsed by Felix Steiner):

A very poor quality image of Fritz Bunse taken after his award of the Knight's Cross. Despite his early entry into the *SS* and his subsequent career, clear images of this soldier are very hard to come by.

SS-Sturmbannführer Bunse has, since 12.1.44, occupied a blocking position in the forest southeastward of Poroshki with *2.* kompanie from his II Pioneer Battalion. Their occupation was in place by the 14th, as per his orders, despite the time of year. On 14.1, a Russian attack started on this small blocking position. He was under the verbal command of the commander of *9. Luftwaffe Field Division*. Compared to the attack on Poroshki, the enemy attack collapsed and hardly indented his position. He started here, with the left and right wide open, against a vastly superior enemy who attacked his right flank in the forest simultaneously. On his own initiative, he attacked the enemy using his right kompanie and fought to take back this blocking position.

His people had been physically battered by the attacks through deep snow, against their insufficient positions, only partially dug snow holes—eight of which were under the most heavy artillery fire (drum beat and salvo fire)—and mass attacks from tanks supported by guided aerial attacks. These attacks from the far superior enemy resulted in high bloody losses for them and significant losses to our own men. During the final two attacks the two neighboring positions were overrun. The strength displayed by his young troops (60% new young men in this position) has only been possible because of his personal actions in the foremost lines. His courage was a model of exemplary bravery. His battalion, by this and as a single unit, held the position through two long days.

After the enemy had broken into the position with tanks, on the evening of 15.01, he used a combat patrol to push it back and recover the wounded, leaving the last of his men in the position with machine pistols. In this southeast position they were good from there to the village of Lewolowo.

Here he defended, moving from the left and right of two kompanies of Infantry Regiment 176 with a further 1 leader, 1 NCO, 11 men (the rest of his battle group had either fallen or were wounded) through another two night attacks by the Soviets.

Against these measures the enemy was forced to learn of the toughness of *SS-Panzer Pioneer Battalion 11*, which they learned from analyzing radio traffic.

Through the exemplary self sacrifice of the battalion encouraged to the highest achievements by his exemplary commander, *SS-Stubaf.* Bunse, it was possible for the group "*Schwerstes Flachfeuer*" to effect a withdrawal of the hostile enemy.

In addition to this formal recommendation there is a detailed two-page typed document that is a record of a radio conversation that took place over two days of the battle. This document refers to the "Battle of the Bucket," which covers the area where Bunse and his men fought. The document finishes by stating that at the end of the fighting there were only forty of Bunse's men left standing.

This recommendation was approved on January 30, 1944, and gave *11. SS-Panzergrenadier Division Nordland* their first of many Knight's Crosses.

In June, he was promoted to *SS-Obersturmbannführer*. At the end of the following month he was temporarily leading *SS-Regiment "De Ruiter."* He is listed as being on the reserve officer's list from December, potentially following an earlier wound in October. He attended a regimental commander's training course between February and March 1945. He is also listed as spending time with the staff of *VI. SS-Freiwilligen* korps *(Lettisches)* and the *V. SS-Gebirgs Korps*.

Fritz Bunse survived the war and died on September 14, 1970, in Herne.

Name: Michael Wittmann
Date of birth: 22.04.1914
SS Number: 311 623
Award: Knight's Cross with Oakleaves

We have already featured this soldier as the second person awarded the Knight's Cross in 1944. This further award was approved only sixteen days later, on January 30, 1944. It is not the first time the same soldier has been featured twice in the same volume, but it *is* the first time a soldier has been featured twice in the same chapter of one volume!

There does not appear to be a telex from Wisch this time, or if there was, it does not survive in his file. There is an official communiqué:

> On 30/1/44 *SS-Untersturmführer* Michael Wittmann, who was named in the Wehrmacht communiqué on 13/1/44 and decorated with the Knight's Cross, platoon commander in an SS Panzer regiment of the *Leibstandarte SS Adolf Hitler* from Ingolstadt on the Danube, became the 380th soldier to be decorated by the Führer with the Knight's Cross of the Iron Cross with Oakleaves. The Führer sent him the following telegram:
>
> In grateful appreciation of your heroic action in the struggle for the future of our people, I award you as the 380th soldier of the

Part of my own collection, this hand-signed image of Michael Wittmann captures him in Normandy while wearing the Oakleaves to his Knight's Cross. He is the first of two soldiers that will appear twice in this volume.

> German Armed Forces the Knight's Cross of the Iron Cross with Oakleaves. Adolf Hitler.

Why was there this unprecedented and incredibly short time frame between both levels of this, the highest bravery award within the German armed forces at that time? While Wisch was sending his first telex and the Führer was considering this, Wittmann was kept busy with major enemy tank attacks. Even on the day he and Bobby Woll were presented their Knight's Crosses the fighting was continuing, and after that. By the closing days of January 1944, Wittmann (and Woll) had inflicted huge levels of destruction on their Soviet enemy, with 117 enemy tanks to Wittman's name. His skill was unquestionable and helped to cement his legend as the best Germany had to offer, especially when put in control of their best fighting vehicle.

The fact Wittmann was nominated and approved for this second level award meant he was the lowest ranking holder of the Oakleaves to the Knight's Cross. This quickly changed, as on January 30 Wittmann was promoted to *SS-Obersturmführer*. He was sent personally to meet the Führer to receive his Oakleaves. This presentation from the head of the armed forces would not end Michael Wittmann's connection to this medal; for now, just consider his accomplishments and the fact that this man was approved for the first two grades of the Knight's Cross within sixteen days of each other!

CHAPTER TWO

HOLD NARWA, ESCAPE KORSUN! - FEBRUARY 1944

The northern push was meant to remove the Germans from that sector of the USSR and roll up the Baltic countries too, but Steiner's *III. (Germanisches) SS-Panzer-Korps* had other ideas. Let's detail the actions that prevented the realization of Soviet ambitions at the time.

11. SS-Panzergrenadier Division Nordland

Their arrival at Jamburg the final day of January was meant to be a blocking move and a strong position, using the river as a natural defensive line. The Soviet advance reached that location around the same time and Jamburg had to be given up quickly, with orders issued to move to Narwa. The fighting at Jamburg on the last day of January and first two days of February would place great strain on the defensive efforts of *SS-Division Nordland*, but would also provide opportunities for the soldiers of that division to add more Knight's Cross wearers to their ranks. One of these was to Divisional Commander *SS-Brigadeführer* Fritz von Scholz, who would receive the Oakleaves to his existing Knight's Cross. *SS-Obersturmbannführer* Arnold Stoffers and *SS-Sturmbannführer* Hanns-Heinrich Lohmann would be awarded the Knight's Cross.

The move to the defensive line at Narwa brought the *Waffen-SS* troops in the northern sector of the eastern front into the boundaries of Estonia; their two-and-a-half year occupation of that area of the Soviet Union was now at an end. This was also the first "friendly" country they would find themselves defending against the onslaught of the Soviet military machine; it would certainly not be their last, as Berlin was a mere 1,000 miles away! They did not have time to dwell on the fact, as they were too busy focusing on trying to halt the enemy along the Narwa River line. That line ran north to south from Hungerburg on the coast and to the top of the Narwa Reservoir in the south, with the city of Narwa being the focal point of defensive efforts; that defensive line came under almost immediate attack as February began to unfold.

SS-Regiment Danmark held the southern portion of Narwa city, while the battered remnants of *Norge* were placed along the line. Elements of that regiment, under the command of *SS-Sturmbannführer* Albrecht Krugel, battled against the enemy around Vepskula and Ssivertsi from February 12. The fighting became the focal point of the enemy activity at the time and as such, the intensity was strong. Krugel played his part holding these vital areas, fighting alongside the pioneers from *Nederland* until he was wounded, earning Krugel the Knight's Cross. The fighting continued through to the end of the month, with the Estonian SS men joining the battle too; their actions will be detailed.

Nordland's Aufklarung's Battalion fought an enemy coastal landing at Merekula. The fighting took place on February 14–15 and resulted in the complete defeat of the Soviet raiding battalion.

In the final week of February, additional elements of *Nordland* were sent to the southwest at Waiwara. The enemy was pushing in from that direction with the aim of linking with their westerly advancing comrades north of Narwa. On February 25, the *Norge* soldiers under *SS-Obersturmbannführer* Arnold Stoffers pushed against the enemy. Stoffers and some of his men were killed in this fighting, which succeeded in halting further enemy advances at that time. Stoffers's approval for the award of the Knight's Cross would come just over two weeks later and was for his actions at the start of February.

4. SS-Freiwilligen-Panzergrenadier Brigade Nederland

As January came to a close, the men of *Nederland* had already been ordered to move to Narwa. They took up their positions as February opened, with the bulk of the brigade in the northern sector of Narwa and also farther north. They strengthened their line as best they could while the enemy continued to probe along the river line.

February 12 saw a peak in the enemy's efforts around Ssivertsi. *Nederland's* pioneers held that place against the Soviets with the assistance of elements of *SS-Regiment Norge*. The fighting raged for the remainder of February, with the *SS-Estonian Division* joining the fray during the final week or so.

20. Waffen-Grenadier Division der SS (Estnische Nr. 1)

The general Russian offensive that began in early January would imminently hit Estonian territory, so the existing men from the *Estonian SS* were sent north from Idritsa to the Narwa front area the first week of February. En route, the advance units under *SS-Sturmbannführer* Haralt Riiplau were diverted and took part in a short engagement with the Russians on the western bank of Lake Peipsi, east of Tartu. That fighting lasted from the fifteenth through to the seventeenth. They then carried on northward to their Estonian kameraden who were arriving in the Narwa area. Their arrival placed them under the command of *Steiner's* korps and gave him another SS division to bolster his numbers. The addition of the Estonians increased the "range" of the foreign volunteers within the ranks of the *"Germanic" SS-Panzer* korps even further.

They took up positions around Vepskula and prepared to attack the Soviet bridgehead there. As February closed, the Estonians engaged the enemy for the first time and that first taste of action resulted in their first Knight's Cross holder.

To the southeast . . .

VI. SS-Freiwilligen korps *(Lettisches)*

This recently raised *SS-Korps* arrived in the Velikaya River area in late February and assumed command of the *15. Lettische SS-Freiwilligen Division*, which was joined by the *2. Latvian SS-Freiwilligen Brigade.* That brigade was upgraded to the *19. Waffen-Grenadier Division der SS (Lettische Nr. 2)* at the same time. The command of this *SS-Korps* was under the control of *SS-Obergruppenführer* Karl von Pfeffer-Wildenbruch. Let us detail what this second *SS-Korps* operating in the north of Russia in early 1944 had to contend with.

15. Waffen-Grenadier Division der SS (Lettische Nr. 1)

Moving into the Belebelka area would soon give them their second engagement with the enemy, which took place on February 5, around Kholodovo, and lasted four days. Their next fight came in the middle of the month, when the Latvians were positioned east of Dedovichi, at Belebelka. That short battle lasted two days and resulted in the defeat of the Soviet attackers, who came from two directions. Just after this, they were ordered around 10 km

(6.2 miles) westward, back to the Polist River. At the same time their commander was changed when *SS-Oberführer* Nikolaus Heilmann took over for *SS-Brigadeführer* Puckler-Burghauss. In the closing week of February, the Soviets pushed against these Latvians as they moved towards their new positions during a heavy snowstorm. Those moves were complete by the end of the month.

They were now around sixty miles to the southwest, on the Velikaya River, and had been titled the Panther Positions. Their headquarters was at Kruki, with their newly arrived *19. SS Latvian* kameraden to the north at Voronkovo.

The recent change in name for their *19. SS-Division* kameraden resulted in a renaming for them also.

19. Waffen-Grenadier Division der SS (Lettische Nr. 2)

During February, they continued to move in a general southwesterly direction that took them through Kutkova, Kostrin, Gorodnja, Rusenye, Bol. Utorgosh, Borok, Gorodok, and Dubrovno. They were harassed the entire way and had to move through enemy groups backed by partisans. Losses mounted, but determination to reach friendly lines urged them on. Those friendly lines were crossed on February 26, 1944. The following day, what was left of this new SS "division" was loaded onto rail transports and sent towards the Velikaya River, where they were to be positioned close to the area of their sister formation, the *15. SS-Division*.

To the northeast . . .

Kampfgruppe SS-Polizei Division

They continued to move away from the enemy until early February, when they became encircled again at Oredesh. By the second half of the month they were southwest of Nikolajewo. It was in these positions that *SS-Sturmbannführer* Traupe was presented with his Knight's Cross by Gen. Speth. By the end of February they were southeast of Pleskau, between Krakuscha and Twerdunowo.

As the *Waffen-SS* soldiers in the north held the Narwa front and contended with attacks in other areas, their southern kameraden were fixated on the impending disaster of the Korsun Pocket. Let's see what took place during February 1944 in Army Group South.

5. SS-Panzer Division Wiking

The Korsun Pocket had been closed up in the last few days of January 1944. During the first week of February 1944, these *SS-Wiking* soldiers resisted the enemy and played their part in holding the pocket, albeit across a smaller area of ground, thereby avoiding destruction. *Wiking* was in the southeast sector of the pocket at that time and on February 2, *SS-Oberscharführer* Fritz Biegi conducted actions at Orlowez that would result in his later award of the Knight's Cross. The fighting at Orlowez would also contribute to Hans Dorr's later Swords award (both covered in volume 5).

On February 2, *SS-Unterscharführer* Gerhard Fischer defended Burty with his self-propelled guns; it was the main security line then and lay about twenty miles directly south of Goroditsche. Fischer's actions resulted in him receiving the Knight's Cross.

On February 7, after realizing the holding of the pocket would be impossible, orders were issued for the men to break out to the west and link with friendly forces. This seemingly straightforward task on paper was a world away in reality, and the time in between orders and their completion would require a huge exertion of effort from the men of *Wiking*, but would also result in further Knight's Cross related actions. The "breakout" task involved the men within the pocket to move collectively westward and retake positions that had been under their control only days earlier. This retaking would have to be done against a formidable enemy. *Wiking* itself was considered a strong force within the pocket, despite the exertions it had undergone in the past couple weeks. Therefore, they were moved from their positions at Goroditsche and sent farther north to Korsun, so they could help lead the punch out of the Soviet ring around them; they would be fighting alongside their *SS-Walloon* kameraden in this upcoming action.

In preparation for the main breakout movement westward some key locations had to be taken and held; some of these were assigned to the men of *Wiking*. During the second week of February 1944, Schanderowka and Nowo-Buda came under control of *Wiking*, while the northern and southern extremes in the east of the pocket had to be defended against. Over February 8–9, *SS-Obersturmbannführer* Manfred Schonfelder defended Goroditsche, resulting in his award of the Knight's Cross. Over February 10–12, *SS-Obersturmbannführer* Joachim Richter defended against enemy thrusts farther north at Korsun, which also added him to the ranks of *Waffen-SS* Knight's Cross holders. While this was going on, *SS-Obersturmführer* Werner Meyer was conducting his Knight's Cross actions at Schanderowka between February 11 and 13. Also on the thirteenth, *SS-Obersturmführer* Kurt Schumacher was fighting in Nowo-Buda, which would result in him later becoming a *Waffen-SS* Knight's Cross holder. All of these awards took place over a period of a few days at the various extremes of the pocket. They are testament to the intensity of the fighting, the German defenders who were intent on reaching friendly forces, and the Soviets, who were equally determined to inflict another bloody defeat on enclosed enemy troops just as they had done one year earlier at Stalingrad. The fighting was continuous for all of these men and their *Heer* kameraden with one notable casualty on February 13: *SS-Wallonien* commander *SS-Sturmbannführer* Lucien Lippert was killed at Nowo-Buda.

By February 16, the conditions were considered right and the necessary locations were under control for the main push westward. From outside the pocket, the relieving forces had been moving eastward against strong Soviet forces, battling the weather and resulting poor "road" conditions; they now stood less than eight miles from one another. The *SS* men held the southern sector of what now constituted the pocket. *Wiking* was located between Schanderowka and Komarowka, with their *Wallonian* kameraden to their rear towards Nowo-Buda. The main focus of the relief effort would be Hill .239, close to Oktyabar and northeast of Lissjanka.

Wiking's effort would be led by the reconnaissance battalion under the command of *SS-Obersturmführer* Heinrich Debus; he had to lead the SS breakout attempt through enemy held positions in Dshurshenzy to the north and Potschapinzy to the south—a gap of about two miles! His advance towards Lissjanka and battle with opposing forces during February 16–17 would later earn him the Knight's Cross. Lissjanka was also where Walter Schmidt displayed further bravery; the fighting on his part would make up the final aspect of his subsequent Oakleaves recommendation. The push westward was made during the night of February 16–17, 1944. This movement was under the dominant view of the Russians, who held the height of Hill .239. The Soviet tanks rained further death upon these men, as they could see the line of safety within their reach: the Gniloi Tikitsch River.

This natural barrier represented a final test for the men of *Wiking* and *Wallonie*, one that some of them would not pass, as they lost their lives in their attempts to cross the ice cold swollen water obstacle. One man that made it across was *Wiking* Commander *SS-Gruppenführer* Herbert Gille. Former *Waffen-SS* soldier Ferdinand Kaisergruber was near Gille when he made the crossing.

Gille and the remaining men of *Wiking*—numbering just over 7,000—continued westward until they reached the lead elements of their *Waffen-SS* kameraden from the *Leibstandarte*. Rear elements crossed into the hands of the *LSSAH* over the following day, too. As the lead elements were reaching

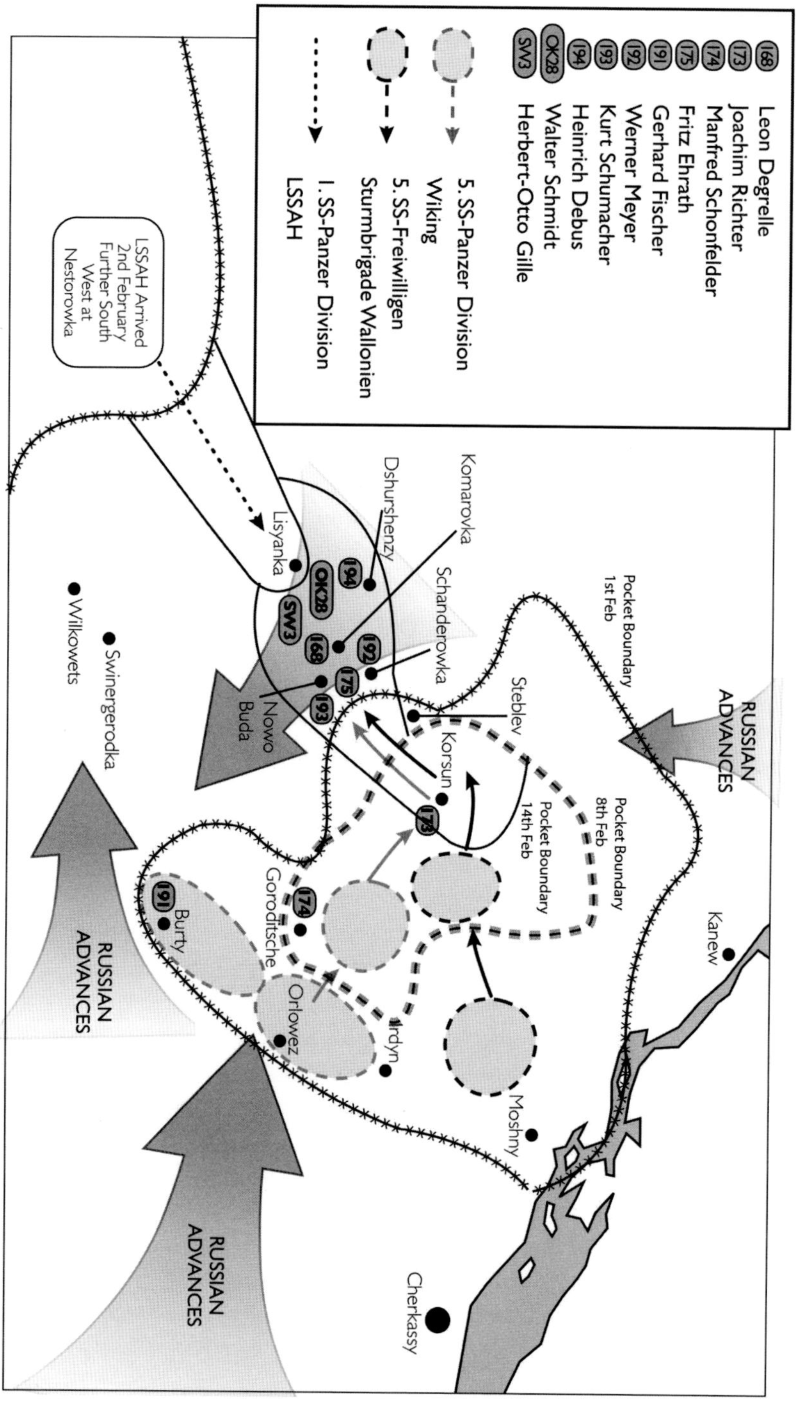

Map 10 – Korsun Pocket Tightens and the Breakout: February 1944

friendly troops, the rear of the pocket still had to be held to allow as many people as possible to escape Soviet capture or worse. One such rear guard action took place at Schanderowka, under the command of *SS-Obersturmbannführer* Fritz Ehrath. His would be the first of the "Cherkassy" Knight's Crosses awarded after Gille's Swords and will be detailed in this volume.

5. *SS-Freiwilligen Sturmbrigade Wallonien*

Hemmed within the recently closed Korsun Pocket at the start of February, the *Wallonien* men began moving towards Nowo-Buda, within the northern sector of the pocket. The enemy was not long in arriving, and on February 13, the Belgians were hit by a combined tank and infantry assault; Commander *SS-Sturmbannführer* Lucien Lippert was killed by an enemy sniper that day. They could not withstand the enemy onslaught, so orders were issued for the evacuation of this location and an attempt to break out westward was decided upon and set for February 17, 1944.

The above coverage of *Wiking* pretty much reflects the experiences of the men from *Wallonie*. They moved towards the Gniloi Tikitsch River under constant attack. The body of their former commander was initially taken with them, but an enemy shell put paid to his remains in the final stages of the breakout. The remnants of *Wallonie* made it across the river; just over 600 Belgians survived, but they left behind over 1,000 kameraden; their new commander was *SS-Hauptsturmführer* Leon Degrelle. For his actions in this particular battle, Degrelle was awarded the Knight's Cross on February 20, 1944—personally presented by Adolf Hitler.

> Here are the recollections of a former *SS-Wallonien* soldier; at the time of the fighting in Korsun he was *SS-Rottenführer* Ferdinand Kaisergruber; I visited him at his home in 2006. During the breakout attempts he received a wound from a Russian shell splinter; the force of the blast broke his tibia and forced it through his skin. He started to crawl along on his elbows—the fear of being captured by the Soviets was too great! After 150 meters (492 feet) the elbows of his coat had worn through and the pain became too great. Kaisergruber contemplated suicide with his pistol at this point, but then a savior came along.
>
> A *Wehrmacht* kameraden came by and offered to help him. The enemy gunfire had broken a pack of horses free and they were moving in a line and the *Wehrmacht* soldier was on the back of one of these horses. He helped Kaisergruber onto the back of another

horse and they continued westward together. A little while later, a Russian machine gun bullet went through the neck of the horse and it fell over dead. The fall took Kaisergruber with him and unfortunately trapped his good leg underneath. While lying there he noticed blood oozing out and realized the bullet that had killed the horse had also penetrated his own arm; the extreme cold was preventing him from feeling the pain. Due to this he decided to remove the bullet with his teeth, as the cold was starting to freeze the oozing blood!

His army friend helped him once again onto the back of another horse. That horse was later killed by an anti-tank round, so Kaisergruber had to move to a third horse. When they finally reached the Gniloi Tikitsch River, Kasiergruber watched in disbelief as *SS-General* Gille stripped naked, tossed his clothes to the opposite bank, and then entered the freezing river. Gille retained his cap on his head, but it initially started to float away. He grabbed it and placed it back on his head and carried onto the opposite bank, where he then redressed. This unusual decision may seem odd to some readers—why cross an ice-cold river naked—but it ensured Gille had dry clothes to wear once on the opposite bank, which probably saved his life in the sub-zero weather! Kaisergruber recalled the temperature was around -8 or -9 degrees. He himself made it across the river, but the opposite bank was one-and-a-half meters (five feet) higher and he only made it up this bank with the help of more kameraden; his third horse could not make it up. He tried to move his arm but the jacket was frozen, so he had to break the sleeve to be able to move his arm. Kaisergruber was promoted to *SS-Unterscharführer* later in 1944 and held the Second Class Iron Cross, Infantry Assault Badge, Silver Wound Badge, and Close Combat Clasp in Silver.

The enemy attempts to destroy the men within the Korsun Pocket had not borne the fruit they had aimed for. Out of the 60,000 men trapped, around 40,000 escaped to fight another day. This had been portrayed as a second Stalingrad for the Germans by the Soviets and Western governments, but the facts of their claims did not back up the reality of the situation. It was an utter defeat for Hitler's troops, but the appearance of Degrelle and Gille in the weeks after this fighting only gave their enemies embarrassing changes of "story" to explain. This was small comfort for the survivors and the wider German situation. The survivors focused on resting and being part of a refit of their respective units. Hitler and his generals had the realization that the enemy was even farther westward than they were when 1944 began, and now there were even less troops to face them.

1. SS-Panzer Division Leibstandarte SS Adolf Hitler

The worsening situation within the Korsun Pocket required a relief force, part of which was to be the *Leibstandarte*. They had moved fifty miles to the area around Nesterowka by February 2. They closed up over the next two days and then, in the final hours of the fourth, they began their moves. They initially went to the northeast toward Krassnyj and then farther northward to Tinowka, which took them to the seventh, by which time the high command had issued orders for the trapped forces within the Korsun Pocket to link up with friendly forces. That was initially to be Lissjanka to the east, but before getting there, the men of the *LSSAH* had to hold off the Soviets pushing down from the north in combination with Heer units.

The second week of February was spent in this sector, with a focus on extending the line slightly to the east as far as Repki and Tatjanowka. The enemy was pushing against them, but the line was held. It was during that second week that further Knight's Cross related approvals were given for *Leibstandarte* soldiers. Three of those were on February 12: to *SS-Oberscharführer* Fritz Henke (for his actions on December 29, 1943, at Bol. Moschkowzy) and *SS-Untersturmführer* Helmut Wendorff (for his actions during December 27–28, 1943, at Korosten), both of whom were awarded the Knight's Cross; and to *Leibstandarte* Commander *SS-Brigadeführer* "Teddi" Wisch, who was awarded the Oakleaves to his existing Knight's Cross in recognition of his actions between March 1943 and January 1944. Those three awards were followed the next day by the approval of the award of the Knight's Cross to *SS-Sturmbannführer* Herbert Kuhlmann for his leadership of the Panzer Regiment's I Battalion between early November 1943 and January 29, 1944.

As the men of the *LSSAH* continued to hold the line between Tinowka and Repki, their kameraden inside the Korsun Pocket were continuing their efforts to push to the west and link up. This brought about another change in orders for the *LSSAH* starting on February 16: their positions began to be taken over by the *Heer's 34. Infantry Division*, so the *Leibstandarte* could move eastward toward Frankowka, with advanced elements reaching that location later the same day under difficult "road" conditions. From there, they pushed further eastward to Lissjanka and Oktjabr (reached on the seventeenth); that was the same day the first men within the Korsun Pocket group made contact with soldiers from the *Leibstandarte*, with the first men being from the *5. SS-Panzer Division Wiking*. That began a flow of men out of the pocket and into friendly held territory. The enemy continued to exert pressure from the north and south, but the line held against these assaults, with the *Leibstandarte's* focal point of defense around Lissjanka.

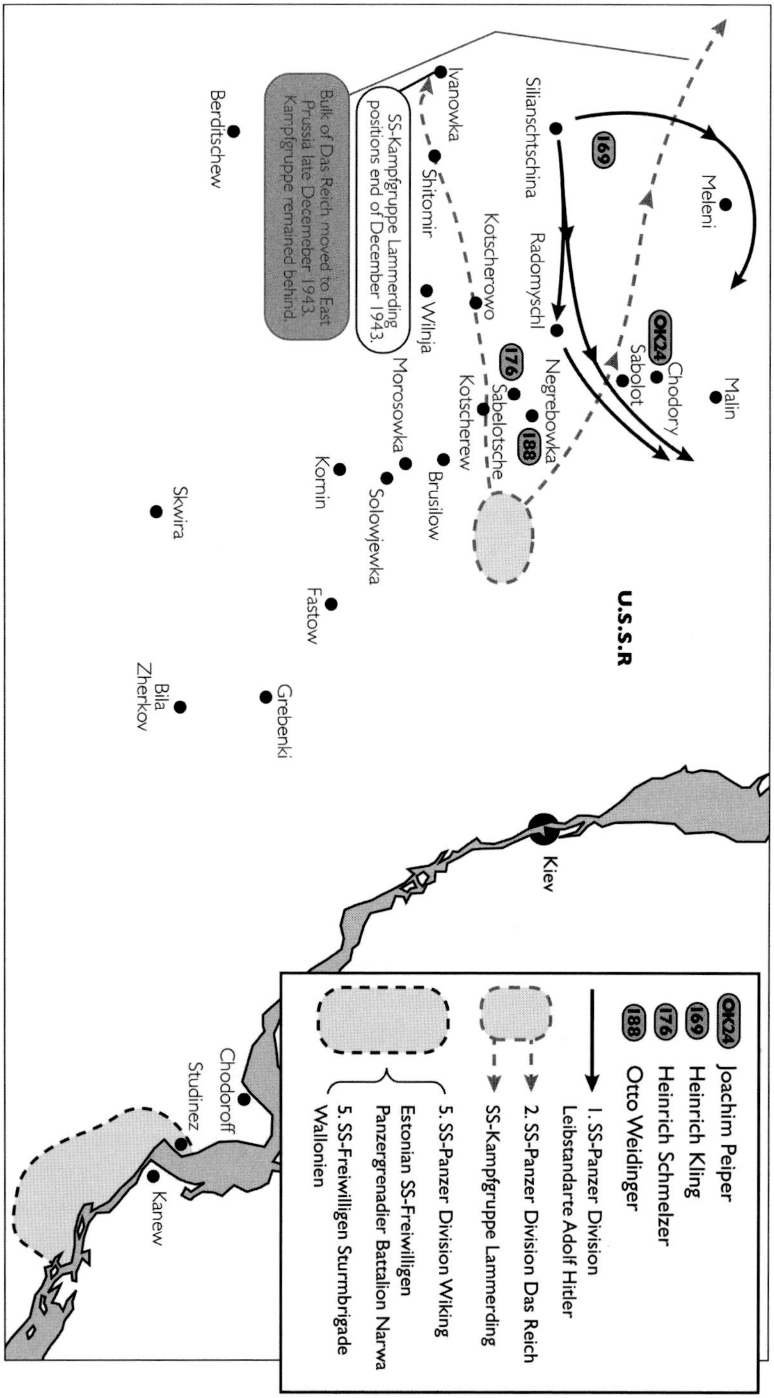

Map 11 – Dnjepr River North: December 1943

Further arrivals helped to bolster the strength of the *LSSAH* defenders. Tens of thousands of German troops made it out of the Korsun Pocket, but they left behind many thousands of their kameraden and almost all of their equipment.

Leibstandarte held their area until February 23, when they began their move back westward. They had certainly played a significant part in the relief efforts to rescue the men from the hell of the Korsun Pocket. The actions at Lissjanka were under the command of existing Knight's Cross holder *SS-Sturmbannführer* Sandig. It was also on the twenty-third that a further series of Knight's Crosses were approved for the *LSSAH*: to *SS-Hauptsturmführer* Heinrich Heimann (for his actions between July 1943 and January 1944); to *SS-Hauptsturmführer* Heinrich Kling (for his actions on December 20, 1943, at Korosten); and to *SS-Obersturmbannführer* Rudolf Lehmann (for his actions on December 29, 1943, at Berditschew). It would be a further ten weeks before more *Leibstandarte* Knight's Cross approvals joined them.

In the closing days of February 1944, the remaining men of the *Leibstandarte* focused on moving westward towards Krassnyj, before they were sent around thirty miles southeast to Talnoje. They were to be loaded onto trains and sent around 175 miles northwest to the Proskuroff area. That move brought them just over 200 miles east of the former Polish border they had crossed in the summer of 1941. They were to be used as part of a larger group to help hold this area against one of the Soviet thrusts farther westward. They moved into their assigned locations as February ended and the first days of March began.

SS-Kampfgruppe Lammerding

Their defensive area—begun in mid-January—was farther to the west and centered around Grinowzy. There was limited fighting while in that area, but nothing near the intensity of the preceding battles. Starting on February 18, they began a move fifty miles to the northwest toward Isjaslawl; it had to be fought for, but was secured on the twenty-second. Emphasis was then shifted to extend the area under their control and holding it. *Langemarck* was fighting in close proximity during those days. Their area was defended heavily against an increasingly strong enemy through the remaining days of February and the first few days of March 1944—then things got a bit more serious!

6. SS-Freiwilligen Sturmbrigade Langemarck

By mid-February, they were moving towards Jambol and heading to Shepetowka. In the third week they fought increasingly heavy battles from Zaslav, Klembovka, and Bjelgorodka. Jambol was reached at the end of February 1944, but the Russians were there and heavy fighting ensued (see chapter 3).

The eastern front still held the main focus for German armed forces, but activity in Italy and the Balkans began to intensify too, so let us see how that tested some of the additional *Waffen-SS* formations there.

16. SS-Panzergrenadier Division Reichsführer-SS

In the last chapter we touched on the fact that a battle group was sent to Cisterna. Those soldiers took part in the fighting during the second half of February. Although the landings were successful, the advance from the beachhead did not materialize and the Germans hemmed the Allied troops within a small area. These *Reichsführer-SS* men played their part in that halting of Allied intentions at that time.

SS-Karstwehr Battalion

They fought a series of further anti-partisan operations in the general Gorizia area, continuing in February, then March, April, and also May 1944. There were sizeable partisan forces in this area and the frequency of operations mounted will give some indication as to the threat they posed to the *Waffen-SS* men of *Karstwehr* and the steps they had to take for their own security. They counted hundreds of dead partisans throughout this first half of 1944 (see the next volume for more of their story).

V. SS-Gebirgs Korps

In Bosnia they oversaw the use of mainly SS mountain troops in this region—including the *Prinz Eugen Division* as 1944 opened—alongside Wehrmacht units. This changed in February with the inclusion of the *13. SS-Division*.

7. SS-Freiwilligen-Gebirgs Division Prinz Eugen

In February, the division moved again to an area around Sarajevo. Kumm's immediate focus was to secure this wider area and ensure it was free of partisans. To this end, smaller, localized operations were conducted during February and March 1944.

13. SS-Freiwilligen Bosnien-Herzegowina-Gebirgs-Division (Kroatien)

The training period for the men of this unit came to an end in early February, despite the overall formation lacking officers and NCOs. These Balkan SS men returned to their homeland during the second half of February 1944, moving into Croatia. They were centered around Vinkovci in the southeast, with the various units positioned to the south. They were sent to this region to help control the northeast section of Bosnia against the increasing menace of partisans. They were placed under the control of *V. SS-Gebirgs* korps around this time and readied themselves for their first combat activities.

18. SS-Panzergrenadier Division Horst Wessel

Alongside the men of the former *1. SS-Infantry Brigade (mot.)*, Hungarian and Romanian volunteers were being gathered together in southeast Slovenia between Cilli and Rann. In February, former *1. SS-Infantry Brigade (mot.)* men moved southward and joined their new kameraden in Slovenia. This placed another SS formation in the southern sector of Europe. They were attached to the *LXIX Armee Korps*.

Away from the front lines changes were taking place for some the units still in their training and formation stages.

9. SS-Panzer Division Hohenstaufen

They also had to conduct a move when, in early February, they were relocated from their northern French location north of Amiens to southern France, centered around the Nimes area.

14. Galizische SS-Freiwilligen Division

Although the main division was focused on training during the opening months of 1944, in the second half of February, a sizable battle group of around 2,000 men began an anti-partisan operation not far from Lemberg and close to Cholm under the command of *SS-Standartenführer* Beyersdorff. This operation lasted around one month, with the fighting centered on Frampol, and cost the unit their first combat losses.

As the men were engaged in their operation, the remaining *Ukrainian* SS men were relocated to better training facilities at Neuhammer, in the extreme west of Poland; training continued as much as equipment allowed. Heinrich Himmler made an inspection in mid-May (read more in volume 5).

Ostturkischen-Waffen-Verband der SS

In February 1944, they were moved to Belorussia, close to Minsk, and continued their limited training. They were also assigned to assist the anti-partisan operations in this area.

Schwere SS-Panzer Abteilung 101

Exercises took place in February that were observed by Sepp Dietrich. One of the men who joined this unit in Mons was Oakleaves holder Michael Wittmann.

Schwere SS-Panzer Abteilung 103

In February they were moved to Paderborn and also received the first of six Tiger tanks.

This details all significant actions or changes that occurred during February 1944 for the soldiers of the *Waffen-SS*. Following are the fifteen men who were approved for the award of the Knight's Cross or its higher grades during the month.

Name: Woldermars Veiss
Date of birth: 07.11.1899
SS Number: None assigned
Award: Knight's Cross

Born in Riga, Latvia, his military career started on Christmas Day 1918 with the Latvian Army. By late May 1919, he had obtained officer rank, which then progressed further to 1st lieutenant during February 1920. He was promoted to captain in 1935 (after spending three years at the Riga war academy) and then in 1937 was holding lieutenant-colonel rank. He served in Finland and Estonia in 1939. From June 1941, he was actively fighting partisans with the Latvian *Schutzmannschaft* units under the overall control and command of the Germans.

When Latvian units were being raised for the SS in April 1943, Veiss transferred with his Latvian Army rank and became a *Waffen-Obersturmbannführer der SS,* which quickly changed to *Waffen-Standartenführer der* SS in August. He was given command of the *1. Lettisches SS-Freiwilligen Regiment.* He had been fighting on the Wolchow front near Leningrad since early May 1943. The award of the Second Class Iron Cross came on July 20, with the First Class Iron Cross being awarded in September. On January 27, 1944, Hinrich Schuldt, commander of the *2.*

Latvian *SS* commander Voldemars Veiss after his award of the Knight's Cross, the first to the *Waffen-SS* Latvian units. He is also wearing a reversible *Heer* parka.

Lettisches SS-Freiwilligen Brigade, penned a recommendation for the award of Veiss' Knight's Cross that read:

> *SS-Standartenführer* Veiss, as the leader of *Kampfgruppe Veiss*, has been fighting the enemy in the most difficult manner and prevented them from taking Nekoschowo following exceptional defense by his troops at Podporesje. Through daring advances along the railway line and railroad station at Tatino, moving southward, he broke through enemy attacks and inflicted severe destruction on them. After days of fighting in the swamps and forests he attacked Dolgowo using his own initiative. He also held Tatino for several days and therefore held the advance of strong hostile groups moving against the open left flank of *KG "General Speth,"* significantly weakening and delaying them. By these attacks done under his robust personal leadership the enemy suffered heavy losses.
>
> These battle successes of the *Latvian Brigade* were crucial for the heavy defensive battles of the *XXXVIII. Army Korps*. Influenced by his outstanding attitude, personal bravery, and hard determination, all obstacles have been overcome; he cleverly moved his troops forward. *SS-Standartenführer* leads the brigade during this time. He has maintained the highest efforts in defense and attack in the final days. The commander in chief has verbally spoken of his appreciation through the commanding general and personally in writing.
>
> I recommend *SS-Standartenführer* Veiss, in agreement with the warmest support from the *XXXVIII. Army Korps*, is awarded the Knight's Cross of the Iron Cross.

This proposal was backed up with a letter written on February 4 by Gen. Herzog, commander of the *XXXVIII. Army Korps*. The letter highlighted Veiss and the bravery displayed by the men under his command. It also mentions the tenacity of the Latvians, the fact that Veiss was always at the head of his men, and specifically points Veiss out as an example of a great fighter.

Himmler supported the Schuldt recommendation with a short addendum to the typed version of the recommendations dated February 8; this multi-level suggestion was approved the following day. The approval gave the *Latvian* SS units their first Knight's Cross; it would be one of two awarded in this time frame (but not the first Latvian-born *Waffen-SS* Knight's Cross holder, as Berndt Lubich von Milovan preceded him by almost four months and Heinrich Sonne by two months). When proposed, the unit was titled the *2. (Lettisches) SS-Freiwilligen Brigade*, but by the time of approval they had been renamed the *19. Waffen-Grenadier-Division der* SS *(Lettisches Nr. 2)*, so it is that unit we will "count" this award under.

Veiss was given command of *Waffen-Grenadier Regiment der* SS *42* within the *19. Waffen-Grenadier-Division der* SS *(Lettisches Nr. 2)* during March 1944. Back at the front, Veiss was heavily wounded by grenade shrapnel on April 7. He was evacuated by air to Riga, but died on April 17, 1944, due to the severity of his wounds. He received a full military burial, with his coffin being transported on the back of a Marder III self-propelled anti-tank gun.

Name: Helmut Wendorff
Date of birth: 20.10.1920
SS Number: 365 017
Award: Knight's Cross

Born in Grauwinkel, he became a member of the Hitler Youth during mid-March 1933, and remained there until early September 1939. He joined the SS at the same time and was posted to the *Leibstandarte*, initially with *11. Kompanie*. In early June 1940, he was placed with the newly created *Sturmartillerie Batterie* (later the *StuG Battalion*). His first action was in the Balkans in early 1941, followed by fighting in the early stage of Barbarossa up to the end of October. *SS-Sturmmann* Wendorff had earned the Second Class Iron Cross on September 14, as well as the Tank Assault Badge.

At the start of November, he went to Bad Tolz for officer training, holding the rank of *SS-Oberscharführer* at the time. That training was completed at the end of April 1942, when he returned to the *Sturmgeschutze Battalion*. His promotion to *SS-Untersturmführer* followed on June 21. In December 1942, he moved to the 13th (Heavy) Company of the *Leibstandarte's* Panzer regiment, training in their Tiger tanks at Fallingbostel. He returned with that kompanie to the Russian front in February 1943, around Kharkov, commanding III Platoon, Tiger tank number 435.

The Kharkov battles gave Wendorff a chance to put his training to the test and, along with his *13.* kompanie kameraden (Heinz Kling, Michael Wittmann, and others), they acquitted themselves very well against the Soviets. His next test was the short but intensive Kursk battle. He had moved to command II Platoon and was now in command of tank number 1321. He was lightly wounded in the opening phase, but it did not require him to

Helmut Wendorff, one of the growing number of *Waffen-SS* Tiger tank related Knight's Cross awardees.

leave the front. That campaign was succeeded by the *LSSAH's* move to Italy in August; while there, Wendorff was awarded the Black Wound Badge (September 4—the same day he was married) and the First Class Iron Cross (September 16). They focused on training the men and getting ready for their next engagement, which turned out to be back in Russia in November 1943. As they were on their way, Wendorff was given command of I Platoon, in Tiger tank number S11. His tank sat amongst the men of the *LSSAH*, supporting them during the challenging fighting that ensued during these closing stages of 1943.

It was in the last few days of the year that Wendorff conducted the actions that led his regimental commander to put him forward for the Knight's Cross award. The proposal was written on January 17, 1944, by Joachim Peiper and detailed the following:

> *SS Ustuf* Wendorff has, as a platoon leader in the *13.(s)/SS-Panz. Rgt. 1 "LSSAH,"* in all of the fighting of the kompanie, acted with resolute and excellent composure. Even in the most critical moments he was quiet and acted with caution. With his dynamic approach and exemplary use of tactics with his platoon he mastered all of the situations put to him.
>
> In the Christmas days, the division was in the area of Korosten, in a forced march in the area southeastward of Shitomir, moving in a line including Staroselye - Staraya-Kotelnja, including the railway line between Zhitomir – Fastow, providing short security points on the right flank. In the early morning hours of 27.12.1943, *SS-Ustuf.* Wendorff, who was in Ivankovo with his platoon (4 Tiger), was instructed to intercept and destroy the Russian armored spearheads advancing out of the forest north of the main road to protect the division's withdrawal into the area south of Gujwa during the night. In the course of a series of attacks against these armored spearheads, *SS-Ustuf.* Wendorff distinguished himself through exceptional daring and outstanding bravery. He positioned himself in an ambush location at the crossroads north of Ivankovo. After destroying two Russian T-34s he allowed to approach before opening fire, he was instructed to carry out a driving attack on a strong armored group in Tschubarowka.
>
> In a dashing approach along the railway line he drove into the village from the northeast and destroyed eleven T-34s there. After his return, he was sent against enemy tanks that had broken out of Jusefowka and destroyed three more enemy tanks there. In the

> afternoon, the enemy broke into Staroselye and seized the bridges in the area; the only avenue of retreat for the division's heavy weapons was through Ivankovo. Attacking with several armored spearheads, the enemy attempted to seize these crossings as well, thus threatening the withdrawal of the elements of the division positioned in the Wolossowo - Staraya – Kotelnja area.
>
> This advance of the Russians was held by *SS-Ustuf.* Wendorff, standing with his remaining three Tigers. It allowed the artillery battalion and one of the P.G.W. battalion to retreat and also allowed some of our damaged tanks to be recovered from the main battle line. As the last one to disengage from the fighting, around midnight, he brought his three vehicles to the south bank of the Guiwa.
>
> On 28.12.1943, strong enemy groups of armor advanced on the security force in Antopol - Boljarka and broke into the town. With four Tigers—some of which were barely serviceable—*SS-Ustuf.* Wendorff threw himself against these enemy tanks. He shot up eleven T-34s during the heavy tank fighting, preventing the enemy from breaching the division's flank.
>
> On 27. and 28.12.1943, Wendorff shot up a further ten T-34s with his battle tank, raising his personal total of destroyed enemy tanks to fifty-eight.

This proposal was endorsed by "Teddi" Wisch, who summarized the actions above and echoed the view of Wendorff as an outstanding and brave commander. As this recommendation was being considered Wendorff was away from the immediate front area, leading an NCO training course for some of the men. He received a promotion to *SS-Obersturmführer* on January 30, and was also given command of the *13. Heavy Kompanie*. He returned to his men in the first days of February 1944 and led the few remaining serviceable Tigers in the successful relief operation at Cherkassy.

Wendorff was approved for the award of the Knight's Cross on February 12, 1944.

In mid-April 1944, Wendorff arrived in Belgium with his remaining men. He was given a spell of leave before being posted to the role of adjutant of II Battalion in Peiper's Panzer regiment. In mid-July 1944, he was moved to the *101st SS-Heavy Tank Battalion*, assuming command of *2. Kompanie*. For the next month, Wendorff played his part in the fighting against the western enemies. Moving against enemy tanks near Merzieres on August 14, 1944, Wendorff's tank received a direct hit at point blank range, killing him instantly. There was initial confusion as to what had happened due to the fact the location came under enemy control; confirmation followed later. At the time of his death, Wendorff was credited with the destruction of eighty-four enemy tanks.

Name: Fritz Henke
Date of birth: 21.06.1921
SS Number: None assigned
Award: Knight's Cross

Born in Welsede in Hessisch-Oldendorf/Weser Schauburg county, in the district in Lower Saxony, he was the son of a foreman. Joining the Hitler Youth from 1933, he stayed there until 1938, when he moved to the *Allgemeine-SS*. On September 4, 1939, he moved to the *SS*. Henke was initially placed with the *2. Replacement* kompanie of *SS-Regiment "Germania"* in Hamburg-Langenhorn, where he received his basic infantry training.

From there came a transfer to the *2. Replacement* kompanie of the SS Signals Battalion in Unna / Westphalia, where he remained until May 1940, learning to be a radio operator. Then he came as a radio operator to the new SS-Assault Gun Battery of *Leibstandarte* SS *"Adolf Hitler,"* with which he took part in the Balkans campaign in 1941. Henke was promoted to *SS-Sturmmann* in June and then moved to Russia soon after. At the start of October, he was promoted to *SS-Rottenführer* and then, in the closing days of the same month, received the Second Class Iron Cross. The Tank Assault Badge was awarded on February 26, 1942. A move to *SS-Unterscharführer* was made at the start of August following an NCO training course, and it was also in 1942 he received the Russian Front Medal.

Henke was in command of his own vehicle during 1943, and for his actions during the Kursk fighting he was awarded the First Class Iron Cross on July 13. Towards the end of 1943, the *Leibstandarte* found themselves around the Shitomir area, where they stayed until early 1944. A promotion to *SS-Oberscharführer* had taken place in late 1943, as had a move to platoon comander in the *3. Batterie* of the renamed *SS-Sturmgeschutze Abteilung 1*.

Back on December 29, 1943, Henke was operating near Bol. Moschkowzy, south of Shitomir. He positioned himself on Hill 228.1 and helped protect the infantry. He initially stopped a small enemy tank incursion, but later the same day a larger enemy thrust was made. Initially destroying two of the enemy tanks, he then had to use his skill and expertise with all of his might! The accompanying infantry had taken up flanking positions close

An autographed image of Fritz Henke capturing his pleasure at becoming a Knight's Cross holder.

to the village of Stawitsche. Constantly changing his firing position, Henke defeated the infantry lead squads and also managed to knock out the remaining six enemy tanks. A further enemy tank attack was made the same day, this time by eleven tanks; Henke had no time to rest and got to work once more. Identifying a commander's tank, he focused his fire on that vehicle, bringing it to a halt. Although the enemy commander survived his tank being hit, he did not survive a well-aimed pistol shot by Henke! During this fighting he was credited with destroying nineteen enemy tanks and eleven anti-tank guns.

It is not known who wrote the recommendation, or when, but on February 12, 1944, he was approved for the awarding of the Knight's Cross. The medal itself was presented by "Teddi" Wisch the same day during a small ceremony. Henke did not know why he had been summoned to the command post, but he went there without changing his filthy uniform or washing his grubby hands! This fact did not deter Wisch, and Henke returned to his kameraden with his new award hanging from his neck.

He received a promotion to *SS-Hauptscharführer* on November 9, 1943, which may have been backdated and connected to his Knight's Cross approval. The Panzer Assault Badge "25" was awarded on November 9, 1944, with the Panzer Assault Badge "50" being awarded on April 15, 1945. Henke was given a field promotion to *SS-Untersturmführer* on April 20, the same day he received his first wound of the entire war. He survived the war and died on November 15, 1999; he was buried five days later in Moisburg.

Name: Hans Joachim Ruhle von Lilienstern
Date of birth: 09.01.1915
SS Number: 151 372
Award: Knight's Cross

Born in Fritzlar, he was in the Hitler Youth from June 1932 until November 1933. He then had a stint with the *R.A.D.* from May to October 1934, immediately followed by a move to the Heer in November 1934. Prior to the outbreak of the war he achieved the rank of *leutnant* in 1938.

In the first stages of WWII, he served as part of an MG replacement kompanie and then a Pak kompanie. The award of the Black Wound Badge came in 1939, then in May 1940, he moved to the SS as a war correspondent. By October, he was with *Totenkopf*, and on November 9 was promoted to *SS-Obersturmführer*; this was the same day he was awarded the Second

Class Iron Cross. In early November 1942, he was promoted to *SS-Hauptsturmführer*; the same year he received the Russian Front Medal. By March 1943 he was a kompanie commander within the *Nederland Brigade* and then, in early November, he became I Battalion commander of *SS-Rgt. 48 "General Seyffardt."*

On January 22, 1944, he was awarded the First Class Iron Cross, but then three days later the *Nederland* commander, *SS-Oberführer* Jurgen Wagner, wrote a Knight's Cross award recommendation for Ruhle von Lilienstern:

> Recommendation for the award of the Knight's Cross to the Iron Cross for *SS-Hauptsturmführer* Ruhle von Lilienstern.
>
> On 20.1. strong enemy forces threatened to penetrate the newly erected battle front in the area Witino – Głuchowo on both sides of the main road from Narwa - Leningrad. Battalion Battle Group Nederland, under the command of *SS-Hstuf.* Ruhle von Lilienstern, was ready and awaiting orders as operational reserve in the area Witino.
>
> Elements of the battle group arrived at the front, where the enemy had already breached Witino with strong numerical superiority. Using his own initiative, *SS-Hstuf.* Ruhle von Lilienstern immediately launched a surprise attack through the enemy with vehicles. He threw back the enemy and inflicted high losses on them, therefore closing the gap. For three days the battle group held their own, under the heaviest of losses, and struggled alone during the night from 22 to 23.1. against regiment-strength attacks by the enemy. At the same time, the battle group leader personally gathered with his messengers, led seventeen attacks against enemy breaches, and cleaned up his own sector, as well as the neighboring sectors to the right and left. Here, too, the enemy suffered high losses. Crucial to this success was the attitude of *SS-Hstuf.* Ruhle von Lilienstern, present in all of the focal points within his area and, through his unparalleled personal conduct, inspired in his men the highest will to resist.
>
> Himself being wounded, he led his battle group through the fulfillment of his orders and decisively delayed the further penetration of a far superior enemy. After more than six days of ceaseless fighting against frontal and flank attacks, Battle Group Ruhle was still the bulwark of the road from Leningrad – Narwa. His sacrifice prevented the tearing open of the entire korps front on both sides

A poor quality image of Hans-Joachim Ruhle von Lilienstein seen with his Knight's Cross.

of the main road, which in turn contributed decisively to ensuring the construction of a new front.

This recommendation was warmly approved by *SS-Obergruppenführer* Steiner, which helped ensure it was approved and awarded on February 12, 1944. At the start of September, he received a promotion to *SS-Sturmbannführer*. During the following month he moved to Bad Tolz as an instructor and, as such, found himself part of the *38. SS-Division Nibelungen*; the last *Waffen-SS* Division to be formed during the conflict. Ruhle von Lilienstern was placed in command of IV Battalion within *SS-Regiment 95* in March 1945. He survived the war and died on November 26, 2000, in Frankfurt.

Name: Theodore Wisch
Date of birth: 13.12.1907
SS Number: 4 759
Award: Knight's Cross with Oakleaves

"Teddi" Wisch's history has been touched upon in volume 1, when he was approved for the award of the Knight's Cross on September 15, 1941, becoming only the fourteenth *Waffen-SS* soldier to receive the award. He was recognized then for his abilities during mid-July 1941, in the opening days of Operation Barbarossa.

On the back of the award of his Knight's Cross he received a promotion on September 27 to *SS-Obersturmbannführer* and continued to lead II Battalion until March 1942, when health issues removed him from the front line; Wisch had been awarded the Infantry Assault Badge on March 2. He returned to the *LSSAH* in the summer, when they were in France being refitted and expanded. That expansion resulted in him being given command of the newly raised 2nd Regiment. He received further awards while in France: the first was the Russian Front Medal on August 25, and the second was the Romanian Crown with Swords on September 3. In January 1943, he attended a regimental commander's course that helped his promotion on the thirtieth to *SS-Standartenführer*. He took his regiment back to Russia around then, arriving in the Kharkov area. The bravery and capabilities he displayed in that battle earned him the German Cross in Gold on February 25.

In early June 1943, Wisch was given command of the *Leibstandarte Division* following Sepp Dietrich's move to command the *I. SS-Panzer Korps*. Wisch was promoted to *SS-Oberführer* at the start of July, just days prior to the start of the Kursk battle. He led his division in that struggle, led them into Italy in the late summer, and then back into Russia for the hard, defensive fighting that ensued in the closing weeks of 1943. It was this difficult fighting that made up the final part of Wisch's Oakleaves recommendation; the extensive document was compiled by Sepp Dietrich in early February 1944. Before detailing its contents, we need to highlight Wisch was promoted to *SS-Brigadeführer* on the last day of January 1944.

The document begins by making reference to the award of his Knight's Cross back in September 1941:

> I. In the battles of the Russian campaign of 1941, especially in the mopping up of the Nogai steppe in September 1941, in the capture of Mariupol, and in the defensive battles in and west of Rostov, the high qualities of leadership and the personal bravery of *SS-Brigadeführer* Wisch have been repeatedly proven. With his battalion widely separated from the division and often operating independently without any contact, he has accomplished excellently the tasks assigned by the division with great security and evident instinct for the enemy's weaknesses, mostly after personal reconnaissance of the front lines, and achieved great successes, as much in the tactical aspect as through the annihilation of large quantities of men and equipment.
>
> II. During the winter campaign in February / March 1943, *SS-Brigadeführer* Wisch, as commander of the *SS-Panzer-Grenadier-Regiment 2 "LSSAH,"* is credited to the utmost as a leader and champion of his men. Under personal action he was able, along with his men, to repel all attacks of the Russians on the thinly occupied security line eastward from Charkow, and to cushion massive enemy assaults during the planned disengagement movement of his regiment. He succeeded in picking up the 298th and 320th Infantry Divisions from the foreground of the main fighting line and, through violent counter-thrusts carried out by his III. (armored) Battalion, in weakening enemy forces to a considerable extent. The counterattack that began on 2.3.1943 was led by *SS-Brigadeführer* Wisch personally. With the spearhead kompanies he forced the bridgehead by Bridok in hard offensive battles by *Hf. Ljachowa*, and in an enveloping operation of his armored battalion created conditions for the taking of Walki. Again leading personally, in the following days *SS-Brigadeführer* Wisch achieved the capture of

Ogulzy and Ljubotin, the departure point for the attack on Charkow. Engaged with his regiment during the battle for Charkow in the right open flank, on the first day of the attack (10.3.1943) he penetrated as far as the railway station installations. He took, after eliminating the intense flank menace from the high wooded south part of Charkow, first the city center and in the next two days the east edge of Charkow.

The capture of Bjelgorod in a surprise attack in March 1943 was begun with the furious attack of his regiment. He again led from the front-most lines prepared by a pursuit in a wide area. After breaching the early fierce resistance he carried out in an ideal manner through the battle tasks assigned personally in the precise moment to III. Battalion of his regiment.

III. During Operation "Zitadelle," *SS-Brigadeführer* Wisch, as commander of the *1. SS-Panzer-Grenadier-Division "LSSAH,"* again showed himself a soldierly leader with high military qualities, strong energy, and hardness. With a permanent personal commitment, he has led these hard offensive and defensive battles from the front line. The successes of the attack days are thanks to his personal intervention. The armored personnel carrier of the divisional commander in the middle of the tank attacks, or the attacking grenadiers, or rushing across the battlefield from command post to command post, were images constantly repeated during these days. His fair evaluation of the situation, his measurement of the weight of our offensive battles, and his permanent presence on the front lines are to be thanked for the successful defense on 12.7.1943, through the operative defense carried out by *SS-Panzer-Regiment 1* and the assault gun detachment, against the surprise outflanking enemy attack with two tank corps. In two hours they knocked out and destroyed 130 enemy tanks using our tanks, assault guns, and close combat troops.

IV. After the conclusion of the disarmament of the troops all over the plain in upper Italy, *SS-Brigadeführer* Wisch, with his division, stands since 1.11.1943 engaged incessantly in large battles in the areas Shitomir, Korosten, Berditschew, and southwest of Pogrbischtsche. In each one of these five large offensive operations—executed to the moment in these areas—as well as in the defensive battles eastwards of Shitomir and Berditschew, *SS-Brigadeführer*

Leibstandarte commander Theodore "Teddi" Wisch (autographed) seen with his Oakleaves; the fourth and last Oakleaves award in this volume for an *LSSAH* soldier.

Wisch, with his permanent personal commitment to the front lines, was the soul of the fight.

During the assault from 14.–18.11.1943—in the deep flank of the enemy from Kornin over Ssolowjewka towards Kotscherowo in the road Shitomir-Kiev—after the breakthrough of the armored group, strong enemy forces interrupted the advance route, settled down around Ssolowjewka with the mass in Brussiloff, and tried to hinder the advance of the division through counterattacks. Through an offensive flank cover by elements of the 2. Regiment and the *Aufklarungs Abteilung*, the division managed to secure the ground gained toward the east. During an enemy breakthrough from the west on 26.11.1943, *SS-Brigadeführer* Wisch, just returned from a reconnaissance, dispatched several assault guns and elements of the *III./SS-Panzer-Grenadier-Regiment 2,* and in a counterattack he personally led and annihilated a battalion strength enemy group and with it, prevented the foreseen taking of the road. Next to this breakthrough toward the road, the division was assigned the task to destroy several strong enemy infantry groups through the wooded area east of Radomyschl.

Without waiting for the assembly of the "*Leibstandarte*"—slowed by bad road conditions—*SS-Brigadeführer* Wisch put into combat all of the assault guns ready for action with riding infantry. With them, together with another kampfgruppe deployed further to the northeast, he quickly gained ground. The union of both *kampfgruppes* to the rear of the opponent took place within a few days, and with the frontal engagement of the remaining elements of the division a pocket was built and the enemy destroyed.

Since 5.12.1943, the division had battled in the area eastward from Tschernjachoff with the task of establishing contact between the *XIII. Army* korps and the *LIX. Army Korps*. The troops fought eastward from Korosten, throwing and annihilating the enemy troop groups that had advanced from the area of Radomyschl.

SS-Brigadeführer Wisch began this undertaking with a wide assault by a strong armored group 30 km [18.6 miles] deep to the rear of the opponent laying in front of the *XIII. Army Korps.* Without regard for the destructive fight of the *XIII. Army* korps then developing in the rear and flanks of the division—in an additional daring assault of the amored group—*SS-Brigadeführer* Wisch smashed the operational bridgehead of the enemy by Radomyschl.

The success of this undertaking, for which the commander in

chief of the *4. Panzer Army*, *General der Panzertruppen* Erhard Raus, personally expressed his special recognition during his presence in the divisional command post; must be thanked, besides the boldness, bravery, and almost superhuman tribute of their full forces by the tankmen and grenadiers, in a large scale to *SS-Brigadeführer* Wisch. With his armored personnel carrier he traveled daily to the front and led his troops.

On 20.12.1943, the division, together with the *1.* and *7. Panzer Divisions*, received the task to move forward from the area east of Korosten towards the east to repel and destroy the opponent. Because of the tangled, swampy, and bushy terrain, the attack spearheads of the divisions, after throwing the enemy out of their field positions during hard combat, went off their original attack routes. Before an even larger confusion happened, *SS-Brigadeführer* Wisch, with compass in hand, personally assumed command of his forward grenadiers and tanks.

As in the partisan area, the leadership of the *kampfgruppes* from the divisional command post was almost impossible because of permanently interrupted telephone communications. During these day and night attacks *SS-Brigadeführer* Wisch always remained close to the forward elements. In the period of the defensive battles against the mass of the 3rd Guards Tank Army, *SS-Brigadeführer* Wisch has proven, besides his evident command qualities, his special bravery.

In spite of the unfavorable tank situation due to the long march from the Korosten area to east of Shitomir, *SS-Brigadeführer* Wisch, through quick concentration of the tanks at the focal point, managed to considerably hold up the massive assault of the enemy tanks. Through the building of anti-tank fronts with tanks under repair he destroyed the enemy tank forces.

Mention of the division in the Wehrmacht report of 21.12.1943 and in a personal teletype sent by *Generalfeldmarschall* von Manstein on 15.1.1944 found their acknowledgement of these hard battles in the area eastward and southwest of Berditschew.

V. Under the command of *SS-Brigadeführer* Wisch, in the course of the actions in Russia 5-12.7.1943 and from 6.11.1943 to 31.1.1944, the *1. SS-Panzer-Division "LSSAH"* has captured or destroyed:

1,124 T-34
12 KW

5	armored scout cars
89	other (small tanks)
6	guns 7.62 cm
34	guns 12.2 cm
5	anti-aircraft guns
7	automatic guns
97	other guns
227	medium anti-tak guns (3.7 cm to 4.5 cm)
1,056	heavy anti-tank guns (7.62 cm)
12	grenade launchers of 50 mm
45	grenade launchers of 82 mm
73	grenade launchers of 122 mm
553	anti-tank rifles
638	machine-guns
575	machine-pistols
2,003	rifles
	nine set up flame throwing barriers
37	aircraft
334	vehicles
98	animal-drawn vehicles
2,953	prisoners
16,541	enemy killed

Because of his permanently proven bravery, his never-ending high proof of worth, and the excellent leadership of his division, I consider *SS-Brigadeführer* Wisch worthy of the high award of the Oakleaves to the Knight's Cross of the Iron Cross.

This proposal was rapidly approved, and on February 12, 1944, "Teddi" Wisch added the Oakleaves to his existing list of awards. He still had more to add, but we will continue with his story in later volumes of this work.

Name: Herbert Kuhlmann
Date of birth: 07.04.1915
SS Number: 118 826
Award: Knight's Cross

Born in Harburg, he joined the SS at the start of August 1934. He was placed with the forerunner to *SS-Regiment Germania* and, interestingly, was given the rank *SS-Unterscharführer* from the outset. There is no prior service listed in any organization, so we have no insight into why this was the case. From mid-June 1935, he was sent to the officer's school at Braunschweig (other attendees there at the time were Joachim Peiper and Karl Sattler). He was promoted to *SS-Standartenoberjunker* in late December. His stint at Braunschweig was immediately followed with a platoon leader's course at Dachau lasting up to June 20, 1936, when he moved to the rank of *SS-Untersturmführer*. It would appear he spent time with *SS-Oberabschnitt "Elbe"* and *"Nordsee"* in the prewar years. During 1938, he is listed as taking part in the Austrian and Sudetenland campaigns. He received a promotion to *SS-Obersturmführer* at the end of January 1939. In June, he moved back to *SS-Regiment Germania*, this time with the reconnaissance battalion. It was with this unit he began actions in WWII.

While fighting in Poland he earned the Second Class Iron Cross on September 20. Remaining with Germania, he went west in 1940. He is listed as being with the motorcycle replacement battalion in December 1940, and then, in January 1941, moved to *2.* kompanie within *SS-Regiment "Nordland."* He was awarded the First Class Iron Cross on March 14, 1941, and it can be presumed this was for actions in the west during the previous year. On April 20, he was promoted to *SS-Hauptsturmführer*. He fought in Russia in mid-1941 and received a heavy wound in late November that removed him from the front line. From the opening day of 1942, he was listed under the infantry replacement battalion for *SS-Regiment "Westland."* On February 20, he was awarded the Infantry Assault Badge. Before the end of March, he was moved to SS-Panzer Battalion III, which started his involvement in tanks. In October he added the Russian Front Medal and in November the Silver Wound Badge. From November 16 through December 12, 1942, he attended a tank commander's training course at Wunsdorf. On Christmas Eve he was posted to the heavy tank battalion of the *Das Reich Division* and placed as *2.* kompanie commander. His next move was on June 18, 1943, when he was assigned to the *Leibstandarte's* panzer regiment; before the end of the month he was promoted to *SS-Sturmbannführer*. That placed him in command of I Battalion, which was training in Grafenwohr and was re-equipped with Panther tanks. Kuhlmann and his men rejoined the *Leibstandarte* at the front in Italy during August 1943. They returned to Russia in the closing months of 1943 and fought very difficult battles there that lasted into 1944. No doubt these actions caused further injury to Kuhlmann, as he was awarded the Gold Wound Badge on January 30, 1944.

The following day, "Teddi" Wisch recommended Kuhlmann for the award of the Knight's Cross for his leadership of I Battalion, *SS-Panzer Regiment 1*. The basis of that recommendation was as follows:

SS-Sturmbannführer Kuhlmann has been the commander of I. / (Heavy) Panzer Regiment 1 *LSSAH* since 6.11.1943, and with his battalion has always been close to all of the fighting that his battalion had, even if only a few tanks were ready for use. In all these attacks, *SS-Sturmbannführer* Kuhlmann has demonstrated excellent leadership characteristics and always led his panzer men from the front line.

I. For the attack of Kornin, near Ssolowjewka, on 15.11.1943, *SS-Stubaf.* Kuhlmann showed extraordinary alertness, fearlessness, and daring. While the infantry, supported by *sturmgeschutze*, frontally attacked the village and found tough resistance, he took the independent decision to move out far to the west and smashed the completely shocked enemy, throwing them from their positions and moving into Ssolowjewka from the northwest. This enveloping attack meant the enemy could not escape and a heavy tank battle took place into the twilight, during which twenty-four T-34 and eight *sturmgeschutze* were shot up.

II. On January 23, 1944, *SS-Sturmbannführer* Kuhlmann, as leader in the panzer regiment subordinated to the *2. Panz. Gren. Rgt.* and the II Artillery Battalion, was in the area west of Turboff, opening positions of the enemy and pushing through the positions of the *101. Jaeger Division*. From there, they immediately pushed on to the Bila sector and over Hill 316.5, 307.8 and the railway station at Lipowez, obtaining this and securing it.

SS-Stubaf. Kuhlmann has executed this assignment with necessary speed, but under extraordinarily difficult ground conditions and strong anti-tank and heavy artillery and mortar fire. In so doing, the enemy was completely caught off guard by this breach of the armored group. Thanks to the speed of the attack, seven Russian infantry divisions were trapped within the pocket.

After the village of Brizkoje they had to overcome extraordinary difficulties getting over the bridge and to the opposite side. The armored group pushed ahead to Hill 316.5 and shot up twelve T-34s and four assault guns, despite the strongest of flanking fire from Otscheretnia, the onset of a snowstorm, and increasing twilight. They broke into Ganowka and completely surprised the enemy, destroying them and throwing them from their positions.

Due to the extraordinarily difficult ground conditions—balkas and swamps—the village of Najadowka could only be taken frontally.

Herbert Kuhlmann with his Knight's Cross, another *LSSAH* tank-related awardee.

Despite heavy flanking fire from Otscheretnia and a violent defense of Napatowka, the breach by the heavy armored group was achieved with rapid speed into the northern sector. They overwhelmed the enemy and drove them off, with the enemy responding by hastily retreating, leaving behind many weapons in their positions.

One bridge that was prepared for demolition was cleared of mines despite fierce bombardment. It was thus possible for the battlegroup to attack Rossosche and also take the extremely important Hill 292.3. Since this still did not result in taking the place frontally due to the heaviest artillery and anti-tank defenses, *SS-Sturmbannführer* Kuhlmann ordered the tying down of the enemy by the Panzer IV. He then sat at the head of his panther group and circumnavigated the place, breaching it with a flank attack from the west. This was despite the worst visibility and having to halt at the bridge during the night attack in Rossosche. The enemy was also fully overwhelmed here through the surprise, comprehensive attack and left behind a lot of war materiel, including vehicles and tanks.

Due to a lack of fuel and ammunition the planned attack for the next day could not take place. The enemy, apparently aware of the supply situation of Group Kuhlmann, began violent attacks against them. However, through the use of the tanks from Battlegroup Kuhlmann in tank defense points situated around the whole place and with the infantry providing security for them, they managed to defend themselves for a whole day. They managed to repel strong tank and infantry bands and shot up many tanks, often using their last grenade.

The enemy tried to take back the village of Rossosche twice during the night; both times they came up against the personal determination of *SS-Sturmbannführer* Kuhlmann. He rejected them with his tanks, making them combat ready using the last reserves of fuel and ammunition.

On 28.1, Battlegroup Kuhlmann had fresh supplies and they pushed over the railway line at Babin and farther towards Morosowka.

This daring push led *SS-Stubaf.* Kuhlmann to once again completely surprise the enemy, who fled to the south through the forest and left behind significant war materiels.

During this tank attack from 25.—29.1.1944 Battlegroup Kuhlmann captured or destroyed:

> 116 Enemy tanks
> 89 Heavy anti-tank guns
> 11 Guns, 12.2 cm
> 14 Tractors
> 250 Prisoners
> trapped the bulk of 7 Infantry Divisions.
>
> I believe *SS-Stubaf.* Kuhlmann, because of his outstanding leadership of his heavy Panther battalion during all of the combat days since 6.11.1943, his personal courage and being a rousing role model, and the excellent execution of orders in the area southwest of Pogrebitsche is worthy for the high award of the Knight's Cross of the Iron Cross; I please ask that you give him this award.

This document also contained an endorsement by Dietrich, who gave it his warmest approval and highlighted Kuhlmann's personal bravery.

The proposal was approved on February 13, 1944. For a very brief period in March he led the Panzer regiment, but suffered a heart attack not long after that removed him from the front for a while; he returned to command I Battalion when they were in Belgium in May 1944. He continued as battalion commander until early August, when he once again took temporary command of the Panzer regiment. He led for around two weeks, until he was badly wounded on August 20, 1944, during the Falaise Pocket breakout. His command Panther was hit and although he made it out, he suffered shrapnel wounds to his back. He spent time recuperating after the Normandy fighting. On November 8, he was approved for the award of the German Cross in Gold. He was back at the front in time for the fighting in the Ardennes, only this time in command of the *12. SS-Panzer Regiment*. He was promoted to *SS-Obersturmbannführer* at the end of January 1945. He is not listed as being with the *12.* SS in February, when they were in Hungary. His time in the closing weeks of the war is not entirely clear, with some sources stating he was part of the reserve officer list.

He survived the war and made his way to South America. He died on November 9, 1985.

Name: Leon Degrelle
Date of birth: 15.06.1906
SS Number: none assigned
Award: Knight's Cross

Born in Bouillon, Belgium (in the Walloon region), he was a politically motivated activist long before joining the ranks of the *Waffen-SS*. He was a devout Catholic and worked for a religious publication during his twenties. He also held a doctorate of law. His increasingly extreme views conflicted with those of his employers and the Catholic church. With the rise of political turmoil during the 1930s, Degrelle and some of his like-minded colleagues formed their own political movement, titled Rexism. He had high aspirations and made efforts to talk and meet with people he began to admire around Europe. His political party gathered support within Belgium and they gained multiple seats in the prewar elections.

The invasion of Belgium by the Germans in May 1940 gave Degrelle complications, as he wanted to retain Belgian independence but had sympathies with Germany. He was arrested as a collaborator and spent a short period in prison before gaining release with the help of the Germans, who took control of Belgium and the northern sector of France.

In early August 1941, he volunteered for the German Army after their advance in Soviet Russia; Degrelle was keen to play his part in the defeat of Bolshevism. He fought within the newly raised *373. Wallonian Infantry Battalion*—part of the *Heer*—he started out with the rank of private. Although initially held in the rear, they took part in difficult fighting near Dnjepropretovsk in early 1942 (close to the later kameraden from the *SS-Wiking Division*). Suffering heavy casualties, Degrelle was one of the men who made it through. Various forms of recognition followed; he had no military experience, but did have natural determination and repeatedly displayed bravery in the face of the enemy.

He was given the rank *gefreiter* on February 12, 1942, was promoted to *Oberfeldwebel* by the end of the same month, and was awarded the Second Class Iron Cross on March 3, the Black Wound Badge on March 23, promoted to *leutnant* at the start of May, awarded the First Class Iron Cross on May 21, the Russian Front Medal in mid-August, and the Infantry Assault Badge on August 28—a rather busy six months for this militarily inexperienced former politician!

He remained in Russia, as the Walloons advanced into the Caucausus region of the Soviet Union in the second half of 1942, where he once again fought close to the *SS-Wiking* men. He was back in Germany at the start of

An autographed image of Leon Degrelle from the Justin Horgan collection. The *SS-Wallonian* leader is seen with his Knight's Cross and other combat awards.

1943, then the Walloons were incorporated in the *Waffen-SS* at the start of June 1943. Degrelle was given the rank *SS-Obersturmführer*. As we have already covered in the preceding volume, this unit was moved to Heidelager to begin training under the guise of the *Waffen-SS*. During the October 1943 renaming and numbering of various *Waffen-SS* units, the men of *Wallonien* were redesignated the *5. SS-Freiwilligen Sturmbrigade Wallonien*. The following month, they were ready for active service and were sent to the Russian front, placed alongside the men of *Wiking*; their initial positions were within the Irdyn Marsh area at the end of November 1943.

At the start of January 1944, Degrelle was promoted to *SS-Hauptsturmführer*. During February, the *Wallonian Brigade* was caught up in the Cherkassy Pocket battles. As a result of further bravery he displayed there, Leon Degrelle was put forward for the award of the Knight's Cross, with the typed recommendation being penned on February 15. The short document contained the following overview:

> *Sturmbrigade "Wallonien"* served with the units of the army and the *Waffen-SS* that were left by themselves during the week-long battles in the area west of Tscherkassy and were able to repulse enemy attacks by themselves. After the brave commander of the brigade, *SS-Sturmbannführer* Lucien Lippert, was killed on 13.02 by a shot through the chest, Degrelle took over leadership. Degrelle, who had already distinguished himself through numerous acts of bravery, proved his excellent fighting leadership during the decisive break-through battles in the last days. In a loyal comradeship of arms he, along with his brave Wallonians who fought on his side and on the side of the men of the army and Germanic men of the *Waffen-SS*, was able to lead the breakout in an excellent fashion. I recommend the award of the Knight's Cross of the Iron Cross for this brave people's leader.

This recommendation was rapidly approved on February 20, 1944. The various documents in his file list the awards of the Close Combat Clasp in Bronze and the Silver Wound Badge. The dates of these awards do vary considerably between November 1943 and the same date as his approval for the Knight's Cross to the Iron Cross. Although the actual dates may vary, it is certain he held these no later than the same day he added the Knight's Cross to his existing list of awards. We will return to the military career of Leon Degrelle in later volumes.

Name: Herbert-Otto Gille
Date of birth: 08.03.1897
SS Number: 39 854
Award: Knight's Cross with Oakleaves and Swords

Gille was featured in the previous volume when he was awarded the Oakleaves to the Knight's Cross at the start of November 1943. Almost immediately following that award, on November 9, he was promoted to *SS-Gruppenführer und Generaleutnant der Waffen-SS*. He remained with his men in their Dnjepr positions as 1943 came to a close, but as 1944 opened, things took on a whole different dimension for Gille and his *Wiking* soldiers.

His division was caught up in the very difficult fighting in the Korsun Pocket during January and early February 1944. On February 18, 1944, almost immediately following the successful breakout, Gille was flown to Hitler's headquarters (with Leon Degrelle). It was there Gille was presented with the Swords to his existing Oakleaves and Swords. There is no surviving official Swords recommendation in Gille's file, but at least two other documents in his file show that on February 20, 1944, Gille was awarded the Swords to his existing Knight's Cross with Oakleaves. This made him only the forty-seventh soldier to receive this high award and only the third *Waffen-SS* soldier. So what can we determine as the rationale for this high level recognition in the absence of any official documentation? Ernst-Gunther Kratschmer's book states the award was made spontaneously by Adolf Hitler, which would support the lack of official documentation.

The challenges Gille and his men faced during those long days in the Korsun Pocket have been covered, and the success achieved when they managed to breakout also helped save thousands of much needed men for further defensive actions. Gille, as divisional commander of *Wiking*, led his remaining men through all of this and ensured they remained focused and effective during this monumental challenge. It would have been easy to become overwhelmed physically and psychologically during a high-pressure situation such as the occurrences within the Korsun Pocket. This is how military routs come to be and the Soviets were hoping for exactly that. Gille's leadership and example to his men, plus his close proximity to them, ensured this did not take place. His leadership example continued right up to the point of reaching friendly forces on the other side of the Gniloy Tikich River.

The men under his command certainly considered him an excellent leader and his superiors obviously agreed; the lack of an official recommendation

Herbert-Otto Gille photographed in the field after he had been awarded the Swords to his existing Knight's Cross with Oakleaves. It was the first set awarded in 1944.

did not get in the way of ensuring the award was given from the hands of the German head of the armed forces. A fitting endorsement of his capabilities and even this example on the part of Gille would not end his connection to this award; his further history will follow within the pages of this volume.

Name: Heinz Kling
Date of birth: 10.09.1913
SS Number: 39 402
Award: Knight's Cross

Born in Kassel, Kling joined the SS on August 1, 1932, and was placed with the *2. Sturm, 26. SS-Standarte*. In September 1933, he moved to the *9. Sturm, 21. SS-Standarte* and two months later was holding the rank *SS-Unterscharführer* (*SS-Scharführer*). He was moved again in November 1934, to the *4. Sturm, 59. SS-Standarte*; whilst with this unit in 1935, he was promoted to *SS-Scharführer*. In late August the same year he moved to *"Germania's" 7. Kompanie*. He remained with *Germania* up to October 1937, when he was sent to Bad Tolz for officer training, leaving there a *SS-Hauptscharführer*. In August 1938, he immediately followed with a platoon leader's course in Dachau and, while there, was promoted to *SS-Standartenoberjunker*. He returned to *Germania* in September and served as a platoon leader with *10. Kompanie*, III Battalion. His first officer rank (*SS-Untersturmführer*) was achieved on November 9. He remained with *Germania* for another year, seeing action in Poland with them, but by then he was with *9. Kompanie*.

In November 1939, he moved to the role of kompanie commander for the *6. Kompanie, 12. SS-Standarte*. He obtained *SS-Obersturmführer* rank at the start of June 1940, with an award of the Second Class Iron Cross coming on August 20. He served with various *SS-Standarte* up to mid-June 1941, then moved to the *Leibstandarte*. Back in January, he was presented with the War Merit Cross Second Class with Swords. He went with the *LSSAH* into Russia that same month and was soon awarded the First Class Iron Cross on July 16. Before the end of the year he had been promoted to *SS-Hauptsturmführer*. It would appear he was wounded in late 1941 or early 1942, as he spent some time with the replacement battalion of the *LSSAH* from April 1942 (the actual award date for the Black Wound Badge is not listed, but higher grade award dates are). He progressed into their Panzer replacement battalion in June before returning to the *Leibstandarte* in November, initially serving in their II Battalion within the Panzer regiment, but quickly moving to the heavy battalion before the end of the year as *1.* kompanie commander. He was awarded the Infantry Assault Badge back in March, with the Silver Wound Badge following on May 1, 1943. Further recognition of his capabilities followed as 1943 progressed, with the Gold Wound Badge being approved on August 26 and the German Cross in Gold coming on December 30; this was awarded for actions with the *LSSAH*'s *Tiger* kompanie from July through late November 1943.

Despite these various high level awards, his commanders felt he warranted further recognition of the efforts he was exerting and as 1944 opened, his regimental commander, *SS-Sturmbannführer* Joachim Peiper, penned a recommendation for the award of the Knight's Cross to the Iron Cross on January 17. It was short in content:

> *SS-Hauptsturmführer* Kling held himself excellently in all of the previous fighting as commander of the *Tiger-Komp*. He carries a major part of the successes of *SS-Tank Regiment. 1 "LSSAH"* and was awarded the German Cross in Gold for his bravery. Also in the winter fighting in the area Korosten - Zhitomir – Berdichev he once again led his kompanie to success.
>
> With only a few operational vehicles—as always his manner was to drive as the lead fighter—Kling was to be found at all focal points of movement, scoring well in countless hard-hitting battles. On 20.12.1943, he personally destroyed his forty-sixth tank.
>
> Thus, kompanie *Kling* has achieved these proud successes in fourteen weeks of operational fighting:
>
> 343 Tanks
> 8 Assault Guns
> 255 Heavy Anti-tank guns
> 20 Guns of middle and heavy caliber
>
> as well as numerous other war material destroyed.
>
> These unique results are forever connected personally to *SS-Hauptsturmführer* Kling, who was personally willing—although he has already been wounded five times—to use his tank soldiers to push forward.
>
> Kling is a proven worthy, crisis-proof natural fighter and he is fully worthy of this proposed award.
>
> (Signed) Peiper

A signed image of Heinz Kling, yet another *LSSAH* Tiger tank Knight's Cross awardee.

Divisional Commander "Teddi" Wisch added his endorsement to this, stating:

I consider *SS-Hauptsturmführer* Kling for his repeatedly proven leadership, his extraordinary personal bravery, and because of the overall excellent leadership of his kompanie should be awarded the Knight's Cross of the Iron Cross.

For worthiness, I please ask you confer this high award to *SS-Hauptsturmführer* Kling.

(Signed) Wisch

SS-Brigadeführer and *Generalmajor der Waffen-SS*

To finish this multi-level proposal off Sepp Dietrich added a short note:

The proposal is supported by me.

(Signed) Dietrich

This multi-signed recommendation was soon approved on February 23, 1944. He was promoted to *SS-Sturmbannführer* on June 21 and was commanding the *101st Heavy SS-Tank Battalion* by then. In January 1945, he was moved to command I Battalion, *12. SS-Panzer Regiment*, within the *12. SS-Panzer Division "Hitler Jugend."* During March 1945, he was ordered to take over command of his former unit (101st Heavy SS-Tank Battalion)—now the 501st Heavy SS-Tank Battalion—remaining with them until the end of the conflict.

He survived the war and died (drowned) on September 10, 1951.

Name: Rudolf Lehmann
Date of birth: 30.01.1914
SS Number: 111 883
Award: Knight's Cross

Born in Heidelberg, he joined the SS in March 1933 and was initially placed with the *.32 SS-Standarte* before being moved to the recently created *SS-Stabswache Berlin*—the *Leibstandarte*'s precursor—in May. By August, he was holding the rank *SS-Sturmmann* and by April 1934, he was an *SS-Unterscharführer*. He took part in an NCO training course from November 1934 through late April 1935, when he was sent to the officer school at Bad Tolz. This lasted until the end of January 1936, and was soon followed by a platoon leader's course at Dachau that took him to the end of March. On April 20, he was promoted to *SS-Untersturmführer.*

From there, he was sent to *SS-Regiment Germania* and while there had his first taste of a staff officer posting. During late 1937 he was serving with their *15. Kompanie*. In January 1938, he was back with the *Leibstandarte* for a short armored-car platoon leader's training course. Returning to *Germania* in February, he had a further armored car course at Doberitz. He is listed as holding the Austrian Anschluss medal, so it is presumed he took part in that campaign in March. By August 1938, he was with *Germania's 14. Kompanie*, with a promotion to *SS-Obersturmführer* coming in September. He also counted the Sudetenland medal amongst his awards, which took place in October. In the second half of May 1939, he was with the armored car platoon of *Germania*. Among the men under his command at that time was Fritz Langanke, later Knight's Cross holder with *Das Reich*; Karl-Heinz Lichte, later Knight's Cross holder with *Wiking*; and Wilhelm Weber, later Knight's Cross holder with *Charlemagne.* It was with this unit Lehmann entered WWII.

Serving in Poland he earned the Second Class Iron Cross, with the medal being awarded on November 14, 1939. At the start of April 1940, he took over command of *14.* kompanie and went into Holland with them. He was awarded the First Class Iron Cross on June 3. Less than one month later, on July 1, he received a promotion to *SS-Hauptsturmführer*. The award of the Infantry Assault Badge came on November 9. From October 1, 1940, he moved to the *Leibstandarte* and had his second staff position as their ordnance officer. He went into the Balkans with them in April 1941, at the same time becoming acting first staff officer. He advanced into Russia in July and was wounded late the following month; this wound removed him from the front line. When he was considered fit once more, in March 1942, he attended a three-month general staff officer's training course. He then returned to the role of first general staff officer for the *Leibstandarte*. On July 6, he added the Bulgarian Bravery Medal IV Class to his awards. A promotion to *SS-Sturmbannführer* came at the start of September. The award of the German Cross in Gold came at the start of November 1943, following a proposal by "Teddi" Wisch and endorsed by *II. SS-Panzer* korps Commander Paul Hausser, who was also Lehmann's former divisional commander. A promotion to *SS-Obersturmbannführer* came on January 30, 1944.

The following day, "Teddi" Wisch penned a comprehensive proposal for Lehmann to be awarded the Knight's Cross:

Rudolf Lehmann shown after his Knight's Cross award. Lehmann was the first staff officer for the *Leibstandarte* and the divisional historian postwar.

SS-Obersturmbannführer Lehmann is, since August 1942, the *Ia* of the division and was awarded the German Cross in Gold on 2.11.1943 for his outstanding performance during the winter fighting of 1943 at Kharkov and also Operation *Zitadelle*.

SS-Obersturmbannführer Lehmann had greatly contributed to the success of the division through his excellent work as a general staff officer during the continuous heavy fighting since November 1943. With his clear judgement of all situations and his superior calmness, he scrupulously prepared the decisions of the divisional commander. At the same time he fully recognized situations that required independent action.

Before noon on 29.12.1943, *SS-Panzergrendier Regiment 2* was positioned on the riverbank of Guiva, while the rest of the division was in the area east of the line connecting the villages Shitomir and Berditschev. These units were engaged in a hard defensive battle against an enemy with superior tank forces. The division, reinforced only with weak panzer support, had the task of stopping the Soviet 3rd Guard Tank Army, which fully intended on securing the highway between Shitomir and Berditschev. At the same time, we had to foil the attempts of the enemy to surround Berditschev. During these defensive morning battles the division received freedom of action from *XLVIII. Panzer* korps with respect to choosing its own main fighting line. Shortly thereafter the division was forced to completely act on its own, since it had almost completely lost contact with *XLVIII. Panzer Korps*.

The area west of the line connecting the villages Bolschije Moschkovzy and Tschernovaje could only be secured with spaced out strong points secured by *SS-Flak Abteilung 1*, *SS-Panzer Pioneer Battalion 1*, and *SS-Panzer Aufklarungs Abteilung 1*. Aerial reconnaissance revealed an enemy tank attack, so the divisional commander set out to reconnoiter the area in his personal tank. With this decision the responsibility of the division was given to *SS-Obersturmbannführer* Lehmann, who was unable to maintain contact with the divisional commander. At about 11:00 hours, the pressure exerted by the enemy tank forces coming from the north and east became so strong that the only action left to prevent the division from being annihilated was to disengage. The concentrated advance of the enemy tanks on the divisional command post could not be beaten off, nor even stopped by the regiments defending it. The fighting during the early hours of the day revealed the enemy's strategy of retreating from difficult fighting, after which they proceeded to surround our forces.

At about 12:00 hours, *SS-Obersturmbannführer* Lehmann decided to issue the order to disengage, retreat, and form a new defensive line linking the villages Tatarinovka, Solotvin, and Folovykoye. At the same time we held open the village Kaskapna-Mogila, which would serve to secure the disengaging grenadier regiments.

After personally reconnoitering the areas north and northeast on an observation motorcycle, *SS-Obersturmbannführer* Lehmann secured the occupied village by organizing troops of *SS-Panzer Nachrichten Abteilung 1*, a few panzers in need of repair, and several drivers and typists of the divisional staff, as well as remnants of *SS-Panzer Artillery Regiment 1*, which had been overrun by enemy tanks. Lehmann situated these forces to provide an all-around defense. He then gave the command to all of the battle groups to retreat to the new main fighting line.

Even though an enemy tank group of more than thirty tanks was operating on the flank and in the back of the divisional command post—one of which was firing directly at the battle groups—the units were able to hold the village until the entire retreat of men and vehicles was complete.

Through this independent decision, *SS-Obersturmbannführer* Lehmann not only displayed exceptional bravery, but also deserves to be recognized for his exceptional capacity to maintain the fighting ability of the division. He enabled the division on 30.12.1943 and during the following days to hold out during undiminishing heavy Russian infantry attacks and beat back their tanks attacks.

The execution of these retreating movements of the battle groups was, next to the exceptional bravery of the men in these positions, only possible because *SS-Obersturmbannführer* Lehmann led the movements with sovereign calmness and a superior confidence while giving precise orders, as well as personally leading the retreating movements of the division. He also visited his troops positioned in the outer security positions and, with weapon in hand, took over their leadership.

SS-Obersturmbannführer Lehmann has proven himself during all fighting in the area east of Shitomir, near Radomyschl; northeast of Tschernjachoff; east of Korosten, in the area east of the line between Shitomir and Berditschev; southwest of Berditschev; and for a short time south of Pogrebischtsche. His experience, his

> exceptional calmness in war situations and, above all, his sure and clear judgement of the situation, as well as his lightning-quick and energetic behavior, have contributed to each battle. With his exceptional and imaginative general staff work he has to be credited with a large part of the division's successes.
>
> I believe *SS-Obersturmbannführer* Lehmann, because of his excellently maintained attitude every time, his personal bravery, and his outstanding services in the areas of military troop leadership is worthy of the award of the Knight's Cross to the Iron Cross and I please ask that he is given this high award.

Sepp Dietrich also added his thoughts and highlighted Lehmann was personally brave, strong during a crisis, and an excellent leader when having to make decisions. He went on to state that Lehmann's general staff work was especially worthy of this award. The approval followed on February 23, 1944, but this would not end his connection to this medal; we will cover his remaining history in the final volume of this project.

Name: Hans Traupe
Date of birth: 04.05.1913
SS Number: 121 951
Award: Knight's Cross

Born in Kunern, near Munsterburg, he joined the SS at the start of May 1933. Whilst still a member of the SS, he served in the *Reichwehr* from April 1934 to October 1935. By the start of April 1936, he was holding the rank *SS-Unterscharführer* and was sent to Bad Tolz for officer training. Five months later he moved to *SS-Scharführer*. In the second half of February 1937, he was an *SS-Hauptscharführer*; this was the same time he was attending a platoon leader's course at Dachau. On April 20, he was promoted to *SS-Untersturmführer*. He attended a course for junior officers of the *Schutzpolizei* in the first half of 1938. His next promotion came on November 9, when he became an *SS-Obersturmführer*.

With the creation of the *SS-Polizei Division*, Traupe was one of the officers sent to the new unit in October 1940. He initially served as a platoon leader, but in early April 1940, he moved to a divisional staff position; it was also during this month he was promoted to *SS-Hauptsturmführer*. He took part in the western campaign during May and June 1940; the award of the Second Class Iron Cross was made on June 19. In September, Traupe assumed command of *6.* kompanie within the *Polizei's* 1st Regiment. Operation Barbarossa was his next campaign and the award of the First Class Iron Cross was made on September 5, 1941. His men fought in the northern Leningrad sector from the early opening stages and right through 1942 and beyond. He had taken over *8.* kompanie in January 1942, and that year would be a busy one for him! He added the Black Wound Badge on August 2, the Russian Front Medal the following day, the German Cross in Gold on September 25, and the Infantry Assault Badge at the start of November 1942. In the closing weeks of the year he took temporary command of II Battalion.

In January 1943, he was sent on a month-long battalion leader's course; when he returned to the front he took over III Battalion. Promotion to *SS-Sturmbannführer* came on June 21. He remained with that battalion as it became part of the *SS-Polizei's* Grenadier Regiment 3, but was renamed I Battalion of that regiment; this change took place in late October 1943. For his actions leading that battalion during January 1944, existing Knight's Cross holder *SS-Sturmbannführer* Wilhelm Dietrich proposed the award of the Knight's Cross to Hans Traupe in a document dated February 3, 1944:

> On 23.1.1944, *SS-Pol.Gren.Rgt. 3*, after it reached the area of Wolnaja Gorka by rapid transport, was assigned to hold the gap between *Kampfgruppe Speth* (Kromy area) and *Kampfgruppe Schuldt* (Saklinje area). This was to ensure the korps supply road between Sselo Gora – Wolnaja Gorka – Luga was kept open against attacks from the area south of Krasny and via Podberesje, Dolgowo, and the railway station at Tatino being made by the enemy's *310.* and *377. Schutzen Divisions*.
>
> After the enemy managed to take Saklinje with surprising ease—the right-hand cornerstone defense of *Kampfgruppe Schuldt*—they moved to overwhelm the forces ahead of and near Puddubje. During the night of 23. / 24. 44, they attempted to reach the Wolnaja Gorka Welegoschtschi road via Libunizy, which would have made it impossible for the *SS-Polizei-Division Kampfgruppe* to withdraw via Welegoschtschi. It would have allowed the enemy to reach *XXVIII. Army Korps'* retreat road without facing resistance.
>
> *Stubaf.* Traupe, commander of *I. / SS-Pol.Gren. Rgt. 3*, was positioned with his battalion around Libunizy, on the regiment's left wing. They had been given the task to hold Libunizy and prevent the enemy from breaking through to the Wolnaja Gorka –

A signed image of Hans Traupe showing his Knight's Cross, the only such *SS-Polizei* award during 1944.

> Welegoschtschi road until the kampfgruppe were given the order to withdraw by the *korps*.
>
> The enemy, who realized the significance of this position for their further operations, tried from 24. to 28.1.44—with and without preparatory artillery fire, in day and night attacks, and with *kompanie*-strong attack groups or several regiment-strong attack waves—to take Libunizy-Lushkoje time and time again. The enemy wished to turn the flank of the formations employed south of the Wolnaja Gorka – Batizkaja - Luga road (*Kampfgruppe SS-Pol.Div*, *Kampfgruppe Speth*).
>
> The Russians were unsuccessful thanks to the determined and fanatical will to defend, which does justice to the excellent leadership skills of *Stubaf.* Traupe. Traupe was the soul of the defense and was always found in the areas of greatest danger. At first with the reserve platoon, then with the reserve groups, and then with not more than three or four men from his staff Traupe threw them against the attacks. Man to man the intruding enemy was thrown back and Traupe brought the Russian attack to a standstill. Himself wounded, he retained command of his battalion to the last, after a large part of his officers, NCOs, and men had fallen.
>
> Since the beginning of the war Traupe has been at the front and on countless occasions has shown proof of his untiring initiative and daredevil nature that is combined with a great sense of responsibility and leadership qualities.

It is not unusual for endorsements to accompany the initial proposal and this was the case for Hans Traupe. What was unusual for this overall proposal is that the endorsement, written by *SS-Standartenführer* Friedrich-Wilhelm Bock on February 9, detailed a completely new perspective on Traupe's actions during that battle. That document details the same key points: the threat posed by the enemy thrust, Traupe's reaction to it, his initiative and bravery and, last but not least, the result of denying the enemy their objectives. Bock ends the first page by stating how worthy he felt Traupe was for the award of this prestigious medal.

There are further lengthy documents, that go into detail on the day-to-day objectives and results during this period. There is also an ending summary that gives the strength of the kampfgruppe and the resulting losses to the enemy—nearly 1,000 dead and over 150 various weapons—as a result of Traupe's actions. This overall extensive and dual proposal was approved on February 23, 1944. That approval gave *Polizei* their first Knight's Cross award for 1944 and the only one for the time covered in this volume.

As touched on in the proposal document, Traupe was wounded in January, but he remained at the front. For a short period from early March, Traupe assumed command of the regiment due to the wounding of his initial Knight's Cross proposer, Dietrich. In April, Traupe had a spell of leave; then he was given the task of helping gather the returning wounded from his former kampfgruppe at the training grounds in Kurmark. While there, he was promoted to *SS-Obersturmbannführer* on June 21. He attended a regimental commander's course from mid-August through early September 1944, then spent almost a month in the *SS-Führer* reserve, before being posted to *10. SS-Panzer Division Frundsberg* at the start of October. He was given command of the *22nd SS-Panzergrenadier Regiment* and retained it until the end of the war. He survived the conflict and lived in Dresden afterward, dying on June 23, 2004.

Name: Heinrich Heimann
Date of birth: 17.9.1915
SS Number: 323 826
Award: Knight's Cross

Born in Norddinken, his prewar and early-war history is not determined. What is certain is he received the First Class Iron Cross on September 14, 1941, presumably for actions in the opening phases of Operation Barbarossa. He would have been an *SS-Obersturmführer* at that stage, as on April 20, 1942, he moved to *SS-Hauptsturmführer*. In the second half of 1942, he received the Russian Front Medal along with his kameraden. He also held the Black Wound Badge and Infantry Assault Badge, but award dates are not listed. As the Kursk Offensive opened in early July 1943, he assumed command of the *Sturmgeschutze Battalion* (on the sixth). The approval of the German Cross in Gold came soon after on September 6.

His leadership of *Sturmgeschutze Battalion* throughout the remainder of 1943 earned him further high-level praise, when on January 31, divisional commander "Teddi" Wisch recommended Heinrich Heimann for the Knight's Cross:

> *SS-Hauptsturmführer* Heimann has been commander of *SS-Sturmgeschutze Battalion 1* since 07.06.1943.

I. *SS-Sturmgeschutze Battalion 1* took part in all of the combat days during Operation Citadel, in the difficult fighting since 1.11.1943, and in the defensive battles in the area east of Shitomir, Berdichew, and southwest of Berdichew. *SS-Hauptsturmführer* Heimann was, as ever, always close by and leading constantly from his command vehicle. Thanks to his characteristically prominent leadership skills, great experience, and superb attacking spirit that has become self evident for his entire battalion, he could achieve great successes by pushing through each order given.

During Operation Citadel *SS-Hauptsturmführer* Heimann was employed in close support, driving forward at the head of his battalion during the six days of fighting and the armored battle south of Prokurowka on 12.7.1943. Using his own initiative and utilizing his battalion to good effect, he drove off larger-sized attacks from the enemy and shot up fifteen enemy tanks.

II. By the advance of the division into the deep flank of the Russians on 15.11.1943 from Kornin and Kotscherowo along the road Shitomir - Kiev, *SS-Hauptsturmführer* Heimann, along with his battalion, had the order to divide up this armored group. After the taking of Ssolowjewka, the attacking group was to push forward to the northwest. In this attack, which was moved forward during falling darkness, the enemy had reinforced their defenses heavily. They had anticipated an attack from the direction of Ssolowkewka, on their left-hand neighbor, by the lead point of the *1. Panz. Div.*, who felt the full weight of this. *SS-Hauptsturmführer* Heimann, with his self-propelled guns in the lead, realized the town Wodoty was crucial for the rest of the attack. He made an independent decision to drive an attack with his weak infantry forces and vehicles. He eliminated the frontal defense with some of the vehicles after overcoming two anti-tank guns coming from the east. The enemy, who had settled into the village with all-around defense, was completely overwhelmed and destroyed by this energetic attack. They engaged the fleeing enemy on their heels and *SS-Hauptsturmführer* Heimann fought with his last three vehicles and a few grenadiers during the course of the night. He also took nearby Pokryschew, Romanovka, Semenowka, and Sdwischka in his possession. Despite repeated thrusts against them by the enemy, *SS-Hauptsturmführer* Heimann succeeded—through the skillful use of his vehicles and deceiving the enemy while guiding reinforcements—to hold the embattled

The *Leibstandarte's* Heinrich Heimann seen in a poor quality image showing his Knight's Cross award.

villages until the main armored group arrived. This independent decision that demonstrated bravery and resulted in low losses was successful thanks to the thrust by *SS-Hauptsturmführer* Heimann.

III. During the winter fighting (1943/44) from 10.11.1943 to 29.1.1944, *SS-Hauptsturmführer* Heimann and his battalion engaged in nineteen battalion attacks, including some multi-day and night attacks. Since 5.7.1943 he and his battalion had destroyed:

157 Enemy tanks,
189 Anti-tank guns, 7.62 cm and
71 Anti-tank guns, 4.7 cm

From this list, *SS-Hauptsturmführer* Heimann was personally involved with:

9 Tanks
19 Anti-tank guns, 7.62 cm
11 Anti-tank guns, 4.7 cm

SS-Hauptsturmführer Heimann has, during all of the fighting days and in every combat position, time and again ultimately persevered. His standing personal attacks—even if only a small number of vehicles were ready—with him leading these along with his men, is an ideal model.

I consider *SS-Hauptsturmführer* Heimann, with his exceptional leadership qualities proven time and time again on the battlefield, and because of his bravery and outstanding leadership of his battalion is worthy of the high award of the Knight's Cross of the Iron Cross, and I ask you to give him this award.

(signed) Wisch
SS-Brigadeführer und Generalmajor der Waffen-SS'

There was a short endorsement from Sepp Dietrich:

SS-Hstuf. Heimann has remained constant before the enemy and is one of the most deserving leaders of the division.

(signed) Dietrich
SS-Obergruppenführer und Panzergeneral der Waffen-SS

This recommendation was approved on February 23, 1944. It would appear a promotion to *SS-Sturmbannführer* came too, backdated to January 30. He continued to lead this battalion until August 20, when he was killed in action near Chambois, France.

Name: Joachim Richter
Date of birth: 28.07.1896
SS Number: 56 182
Award: Knight's Cross

Born in Magdeburg, his military service started during WWI. Beginning as an officer candidate, he received his promotion to *leutnant* in April 1915. During that conflict he served as an artillery officer, observation officer, liaison officer, battalion adjutant, and battalion commander. He was recognized twice for bravery, earning the Second Class Iron Cross on Christmas Eve 1914 and the First Class Iron Cross on August 9, 1918. He was also given the Honour Cross for Front Fighters. He remained with the army in the immediate postwar period and was part of a border protection unit; he left the army in 1919, pursuing civilian jobs until 1933. He was awarded the Silesian Eagle Badge, 1st and 2nd Class for his postwar military sevice.

In mid-March 1933, he joined the *Allgemeine-SS* and was placed with the *49. SS-Standarte*. A promotion to *SS-Scharführer* (*SS-Unterscharführer*) came at the start of July, followed quickly on August 29 by a move to *SS-Truppführer* (*SS-Oberscharführer*). On January 30, 1934, he was moved to *SS-Oberabschnitt "Sudost,"* based in Breslau. He was promoted to *SS-Sturmführer* (*SS-Untersturmführer*) the same day and began a stint as special duties officer. He was promoted again on May 27 to *SS-Obersturmführer*, and also on January 19, 1935, when he moved to *SS-Hauptsturmführer*. On January 30, 1936, he was moved to staff leader for that *Allgemeine-SS* formation, accompanied by a promotion to *SS-Sturmbannführer*. He spent a one-month stint with the army's Artillery Oberserver Battalion 28 from May to June 1936, utilizing his WWI artillery experience. His next promotion to *SS-Obersturmbannführer* was made on January 30, 1937, and he returned to Artillery Oberserver Battalion 28 the following month for a further short stint. In late April, he was given the army rank *leutnant* (reserve). At the start of October, he moved in the same staff leader role to *SS-Oberabschnitt "Fulda-Werra,"* which was near Arolsen. Between March and April 1938, he was back with the army artillery, this time with Observer Battalion 15. On April 20 he was promoted to the *Allgemeine-SS* rank *SS-Standartenführer*.

He returned to Oberserver Battalion 15 from mid-February through early July 1939.

Immediately after the Polish campaign in September, *SS-Division Totenkopf* was formed and Richter was one of the men selected to join them in October 1939. He transferred to them with the rank *SS-Hauptsturmführer* and took up a post as an artillery battery commander. He did not see action in the west during 1940, as he was with *Totenkopf's* Artillery Replacement Battalion from April through September. He then returned to the main *Totenkopf Division*, leading its II Battalion within the Artillery Regiment. He was promoted to *SS-Sturmbannführer* on April 20, 1941, and it was around the same time he moved to *SS-Division Wiking* as commander of its II Battalion within their artillery regiment. It was with this unit he would see his first action in his second worldwide conflict.

Advancing with *Wiking* into Russia in mid-1941, he rapidly earned further awards for his capabilities: the Clasp to the Second Class Iron Cross was awarded on July 11, and was followed on August 8 with the Clasp to the First Class Iron Cross. In early February 1942, he took over command of IV Battalion and then, on April 20, he received promotion to *SS-Obersturmbannführer*. He added the Infantry Assault Badge to his tunic on May 9. He is listed as being awarded the Finnish Order of the Cross of Freedom, 2nd Class, on April 6, 1943, although why he would receive that award is unclear. At the start of May 1943, Richter took over command of *Wiking's* artillery regiment. His promotion to *SS-Standartenführer* followed on November 9. He was awarded the German Cross in Gold on November 17 for actions stretching back two years. The challenging battles of early 1944 resulted in Gille recommending Richter for the award of the Knight's Cross, dated February 20:

> Since the beginning of the encirclement, *SS-Standartenführer* Richter, commander of SS-Artillery Regiment "*Wiking*," has led a battle group composed of *SS-Panzergrenadier Regiment "Westland,"* the SS-Reconnaissance Detachment, alarm units, anti-aircraft guns and tank detachments with only three Hummels, one self-propelled gun, and one assault gun as heavy support weapons.
>
> The night of 10-11.02.1944, the battle group took defensive positions to the east of Korssun along the Ross sector, with the task of holding these positions until 12.02.1944.
>
> The enemy pushed unceasingly with superior tank and infantry forces from both sides of the Arbusino-Korssun road, trying to force a breakthrough. There were also partisan attacks from the Chut

Joachim Richter shown wearing his Knight's Cross, the first one for *SS-Wiking* in 1944.

> woods in the rear of the weakly occupied position. Deploying continuous counter-thrusts, the breakthrough spearheads were thrown back and the tanks destroyed in close combat. Where danger threatened *SS-Standartenführer* Richter appeared, organizing the defense and carrying out counterattacks. With his personal example he always rallied his men to attack and prevented the splitting of the front in the sector until 12.02.1944.
>
> In an aerodrome close behind the main fighting line there still remained large amounts of gasoline, ammunition, and supplies that could not be removed before 12.02.1944. *SS-Standartenführer* Richter independently decided to halt movement until these important goods were completely taken away and provided to the troops. Not before 13.02.1944 was he ordered to disengage the opponent and take positions in the new main fighting line west of Korssun.
>
> In Korssun itself, there remained long columns of vehicles because of traffic jams, the bad roads, and the conditions of the bridges that would fall in the hands of the enemy when orders to occupy the new fighting line were carried out. *SS-Standartenführer* Richter, on his own decision, ordered the building of a bridgehead to the east of Korssun, enabling an orderly departure of these units toward the west.
>
> I consider *SS-Standartenführer* Richter especially worthy of being awarded the Knight's Cross.

This proposal had an endorsement added by Heinrich Himmler the following day, which no doubt accelerated the approval to February 23, 1944. Richter's next move was to the SS training school at Keinschlag from August 10. Less than one month later he attended a divisional commander's course that lasted until October 7, 1944. In early February 1945, he briefly (less than two weeks) held command of the *32. SS-Freiwilligen-Grenadier Division "30 Januar."* He was placed on the staff of the SS Personal Main Office from that point until the end of the war. One source lists him as receiving a promotion to *SS-Oberführer* on April 20, 1945, although his file does not list this. He survived the war and died on March 19, 1970, in Arolsen.

Name: Manfred Schonfelder
Date of birth: 18.03.1912
SS Number: 59 781
Award: Knight's Cross

Born in Hellerau, near Dresden, he joined the SS in 1932. In late 1934, he was a member of Political Readiness Unit "Sachsen." He was sent to Bad Tolz between April 1935 and February 1936; promotion to *SS-Untersturmführer* came on April 20. He then began service with *SS-Regiment Deutschland.* He was promoted to *SS-Obersturmführer* in 1937, but the exact date is not listed. He held positions as battalion adjutant and kompanie officer during 1938 and early 1939. *SS-Hauptsturmführer* rank came on April 20, 1939.

He took part in the actions in Poland in 1939, earning the Second Class Iron Cross on October 3. Action in the western campaign followed in 1940, and he was awarded the Black Wound Badge on June 10 and the First Class Iron Cross on June 18. In December 1940, he moved to *SS-Regiment "Germania,"* serving as regimental adjutant. He was awarded the Infantry Assault Badge at the start of June 1941 and moved with the initial advance in Russia in 1941, earning the Russian Front Medal in August 1942. Earlier in 1942, he served on the staff of the *XXIV. Army* korps and also took part in a general staff training course. The award of the German Cross in Gold came on June 11, 1942, although the recommendation does not appear in his file. He returned to service with the *Waffen-SS* in September, this time placed with the *SS-Division Wiking*. During the following month he moved to divisional first staff officer, and rounded off 1942 with a further promotion to *SS-Sturmbannführer* in November. He was promoted to *SS-Obersturmbannführer* one year later.

On February 20, 1944, Divisional Commander Gille wrote a recommendation for the award of the Knight's Cross for Schonfelder:

> *SS-Obersturmbannführer* Schonfelder is, since December 1942, the *Ia* (first staff officer) for *SS-Pz. Div. Wiking* and in this time has delivered excellent general staff work. Through his decisiveness and firmness, he has contributed in various ways during all of the crises of the division. At any time he has delivered against the highest demands placed upon him.
>
> His decisiveness was particularly evident in the fighting at Gorodishtche from 8. to 9.2.44. Through rainfall, the roads had become groundless and almost impassable. The initiated withdrawals could, therefore, only be carried out in sections preceded by timely

An autographed photo of Manfred Schonfelder showing his various combat awards. He has listed his posts as Ia of *Wiking* and *IV. SS-Panzer Korps* chief of staff.

measures, so they could figure out positions in the mud for the heavy weapons. The orders for the removal from position "Green" to position "Red" came late, so they only had four hours to do this. Since it was in this crucial moment there was a breach in the southern positions at Petropawlowka, Schonfelder had to decide to go back to the "Red" line or remain for another twenty-four hours with the heavy weapons and secure the gap in the front line created by the removal of his neighbors to the right. He made the decision to remain after a breach occurred at Hof Skiti, and to hold between there and the main battle line (Black). Through this, the opportunity to move the heavy weapons from their positions at Mlejewo to Gorodischtsche was possible, since there was no other street or road present to move to the new "Red" position. He held open the gap in the front via security and alarm units.

Exclusively, and only by the personal intervention of *SS-Ostubaf.* Schonfelder were all of the heavy weapons taken through to Gorodischtsche. This was significant to successfully obtaining the new position.

I therefore consider *SS-Obersturmbannführer* Schonfelder, due to his successful resolve, worthy of being awarded the Knight's Cross.

Heinrich Himmler endorsed this recommendation the following day from his field headquarters. The award was approved a mere two days later, on February 23, 1944.

He is listed as holding the post chief of the general staff for the *IV. SS-Panzer* korps from early August 1944 and remained in that post until the end of the war. Schonfelder survived the war and died on March 4, 1983.

Name: Fritz Ehrath
Date of birth: 09.08.1909
SS Number: 6 605
Award: Knight's Cross

Born in Karlsruhe, he was a member of the *SA* from April 20 through November 1, 1930; he then moved to the SS. This early membership in the SS permitted him to wear the Alte Kampfe Chevron. By January 1934, he was an *SS-Oberscharführer*, but he obtained *SS-Untersturmführer* rank by April 20. He moved to the *Political Bereitschaft Ellwangen* (the forerunner

A signed photograph of Fritz Ehrath clearly showing his Knight's Cross and other combat awards.

to *SS-Regiment Deutschland*), initially serving with *1. Kompanie*, but soon moved to *3. Kompanie*. By the start of 1936, he was serving as the *1b* on the battalion staff. *SS-Obersturmführer* rank was approved on April 20, and by the start of December he was performing the role of battalion adjutant for their III Battalion. At the start of December 1936, he was placed in command of *Deutschland's 11. Kompanie*. On April 20, 1938, he was promoted to *SS-Hauptsturmführer*.

He advanced into Poland and clearly displayed early signs of bravery in action, with the Second Class Iron Cross being awarded on September 23, 1939, and the First Class Iron Cross coming very soon after on October 1! In April 1940, he attended a battalion commander's course. His next action was during the advance westward in May, and he received a wound on the fifteenth; the Black Wound Badge was presented for it.

In early 1941, at the start of February, he became commander of *Der Führer's I Battalion*. *SS-Sturmbannführer* rank came on June 21, just as they were moving into Russia. His second wound occurred on October 16. At the start of April 1942, he attended a regimental commander's course at the Wunsdorf Panzer school. On January 10, 1943, he was approved for the award of the German Cross in Gold for actions going back to late 1941 and early 1942 in Russia. A rise to *SS-Obersturmbannführer* came in April 1943; by October, he was in full command of the *Germania Regiment* in *Wiking*. Besides the awards listed above, by the end of 1943, he also held the Tank Assault Badge and Russian Front Medal.

Caught up in the difficult fighting the opening weeks of 1944 brought, his actions on February 15–16, 1944, resulted in him being proposed for the award of the Knight's Cross on February 20 by a document compiled by Herbert Gille that contained this overview:

> *SS-Obersturmbannführer* Ehrath led a battle group consisting of the *SS-Pz.Gren.Rgt. Germania*, *SS-Pz.Abt. Wiking*, and the *SS-Art. Rgt.* in the cauldron of Korssun. He was protecting the southern part of the cauldron at Schenderowka on 15.2.44 and was without heavy weapons due to the previous heavy fighting and the rough, muddy land. He had only one *Sturmgeschutz* and four Panzer IVs to support his defense and keep this position until all the elements of the *XXXXII.* and *XI. A.K.* had broken through and closed up to the southwest, in the direction of Lysyanka.
>
> On 15.2.44, the enemy began an attack with superior infantry and tank forces from the southern part of Novo-Buda, along the

road Morentsy – Schenderowka, and constantly attacked the positions of Battle Group Ehrath. The enemy tank attack collapsed against their resistance and defense, and groups of enemy retreated back under the counterattack melee of close combat and weapons. *SS-Ostubaf.* Ehrath was the soul of this crucial struggle, and he led from the front line in this clean-up of their front. The goal of the enemy—the splitting of the cauldron—could be seen clearly from the south. Through the tenacious resistance of the battle group they continually made an enemy breakthrough impossible; the enemy attacked until the early morning of 17.02.44.

The enclosed troops then prepared to begin their escape to the west and feed everyone through. This began at 23:00 hours on 16.2.44 and was to be complete by the early hours of the following morning. This schedule was delayed by difficult terrain and enemy actions *SS-Ostubaf.* Ehrath held the position until all of the troops and wounded were set on the march, and only then did he give the order to disengage from the enemy and fight, along with his battle group, through to the relief point.

Due to this brave hold they persevered and repelled all enemy attacks, where twenty-four tanks were destroyed through close combat. It became possible to issue the order to push the mass of the trapped men through the march route.

Signed. Gille
SS-Gruppenführer and Div. commander

Gille's recommendation was supported by Heinrich Himmler and finally approved on February 23, 1944.

By May 1944, Ehrath was commanding the Westland Regiment. In September, he is listed as being on the SS reserve list, which could be the result of wounds. This is followed by a stint commanding *SS-Panzer Grenadier Training and Replacement Battalion 2*, which took him from November 1944 through January 1945. He returned to the reserve officer group and no further details of his activities in the closing months of the war are available. Fritz Ehrath survived the war and died on August 20, 1972, in Neckargemund.

CHAPTER THREE

THE ENCIRCLEMENTS CONTINUE: KOVEL AND KAMENETS, MARCH 1944

The unrelenting Soviets continued their offensive pushes into March and, although they were temporarily halted in places, the advances knew no bounds in others. One of the next places that would become a focus for both sides would be the strategically important Kovel, in western Ukraine. Let us detail how the *Waffen-SS* found themselves fighting there and how this battle would become one of the most famous engagements of the war for that military force.

5. SS-Panzer Division Wiking

The remnants of the *Wiking Division* were collected together in the remaining days of February 1944 and then sent to an area centered in Lublin, Poland, just over 475 miles west of their former location. On the twentieth, Gille was presented his Swords personally by Hitler (the *Wallonian* Commander Degrelle was there too to receive his Knight's Cross). The men were due to move farther west, but the rapidly changing events on the eastern front would impact *Wiking*. Despite their recent ordeal in the Korsun area, they were sent to the city of Kovel, within the Pripjet Marshes. This would take them from their current Polish location back across the border and into the Ukraine; it was a move of around 125 miles east and took them about 375 miles northwest of their former fighting location. The men of *Wiking*, who had been fighting almost non-stop since 1941 and had not left the eastern front in that time, were about to undergo a further test of their fighting abilities. The key to bear in mind is these remnants of *Wiking* had left behind pretty much all equipment in the Korsun area, so they had to be re-equipped with virtually every level of weapon, from machine guns to armored vehicles.

The moves from Lublin to Kovel began in mid-March 1944. Gille flew ahead and into Kovel as his men followed behind in trains. The fast moving advances of the Soviets resulted in Gille becoming cut off in the city as the Russians closed around the outer reaches. The advancing trains of *Wiking* came under fire from these enemy soldiers and had to temporarily halt their advance. This rail advance was made via Cholm and the lead elements managed to make it as far as Luboml, thirty-five miles west of Kovel. From there, the farther moves eastward towards Kovel had to be made on the ground against a mix of Soviet troops and partisan forces. The men of *Wiking* had received some re-equipping while in Lublin in readiness for their commitment at Kovel, but they were mainly light weapons. Heavier support came in the form of *Germania's III* (armored) *Battalion* under *SS-Sturmbannführer* Franz Hack; they had StuGs as part of their order of battle. Alongside this was II Battalion of *SS-Panzer Regiment 5*, who had recently arrived and were equipped with Panther tanks (*8.* kompanie under Karl Nicolussi-Leck).

The initial advances got to Maciejow, eighteen miles from Kovel, by March 21. The advance inched forward to Milanowicze—fifteen miles west of Kovel—and around five miles north of there at Czerkasy (bears a very similar name to where some of these men were a month earlier!); *Wiking* Panthers broke through the defenses there on March 29. This was done under heavy snowstorm conditions and, although they had taken that village, the enemy was still strong. Orders arrived to halt for the time being, but Nicolussi-Leck decided to move ahead with the support of a small group of Heer kameraden. He wanted to take advantage of the momentum they had gained so, against orders, he advanced onward towards Kovel. Further enemy engagements took place with his diminishing group of Panther tanks, but on March 30, 1944, he reached the command post of *SS-Gruppenführer* Gille; this action resulted in Nicolussi-Leck receiving the Knight's Cross and will be detailed in this volume.

SS-Kavallerie Regiment 17

The fighting continued on and off in February, and then started to increase in intensity during the first half of March 1944, as these SS cavalry men moved farther westward towards Kovel. Soviet forces were intent on taking this strategically important rail juncture and *SS-Gruppenführer* Gille was sent to Kovel in mid-March to assume command of the city—just in time for the encirclement to become complete—with *SS-Kavellerie Regiment 17* as part of the troops now trapped inside!

Fighting continuously 200 miles farther to the southeast, the men of *Leibstandarte* and the *Das Reich* battle group would find themselves trapped within another pocket, one that required a rescue force to assist. That rescue force would draw additional *Waffen-SS* units to the Eastern Front, so let us see how March 1944 looked for those soldiers.

1. SS-Panzer Division Leibstandarte SS Adolf Hitler

Now in their new locations around Proskuroff, the first enemy engagements began on March 4 in an area north of Proskuroff, centered round Kupel. Over the next week, they fought the Soviets to the south as the enemy moved strong forces directly southward past Kupel. During this fighting *SS-Hauptsturmführer* Erich Gratz fought around Manatschin; his bravery there resulted in him being awarded the Knight's Cross in the first half of 1944, which will be detailed in this volume. The enemy pressure forced the *LSSAH* southward from Kupel and by the tenth they were fighting along the railway line running west to east near Wojtowzy, around sixty miles northwest of Proskuroff. Enemy movements forced them to continue southwest of there and they continued to fight constant battles, reaching out towards Fedorki over the next week. By the end of the third week of March 1944, they were farther west along the Sbrucz River and less than ten miles from Fedorki.

Enemy advances to the south forced the *LSSAH* to move even farther south. By the last week in March, the *Leibstandarte* were an additional forty miles south of there and now caught within the Kamenets-Podolsky Pocket, which had been closed on March 25. *SS-Sturmbannführer* Gustav Knittel's command of his men during the majority of March 1944 would lead to his later approval for the award of the Knight's Cross (volume 5). It was only a number of weeks earlier that the *LSSAH* was sent to rescue their *Wiking* and *Wallonie* kameraden, but now they were trapped in a pocket of their own!

SS-Kampfgruppe Lammerding / Weidinger

The Soviets launched a major attack on March 3; a push that forced the men of this battle group to move positions once more and took them to the southeast towards Staro Konstantinow, via Shepetowka. The closing of that stage of their fight constituted the final aspect of Heinz Lammerding's Knight's Cross award (detailed in this volume). On March 7, during this difficult move, Lammerding was ordered to join the main division in East

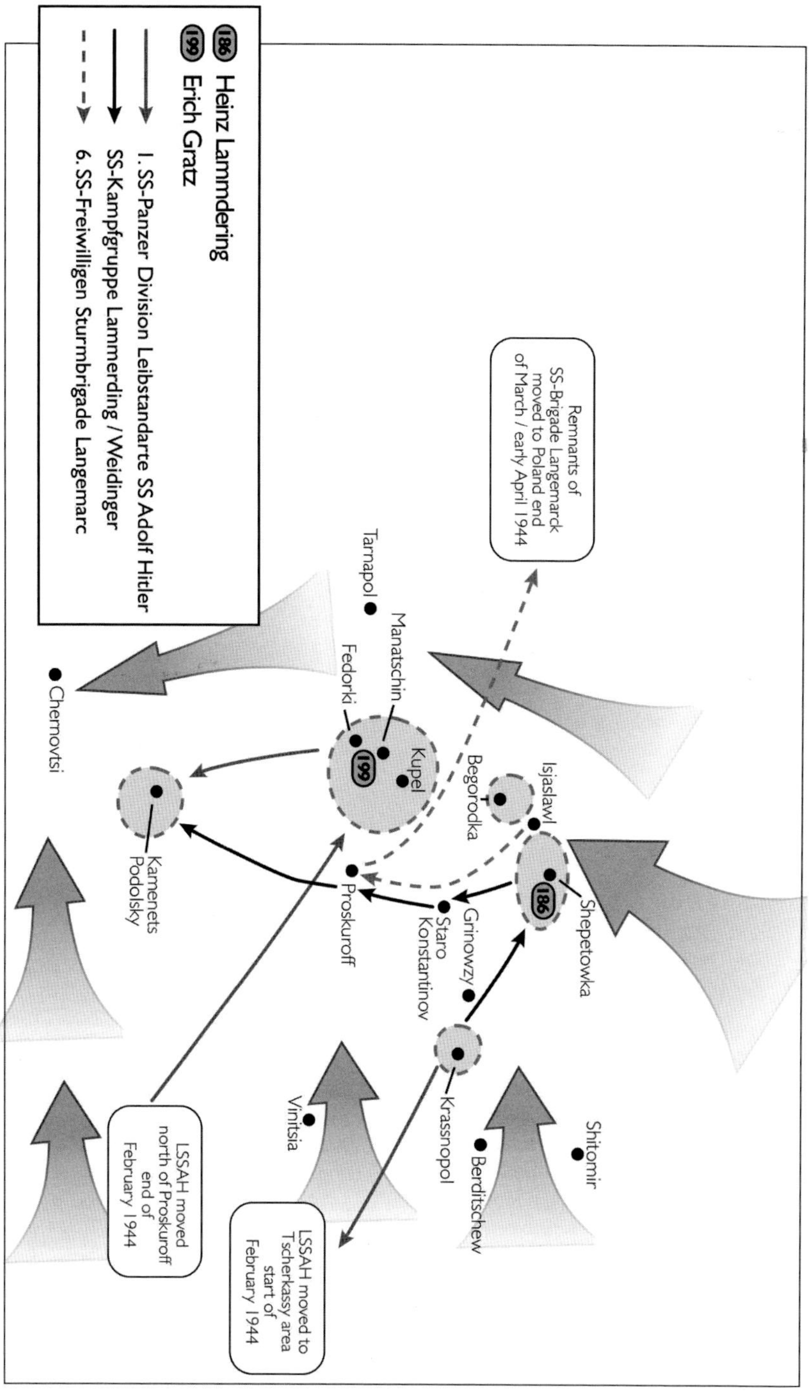

Map 12 – Kamenets–Podolsky Pocket Formation: February and March 1944

Prussia. His replacement was *SS-Sturmbannführer* Otto Weidinger, who had been fighting with the battle group during this whole period. From this time onward, the battle group was known as *SS-Kampfgruppe Weidinger*. On March 11, existing Knight's Cross holder *SS-Hauptsturmführer* Alfred Lex was killed in action; he was one of the key leaders of the recent defensive action over the preceding weeks. The following day brought another notable Knight's Cross-related activity: approval of the award for *SS-Obersturmführer* Heinrich Schmelzer, for his actions back in late December 1943 (detailed in this volume).

Movements were now made to the southwest around the middle of March 1944. Their route took them from Proskurow and onto Lissogorka, due to the pressure from the Soviets and their desire to cut off and destroy any German forces they could. From March 17, they continued through Deraschnia, Slobodka, and on to small Ssewerinowka. By March 21, they had reached Bar and the enemy was in close proximity all of the time. Upon reaching that location they were ordered to hold it against the enemy, but they had to eject some Russian troops from Bar first! This city was important for the withdrawal of friendly troops.

Unrelenting enemy attacks forced constant changes; now operating in the Kamenets-Podolsky Pocket, orders were to move west to link with friendly forces. *SS-Kampfgruppe Weidinger* moved via Daschkowsky and Wonkowzy on March 25. For the remaining days of March, they continued moving westward through dreadful weather and road conditions while contending with the enemy on the move. Stichkowzy, Iwankowy, Ruda Gortschitschanskaja, Donajewzy, Muschkotinzy, Kamenets-Podolsk airfield, Pudlowce, and Sariza were all on their retreat route. At this stage most remaining vehicles were destroyed due to lack of fuel.

6. SS-Freiwilligen Sturmbrigade Langemarck

The fighting around Jambol that began at the end of February lasted until the middle of March and cost the brigade many dead and wounded. One of those was Commander *SS-Sturmbannführer* Schellong; an element had been fighting with a small contingent of *Das Reich* and both of them were overrun and annihilated by the Soviets.

The survivors of the brigade moved to Staro-Konstantinov, but then moved on toward Proskuroff to try to reorganize with their reduced numbers. At the end of March / beginning of April 1944, they were sent westward into Poland. They went to Jaslo, in southern Poland, and then onto Knovitz in Czecheslovakia for another rest and refit. That would take the majority of the men up to mid-July 1944, so we will continue coverage of this unit in volume 5.

By the time of their exit from this area their former *SS-Kampfgruppe Weidinger* neighbors were trapped in the Kamenets-Podolsky pocket farther to the southwest.

II. SS-Panzer Korps

The rapidly declining situation on the eastern front required bolstering forces in that area. The *II. SS-Panzer* korps was to be the main relief force for the trapped "Hube's Pocket" men advancing westward and their meet-up point was Buczacz.

When they arrived, they raised the total number of *SS-Korps* operating on the eastern front to three, joining the *III. (Germanisches) SS-Panzer* korps and the *VI. SS-Freiwilligen* korps *(Lettisches)*. That *SS-Korps* command structure had a total of seven *Waffen-SS* formations under their control out of the eighteen *Waffen-SS* units operating on the eastern front during this time.

The *II. SS-Panzer* korps would soon play their part in relieving some of the *Waffen-SS* kameraden, but let us cover their initial moves from the west to the east during the closing phase of March 1944.

9. SS-Panzer Division Hohenstaufen

Training continued at their new location Nimes until late March, when orders were issued for this division to move to the east. In the closing days of the month, they were loaded onto trains in the Nimes area and began their move to the eastern front. There was an urgent need for additional forces in the east to help stem the flow of enemy troops westward. Their initial destination was Lemberg. They left behind the spring weather of France and were about to exchange it for the harsh cold winter of the Soviet Union. Both divisions of the *II. SS-Panzer* korps were about to bring much needed strength to the hard-pressed Russian front and both of them were almost at full complement; this would add almost 40,000 fresh *Waffen-SS* troops to the fight there.

10. SS-Panzer Division Frundsberg

In late March, they too were loaded on trains and moved eastward, destination Lemberg. From there, *Frundsberg* was sent eastward to Brzezany, southwest of Tarnapol. *Frundsberg* also advanced to the southeast, but farther east than their *Hohenstaufen* kameraden. The progress was slow and the problems of weather and enemy anti-tank positions had to be overcome mile after mile. We will continue coverage of the *II. SS-Panzer* korps in the next chapter.

3. SS-Panzer Division Totenkopf

We last covered them in chapter 1, when they were fighting the enemy in an area northwest of Bobrinez. The fast developing situation and significant enemy advances towards Uman at the start of March forced *Totenkopf* to move once more, this time to try and stem the advance. That move took them around eighty miles west to Kriwoj Osero, which was around 250 miles southeast of where the *LSSAH* was. The movement took them around another two weeks to complete, and engagements with the enemy began as they arrived in their new locations. They pushed westward and for the remainder of March fought in a wide westward arc around forty to fifty miles west of there. The places they fought for at that time included locations close to Balta, near the Romanian border. The fighting there would make up the final portion of the Oakleaves recommendation for *SS-Obersturmführer* Karl Ullrich (the final award featured in this volume). The fighting in that general area was also the basis for *SS-Brigadeführer* Hermann Priess's Swords award to his existing Oakleaves and Knight's Cross, the only award of this level for a soldier within the *Totenkopf Division* during the war (it was approved towards the end of April and will be covered in this volume). *SS-Hauptsturmführer* Hermann Buchner's later Knight's Cross award would also be based on this fighting around Balta (detailed in volume 5).

Now to the northern sector of the eastern front . . .

III. (Germanisches) SS-Panzer Korps

Now around Narwa and containing three separate *Waffen-SS* units (as well as Heer units), they held this key location on the Estonian border against the Soviets. Things would quiet for them for the rest of the period covered in this book, but their baptism of fire had given them an almost instant and hard-earned reputation for their dependability. That hard-earned reputation added no less than a dozen Knight's Cross related awards up to the end of May, with more to follow for actions during that time. That alone testifies to the intensity of what they coped with in this opening phase of 1944; let us now complete their coverage for the remainder of this volume.

11. SS-Panzergrenadier Division Nordland

The fighting at Waiwara continued until March 22, 1944, and was heavily supported by the Tiger tanks of the *Heer's Schwere Panzer Abteilung 502*, under *Leutnant* Otto Carius.

The unrelenting Soviets next focused on Narwa itself as the first week of March 1944 came to a close. The *Nordland* troops were positioned from the center of there and then to the south at Kreenholm, with *Nederland* holding north of Narwa up to Popovka. While elements of *Nederland* held their northern sector, the enemy pushed into the positions held by *Nordland* during March 7–8. *SS-Oberscharführer* Philipp Wild played a significant part in defeating the enemy there; his Panther was put to good use and his fighting skills earned him the Knight's Cross (detailed in this volume).

That initial push along the direct route into Narwa was short but intense, and no further moves were made in that direction, with the main focus being to the north at *Nederland's* positions. The remainder of March through April and May were weeks of relative quiet for *Nordland*. Harassing fire did inflict losses, but no major enemy advances were made. On March 12, no less than seven *Nordland* Knight's Crosses and one set of Oakleaves were approved. More would follow for actions during this opening phase of 1944.

We will return to the story of the *11. SS-Panzergrenadier Division Nordland* in the next volume of this project.

4. SS-Freiwilligen-Panzergrenadier Brigade Nederland

Nederland held the northern sector of the Narwa bridgehead from Popovka. *SS-Obersturmbannführer* Joerchel and the *Frw.Pz.Gren.Rgt. "General Seyffardt"* held the line here and during March 8, Joerchel led a spirited defense against a determined enemy. That defensive action resulted in Joerchel's approval to join the ranks of *Waffen-SS* Knight's Cross holders (detailed in this volume). The enemy continued to press the defenses, moving farther to the south. Lilienbach was a pressure point as the Soviets tried to break through there. The intensive fighting there lasted for two weeks and two men—*SS-Untersturmführer* Helmut Scholz and *SS-Hauptsturmführer* Carl-Heinz Fruhauf—would join the growing list of SS soldiers awarded the Knight's Cross (detailed in the next volume).

With the halting of Russian advances in late March in the northern sector of the Narwa bridgehead, life for the men of *Nederland* took on a quieter feel. They remained there and focused on strengthening their positions. Harassing fire continued, but no additional significant actions took place until June. Wolfgang Joerchel's approval of the award of the Knight's Cross was a high point on April 21, 1944, but with that, we will end coverage of the *4. SS-Freiwilligen-Panzergrenadier Brigade Nederland* and return to them in the next volume.

20. Waffen-Grenadier Division der SS (Estnische Nr. 1)

The Vepskula actions lasted until March 6; during that fighting an NCO named Harald Nugiseks took over lead of his unit following the death or wounding of the senior ranking soldiers. His heroic display earned him the rapid award of the First Class Iron Cross, but that would soon be upgraded to the award of the Knight's Cross (detailed in this volume).

There was a further short fight in the middle of the month for the Estonians, but that too was defeated. That second attempt against *SS-Estonian* held positions was the last for a number of months, as the enemy licked their wounds for the time being. The decrease in enemy activity allowed the Estonians to strengthen their line and their formation. There were no further significant occurrences for the men of the *20th* SS *Division* up to the end of May, except for the approval of the Knight's Cross on April 9 for *SS-Unterscharführer* Nugiseks. He was away from the front then and was not present with his kameraden at the front line to celebrate. We will return to the coverage of the Estonian SS men in the next volume.

To the southeast . . .

VI. SS-Freiwilligen Korps (Lettisches)

This *Latvian SS-Korps* was in the Velikaya River area during March and commanded their two component Latvian SS divisional units. Let us continue with their unfolding story.

15. Waffen-Grenadier Division der SS (Lettische Nr. 1)

In their new "Panther" positions on the Velikaya River with their newly arrived *19. SS Latvian* kameraden to the north at Voronkovo, both divisions were tasked with holding an area from Voronich in the south up to Zhukovo. The Latvians took control of the eastern bank, but as soon as March opened, the Soviets pressed them hard to take this dominant ground. The fighting went on until the third week of the month. The focal point of the battle was Sapronovo.

The fight for the dominant heights renewed on March 25. The determination of the Soviets to take these heights and gain a foothold on the west bank of the river was not diminished, nor apparently impacted, by their recent losses. Aerial and artillery attacks opened these new attempts and were rapidly followed by infantry attacks. The enemy had shifted their emphasis slightly south and pushed against Kusovikha. The result of that push was an enemy bridgehead formed on the west bank, with the Latvian SS men lacking the fighting strength to launch a counterattack. That bridgehead extended slightly south to Sobarovo.

19. Waffen-Grenadier Division der SS (Lettische Nr. 2)

The *19.* SS headquarters was around Voronkovo, with forward positions being directly east and northeast of there from Kupri and up to Podlipenka. Having little time to rest after their recent test farther north, they once again were subjected to attacks by the enemy on the Velikaya River line. They assisted their *15.* SS kameraden holding the domineering hill on the eastern bank for the first three weeks of March 1944. It was during those defensive battles that *19.* SS Divisional Commander and existing Oakleaves and Knight's Cross holder *SS-Oberführer* Hinrich Schuldt was killed by enemy anti-tank fire. The loss of this long-serving and battle-proven SS soldier left a large gap in the Latvian men's capabilities. He was eventually replaced by *SS-Oberführer* Bruno Streckenbach around a month later. The day after Schuldt's death he was put forward for the posthumous award of the Swords to his existing Oakleaves and Knight's Cross. That recommendation was approved and will be covered in this volume.

Closer to Leningrad in the north . . .

Kampfgruppe SS-Polizei Division

In the first couple days of March they were moved to a rear area for a rest. This did not last long, as by March 6 they were back at the forward lines due to unrelenting enemy pressure and advances. They engaged the enemy once again around the Pleskau area, with one notable instance being the death of existing Knight's Cross holder *SS-Obersturmbannführer* Wilhelm Dietrich. On March 12, what was left of this formation was moved to the south, where they enjoyed a longer period of rest around Ostrow.

On the Finnish front . . .

6. SS-Gebirgs Division Nord

As part of the overall Soviet advances elsewhere along the vast front line, they devoted resources to a push in this extreme northern sector. They launched an assault on March 7, hitting the men of *Nord* near Shapkozero. The surprise of the nighttime attack initially caught the *Nord* soldiers unawares, but they counterattacked and restored the situation. A further enemy assault during the day was also defeated with heavy losses for the Russians. *Nord* too suffered losses, and this attack was a portent of how things would be during 1944 in this former relatively quiet sector of the eastern front. Their next battle would come in June, so we will focus on that in the next volume.

For *Nord*, the remainder of March, April, and May returned to the routine they had come to know.

Within Army Group Center . . .

Ostturkischen-Waffen-Verband der SS

During one of their anti-partisan operations around Yuratshki in March, Commander *SS-Obersturmbannführer* Meyer-Mader was killed. *SS-Hauptsturmführer* Billing took over in the short term and was followed in April by *SS-Hauptsturmführer* Hermann. There were no other significant changes for these men (continued coverage in volume 5).

We will leave the coverage of the eastern front and focus now on enemy pressure exerted on other fronts. Moving to the Balkans and Italy, we will detail how that extreme southern front looked during March 1944. We will start with Italy, move into Slovenia, and on to Yugoslavia. A new threat developed in Hungary, so also within this "southern" section we will touch on the units moved to that "new" area; an area that would substantially increase in significance for the *Waffen-SS* as the war progressed and eventually came to an end.

16. SS-Panzergrenadier Division Reichsführer-SS

They were joined by a small contingent of Italian SS men during late March and these two units remained in Anzio until mid-April. Their kameraden in Slovenia were moved to Hungary mid-March to help with the overall occupation of that country. They were initially in the overall Raab area, but then moved to Debrecen.

Italianische SS-Freiwilligen Legion

This new unit was formed in March 1944 and added another country's flag to the existing ranks of the *Waffen-SS*. It was commanded by *SS-Obergruppenführer* Karl Wolff. Elements were rushed to the Anzio bridgehead from their training locations in Turin and Lake Como in northern Italy, and they fought very well during the closing days of March and into April.

To the northeast in Slovenia . . .

18. SS-Panzergrenadier Division Horst Wessel

Now in Slovenia, and despite being in the midst of forming and suffering from the evident equipment shortage at that stage of the war, they were ordered to take part in anti-partisan actions March 5–7, 1944. This was in and around the area where they were being formed, and the operation was aimed at providing better security for them and other German forces in Slovenia. Elements were also attached to Heer forces and used in Hungary.

South, in Yugoslavia . . .

13. SS-Freiwilligen Bosnien-Herzegowina-Gebirgs-Division (Kroatien)

Around Vinkovci since mid-February, their first combat activities came on March 9, when operations began to clear an area to the southeast towards the Sava River. An area from Jamena up to Batrovci and Vrbanja to Morovic was advanced through for the next three days, when the operation was concluded. Battles took place with partisans and hundreds of enemy dead were counted.

Their next operation began on March 15, when they advanced southward over the Sava River and the Bosnian border. Brcko and Celic were among the areas taken by these SS soldiers. The rest of March was spent consolidating their positions.

SS-Fallschirmjaeger Battalion / SS-Fallschirmjaeger Battalion 500

Their training routine was broken in mid-March, when they were sent to an area west of Budapest. They were part of the German forces rushed there in readiness for the forceful occupation of Hungary, ensuring Hungary remained on the side of the Germans as the war situation worsened. This danger was very quickly averted and combat actions did not ensue in that area. At the end of March 1944, they received a name change to *SS-Fallschirmjaeger Battalion 500.* The command of this battalion was now under the control of *SS-Haupsturmführer* Rybka.

8. SS-Kavallerie Division Florian Geyer

Still rebuilding and training, this situation did not last long, as they were needed for action once more. Alongside having to help deal with localized partisan activity, the worsening situation in Hungary called for quick action on the part of the Germans. The main divisional elements were sent northward across the southern Hungarian border and known as Battle Group Streckenbach, under the command of *SS-Oberführer* Bruno Streckenbach. They engaged in occupation activities in the southern part of Hungary during the second half of March.

Now to a couple notable changes for some of the *Waffen-SS* formations away from the front line . . .

5. SS-Freiwilligen Sturmbrigade Wallonien

After their recent and costly fighting in the Ukraine, the surviving Walloon kameraden were permitted a period of leave from the front line. Leon Degrelle started a series of speeches back in western Europe; he was keen to establish himself as the leader of this formation and equally, the Germans were keen to make the most of the foreign volunteer's bravery and obtain further recruits to their ranks. The first speech was in Paris on March 5. Then, at the start of April, a general victory parade was started in Belgium itself (although the battle was a resounding defeat for the Germans, the fact that so many made it out was turned into a propaganda spectacle by the Germans). The *Walloon* men stood before their countrymen and delivered a significant boost to the volunteer numbers for the *Waffen-SS*. As they had no vehicles left, Degrelle and his men utilized vehicles belonging to the *12. SS-Panzer Division "Hitler Jugend."* People such as Sepp Dietrich, Fritz Witt, and Kurt Meyer can all be seen taking part in these parades in Brussels, with no shortage of Knight's Crosses of various grades adorning their uniforms. What is of note in the photos of the parades in Belgium in early-April, Degrelle is seen wearing the rank *SS-Sturmbannführer*, but this rank was not officially made until the twentieth.

The bulk of the *5. SS-Freiwilligen Sturmbrigade "Wallonien"* were sent to the Wildflecken training grounds so they could be refitted after their battle in the Korsun area. Degrelle continued with some of his propaganda speeches while various survivors attended officer training and other specialist courses. We will return to the history of the *Walloons* in volume 5.

Franzosisches SS-Freiwilligen Grenadier Regiment

During March, this formation began to form an artillery component. March was also when conversations began about their increase to a larger unit; this did not officially happen until a few months later. A Flak component began life in April, around the same time the French volunteers moved from their Sennheim camp to Beneschau, south of Prague, to continue their training and formation. We will return to them in the next volume of this project.

Schwere SS-Panzer Abteilung 103

In March, the six Tiger tanks they had received were handed to another unit, putting them behind in their training and formation. Otto Paetsch was reassigned and his replacement, *SS-Sturmbannführer* Kurt Hartrampf, arrived in early March 1944.

That completes the coverage of all combat and non-combat activities for the men of the *Waffen-SS* during March 1944. Before continuing with individual unit activities, let us detail the approval of the month's various awards.

There were a total of ten awards approved: eight of them on March 12 alone. Eight of these awards were approved for men within the *Nordland Division*, which testifies to the intensity of their recent fighting. Those approvals catapulted the division "up the rankings" in relation to total awards held (see appendices). Unfortunately, the posthumous award count also increased during this month, but for now, let us look at the individuals and their actions.

Name: Heinrich Schmelzer
Date of birth: 14.03.1914
SS Number: 21 923
Award: Knight's Cross

Born in Nesselroden, his military career began in 1931, when he joined the *Allgemeine-SS*. He stayed there until June 15, 1935, when he volunteered for the *SS-VT*; he was assigned to *SS-Pioneer Sturmbann*. His first military action was in the west during 1940, with the rank *SS-Scharführer*, where he won both classes of the Iron Cross: the Second Class came at the start of July and the First Class followed on the twenty-seventh.

By the time of the campaign in the Balkans he was an *SS-Oberscharführer*, but before going into Russia, he was serving as part of the *Kradschutzen*. The Black Wound Badge was awarded on October 2, 1941, for a wound received in August. This removed him from the front temporarily, but when he returned, he went back to his former kameraden in the pioneers.

The General Assault Badge was awarded at the end of March 1942 and then, on June 21, he received a field promotion to *SS-Untersturmführer*. He was placed as a battalion headquarters liaison officer. The Russian Front Medal came at the start of August. On October 27, he was approved for the award of the German Cross in Gold for actions near Rshew in late 1941.

With the return to Russia in early 1943 at Kharkov, he was part of *16.* kompanie (Pioneer) within *SS-Regiment Deutschland*, alongside Heinz Macher. Further wounds resulted in the award of the Silver Wound Badge on April 20. He was promoted to *SS-Obersturmführer* on June 21. By

A Heinrich Schmelzer signed image where his impressive collection of awards can be seen, including the Knight's Cross, German Cross in Gold, and Close Combat Clasp.

October 1943, he was commander of *2.* kompanie / *SS-Pioneer Battalion Das Reich*. On December 6, he was awarded the Close Combat Clasp in Gold. He remained in Russia into early 1944 with *SS-Kampfgruppe Das Reich*. On January 13, he was promoted to *SS-Hauptsturmführer*.

On February 5, 1944, *SS-Sturmbannführer* Otto Weidinger compiled a recommendation for the award of the Knight's Cross for Schmelzer (the document listed his previous rank). This document had a front page added by *SS-Oberführer* Heinz Lammerding three days later, so we will start with his short endorsement:

> The proposal is warmly approved by me. *SS-Obersturmführer* Schmelzer is a resolute and prepared kompanie leader each and every time. Through his example and his daring, he pushes every one of his men to the highest fulfillment of their duty, and his nerve never flags during attack or defense.

Now for Weidinger's element of this overall document:

> On the morning of 24.12.43, the enemy advanced from the north on a broad front against the positions of *SS-Panzer-Kampfgruppe "DR,"* attacking them.
>
> After several hours' artillery fire against the bulk of *I. / SS-Panzer-Grenadier Regiment. "DR"* with tank support, and after hours of hard battling, he managed one breakthrough success. At the same time, an enemy force moved west along the road from Kiev-Zhitomir, pushed through, and by evening had already taken Kotscherowo and on toward the road. Thus, the way to the south was closed for all motorized elements.
>
> The pressure of the enemy attacks from the north against Sabelotsche lasted all day unabatedly, so there was only one possibility: to move westward to avoid it. However, here was the Teterev (river), an insurmountable obstacle that offered no possible transit. *SS-Ostuf.* Schmelzer knew there was no other possibility and he gave the order for the bridge to be removed the day before for supply work to quickly be repaired, made stronger, and passable for the heaviest armor and vehicles. Everything depended upon this bridge building; if he did not succeed, all of the battle group vehicles would be out of the game.
>
> Under the most difficult conditions (procurement of the building materials, very poor weather, and lack of labor forces) Schmelzer

succeeded, through ruthless actions, in completing the bridge at 01:00 hours. At 02:00 hours, the vehicles of the battle group and the neighboring division were able to start moving over the bridge and on toward Lenino. The supply trains and troops from all of the various arms could now flow over the bridge from the eastern bank of the Teterew and obtain new positions.

The following day (25.12.43), Schmelzer had the order to blow the bridge immediately after the vehicles had driven over and therefore deny the enemy the ability to move over it. Schmelzer had every intention to follow the order, but the execution of it would demand everything from him. With his kompanie as the demolition commando and bridge security, he had the order to wait until the enemy flood had reached the defensive positions on the eastern shore of the Teterew. While the disengagement from the enemy by each unit went smoothly initially, the enemy soon arrived on the heels of the most recently arrived battalion. Schmelzer was able to throw back weak elements of the enemy who had already arrived at the bridge over the Teterew, but then ensued a dramatic fight near the Teterew, in the moments where the enemy had come forward closer to the bridge. Here, too, Schmelzer threw his kompanie repeatedly against the invading Russians and tossed them back in a counterattack so the last battalion reached the western shore of the Teterev and could withdraw to the new positions. During this time *Kompanie-Schmelzer* suffered the heaviest enemy artillery, anti-tank, and mortar fire. With outstanding toughness Schmelzer held the bridge and calmly threw the opponent back, ignoring all of their fire.

After *Hauptmann* Speidel, commander of *Panzer Pioneer Battalion 19*, arrived as the last one at the bridge, Schmelzer received the order to blow the bridge, but the igniters were damaged. Once again, his pioneers had to fend off the attacking enemy as the cable was back in order. Once the last groups of the *Pioneer* kompanie crossed *SS-Ostuf.* Schmelzer went over.

This proposal was approved on March 12, 1944, but that would not end Schmelzer's connection to the Knight's Cross. We will return to his history in a later volume.

Name: Fritz von Scholz
Date of birth: 09.12.1896
SS Number: 135 638
Award: Knight's Cross with Oakleaves

Fritz von Scholz is another *Waffen-SS* soldier who received further recognition of his bravery to complement his existing level of the Knight's Cross. Like "Teddi" Wisch, he was featured in volume 1 when, on January 18, 1942, he was approved for the award of the Knight's Cross. What were his activities between then and now?

He received a promotion to *SS-Brigadeführer und Generalmajor der Waffen-SS* on December 21, 1942. He was then given command of the *2. SS-Infantry Brigade (mot.)* in late January 1943, staying there for three months. At the start of May he was moved once more, this time to assume command of the newly raised *SS-Nordland Division*. They were raised and trained mainly in Germany (see previous volume) and then, at the start of 1944, were positioned in the northern sector of the eastern front.

They entered the fray almost immediately, as the Soviets launched a major push in their area. Von Scholz's leadership of his untested division during January resulted in Felix Steiner asking for the award of the Oakleaves to his existing Knight's Cross. He penned a recommendation in early February:

> Since 16.1.1944, *SS-Brigadeführer* Fritz von Scholz has been fighting in the northern area of the eastern front and has continued up to this point in time as the divisional commander; he has been a model to his troops during all of the combat.
>
> His division was given the task to move along the road from Kipen-Narwa against superior enemy forces and prevent their attempts to go behind the Narwa.
>
> In the proceeding heavy fighting, the divisional commander set a personal example during the engagements by continuing to surround the enemy and mastered the situation again and again.
>
> 1) On 28.01.1944, the opponent managed to break through between the remains of the *10. Luftwaffe Feld Division* standing south of the Kipen – Narwa route on both sides of Osertizy and the *61. Infanterie Division* to block the route near Gurlewo by advancing toward the northwest. There was a danger of the opponent encircling the *11. SS-Freiwilligen-Panzer-Grenadier-Division "Nordland's"*

Fritz von Scholz shown wearing his Oakleaves, the first set for *SS-Division Nordland*.

Combat Group "Lohmann," which stood near Osertizy, and elements of the *10. Luftwaffe Feld Division*, including its divisional staff, which was neigboring to the south. A nightly counterattack that Divisional Commander *Brigadeführer* von Scholz carried out from Ljalizy via Gurlewo opened up the route again. It threw the opponent back and cleared the way towards Ljalizy for the troops standing to the east and for the *10. Luftwaffe Feld Division's* divisional staff.

2.) On 01.02.1944, *11. SS-Freiwilligen-Panzer-Grenadier-Division "Nordland"* was drawn back from Jamburg to Dubrowka. Strong opposing forces overtook to the north and south, and attacked the divisional elements fighting alongside the route. *Brigadeführer* von Scholz was the soul of the resistance, having realized the remains of the *61. Infanterie Division*, *227. Infanterie Division*, and the *10. Luftwaffe Feld Division*, who were retreating towards the west via Narwa, would need time for this movement. Despite intense attacks by enemy armor, elements of the division succeeded in denying the opponent his pursuit and crushed the continuous attacks carried out at up to regimental strength time and again.

The stubborn hold kept up on both sides of Jamburg, Dubrowka, and Komarowka, as well as the continuous defense against superior enemy forces at a strength of several divisions created the basis for an orderly occupation of the Narwa bridgehead. It also allowed the gathering of forces for the occupation of the northern Narwa position.

Furthermore, the troops' steadfastness and the strict leadership of *11. SS-Freiwilligen-Panzer-Grenadier-Division "Nordland"* made it possible to buy time to bring up *Panzer Grenadier Division "Feldherrnhalle."* Upon gaining additional reinforcements, they led back the remains of the *61.* and *170. Infanterie Divisions*, as well as those of the *10. Luftwaffe Feld Division*, and regrouped them to the west of Narwa.

The troops' achievements and *Brigadeführer* von Scholz's leadership thus created the basis for the continuance of combat on the Narwa Front and are to be considered the decisive factors at this crucial front. *Brigadeführer* von Scholz's personal effort, his example, and his toughness caused the troops to give their very best. He has swept his still-young division towards exemplary steadfastness.

This request was approved on March 12, 1944, and gave *SS-Division Nordland* their first set of Oakleaves to the Knight's Cross. This level of recognition did not halt Fritz von Scholz's association with the various Knight's Cross grades. We will return to his story in a future volume.

Name: Georg Langendorf
Date of birth: 28.07.1920
SS Number: 380 658
Award: Knight's Cross

Born in Grafenhausen, he was a member of the *Hitler Youth* from mid-May 1934. In February 1939, he started training as a construction technician and then an architect. On November 20, 1939, he volunteered to join the SS. His first posting was to the *Panzerjaeger Battalion* within what became *Das Reich* and his role was an MG-Gunner.

He fought in the opening stages of Barbarossa and earned the Second Class Iron Cross at the start of November 1941; that same month he moved to the role of anti-tank gunner. By March 1942, he was part of a self-propelled anti-tank gun crew. The award of the Infantry Assault Badge was made on May 9, with the Russian Front Medal coming on September 13. Langendorf received the First Class Iron Cross on February 8, 1943, and was sent for NCO training the following day. On May 20 he was promoted to *SS-Oberscharführer*. The following month he moved to the *III. (Germanic) SS-Panzer Korps*. Promoted to *SS-Untersturmführer* at the start of November, he was with *5. Kompanie, SS-Panzer Aufklarungs Abteilung 11* as a platoon commander.

The year 1944 would prove to be memorable for this *Waffen-SS* soldier, as he earned half his total awards, along with other changes. This began on February 8, when his battalion commander proposed Langendorf for the award of the Knight's Cross:

> Operating as part of Combat Group "Wengler," *SS-Panzer Aufklarungs Abteilung 11* was assigned to secure the important crossroads at Gubanizy, northeast of Wolossowo.
>
> On 26.01.1944, an attack was mounted against the town by fifty-six Russian tanks, most of them T-34s. With them was a battalion of more than 350 men.
>
> *Untersturmführer* Langendorf, as the heavy *kompanie*'s commander, secured ground in a general northeastern direction towards Torosowo with his anti-tank cannon platoon.

> Despite the fact he had no artillery at his disposal and that our infantry had moved into rearward positions, Langendorf, of his own accord, had his crews manhandle his cannons forward in such a way that he was able to counter the attack in an effective manner.
>
> Two assault guns that carried very little ammunition disengaged after a brief fire fight. Thus, it was up to Langendorf's anti-tank cannon platoon to face the main force of the Russian attack.
>
> Through his reckless personal effort, Langendorf and his cannon platoon managed to destroy twenty-four tanks within two hours—fifteen of them T-34s. An additional six Russian tanks were disabled by hits from Langendorf's anti-tank defense. Eight Russian tanks were destroyed by assault guns.
>
> After having destroyed the initial waves of armor, Langendorf deployed gun-carrying armored halftracks and personally led them to the town's southwestern perimeter, following an advance by straggling tanks. He drove them out again, thus keeping the supply route open in the first stage of the engagement.
>
> Back at the northeastern perimeter, he gathered the weak infantry elements for local defense against Russian infantry and destroyed further incoming waves of enemy armor. On that day, Langendorf's anti-tank weapons destroyed thirty-one enemy tanks (twenty-two of them T-34s) and disabled another six Russian tanks with their fire.
>
> On 27.01.1944, Langendorf successfully hit and destroyed another tank in Lagunovo.
>
> On 29.01.1944, once again two enemy tanks were hit, then personally disabled and blown up by Langendorf.
>
> Thus, within these four days, Langendorf and elements of his kompanie destroyed thirty-four enemy tanks and disabled six.
>
> The overall number of kills made at Gubanizy on 26.01.1944 made it impossible for the enemy to carry out his intentions of pushing through Gubanizy and on to Wolossowo to take that town—an intention that has been confirmed through statements made by prisoners—thus making possible the orderly retreat movement of our own forces at the immediate right.

He joined the ranks of *Waffen-SS* Knight's Cross holders on March 12; the Black Wound Badge came at the end of the month. A move to *SS-Obersturmführer* came on April 20, 1944, the same day he was awarded the Tank Assault Badge. By June 18, he held the Close Combat Clasp in

An autographed image of Georg Langendorf, the first of a series of *Nordland* Knight's Cross awardees on March 12, 1944.

Silver, the Bronze level having been made on the fourth. These various levels of recognition are testament to what Langendorf and his *Nordland* kameraden had to contend with in the first half of 1944. He rounded the year off by assuming command of *5.* kompanie at the start of October.

In the first half of February 1945, Langendorf was recommended for the German Cross in Gold (approved at the end of March) for actions during the second half of 1944 and up to February 1945. He was wounded in mid-April but survived the war. He died on February 28, 1999, in the town of his birth.

Name: Rudolf Saalbach
Date of birth: 18.03.1911
SS Number: 127 697
Award: Knight's Cross

Born in Grossenhain, Sachsen, he entered the *Allgemeine-SS* in July 1932, serving with the *SS-Sonderkommando "Sachsen."* This date of joining allowed him to wear the Alte Kampfer Chevron. Between 1935 and 1937, he was with *SS-Totenkopfverbande "Elbe."* In 1937, he was sent to the SS officer's school at Braunschweig and then, on March 12, 1938, he was promoted to *SS-Untersturmführer*. After Braunschweig he was placed with *SS-Totenkopfverbande "Oberbayern."* He held the SA Sports Badge in Bronze and the Reichs Sports Badge in Bronze. Another promotion came on April 20, 1939, with a move to *SS-Obersturmführer*.

He is not listed as fighting in Poland, but is listed as fighting with the *SS-Totenkopf Division* in the west in 1940. This lasted up to early March 1941, when he moved to the replacement battalion for *SS-Regiment "Germania"*; he stayed with them until January 1942. His next move took him to *SS-Division "Wiking"*; while with them he earned the Russian Front Medal on September 3; the War Merit Cross, Second Class with Swords on September 12; and the First Class War Merit Cross with Swords in November 1942. He also moved to *SS-Hauptsturmführer* on November 9.

The year 1943 would see further significant changes for Saalbach, the first being the award of the First Class Iron Cross on February 19. During May and June, he attended a battalion leader's training course near Paris; following this, he was posted to the command of the reconnaisance battalion of the newly raised *SS-Division "Nordland."* He helped with the raising and training of this new unit throughout the remainder of 1943, then went with them to the Leningrad sector as 1944 opened. In the closing days of

Rudolf Saalbach seen at the front with his Knight's Cross and Close Combat Clasp.

January 1944, he led his battalion as they engaged strong Russian forces in the northern sector of the Soviet Union.

Less than two weeks later, a recommendation came through from the commander of the *Heer's* 366 Grenadier Regiment, detailing the bravery displayed by Saalbach in the January fighting and proposing the Knight's Cross for him. This proposal document was endorsed by Saalbach's own Divisional Commander *SS-Brigadeführer* von Scholz; the document read as follows:

> Deeds of valor of *SS-Hauptsturmführer* Saalbach, *SS-Pz.Aufkl.Abt. 11*
>
> On 26.1.1944, the enemy attacked with a tank brigade (fifty-four tanks) and accompanying infantry at Gubanizy. Saalbach and his subordinate battalion, with all of its heavy weapons, was very effective in repulsing all of the attacks that were put in during this critical day against his battalion. He was always at the focal point of the battle, fighting without care for himself, attacking again and again, and mastering all situations.
>
> With the heavy weapons his battalion destroyed thirty-four tanks this day, twenty-eight of which were type T-34.
>
> On 27.1.1944: the enemy attacked all day long with heavy forces. Saalbach was found repeatedly at the focal point of the fighting, without consideration for risk to himself, and he restored the situation and was a role model to his men.
>
> When the enemy pressed into a point on the main battle line Saalbach arrived there rapidly with a collection of forces and personally restored the situation.
>
> On 29.1.1944, the enemy attacked 2.5 km [1.6 miles] forward of the main battle line in Opolje using strong forces fighting with tank support. Again, Saalbach was always at the focal point of the fighting and fought with his few men, bringing all enemy attacks to a standstill until the other occupied parts of the main battle line were strong enough.
>
> Upon orders, he skillfully positioned himself close to the enemy and because of this two tanks were destroyed; then he managed to withdraw himself from the enemy.
>
> (signed) Wengler: *Colonel* and Regimental Commander'

Opinion of the divisional commander:

Commitment and struggle of Battalion Saalbach, close to the right neighboring division, were crucial factors for the successful battle leadership of *11. SS-Freiw.Pz.Gren.Div. "Nordland"* during these days.

(signed) von Scholz
SS-Brigadeführer und Generalmajor der Waffen-SS.

There was an additional document from the commander of the *227. Infantry Division* written on February 10:

To the *11. SS-Freiw.Pz.Gren.Div. "Nordland"*

The actions of SS *Pz.Aufkl.Abt. 11* were of decisive importance for the activity of *227 J.D.* The personal actions of *SS-Hauptstrumführer* Saalbach deserve special recognition, as he gave a shining example of bravery and fearlessness. Saalbach is most particularly worthy of the bestowal of the Knight's Cross of the Iron Cross.

Signed: (Wilhelm) Berlin
Lieutenant General

This overall proposal was approved on March 12, 1944, and gave *Nordland* their third award of the day, but that would not be the end of Nordland's celebrations.

Saalbach received promotion to *SS-Sturmbannführer* just over one month later, on April 20. He continued to lead this battalion all the way into the titanic struggle in Berlin a year later. He was one of the men that attempted to break through the tightening Russian ring as part of the group that tried to cross the Weidendammer Bridge; he was killed in that attempt. Besides the awards listed above, photographs show him wearing the Close Combat Clasp and the Tank Assault Badge, although actual award dates are not known.

Name: Walter Seebach
Date of birth: 05.11.1920
SS Number: 405 893
Award: Knight's Cross

Born in Heerlen, he was a member of the *Hitler Youth* from March 1933 through March 1937; the next month he joined the *Allgemeine-SS*. In November 1938, he spent a five-month stint with the *RAD*. He entered the armed SS at the start of April 1939. Seebach was placed with *6. Kompanie, SS-Regiment Germania*, but by November, he had been sent to the SS officer's school at Bad Tolz (*SS-Unterscharführer* at that time). He remained there until August 1940, leaving with a rank of *SS-Standartenoberjunker*, meaning he missed out on the actions in Poland and the west in 1939 and early 1940.

He earned the Second Class Iron Cross on March 8, 1941, although what for is not listed; also bear in mind the *Waffen-SS* was not involved in any campaigns then. It can be presumed he moved into Russia in mid-1941, and on November 9, he was promoted to *SS-Untersturmführer* and listed as serving with the *Wiking Division*. The award of the First Class Iron Cross was made on Christmas Eve. The award of the Russian Front Medal came on June 9, 1942. At the start of November, he became the battalion adjutant for *Germania's* I Battalion. In March 1943, he was removed from the front after suffering his fifth wound (not all of the dates of his woundings are listed). This fifth wound earned him the Wound Badge in Gold on the twenty-fifth; three days later he was awarded the Infantry Assault Badge. During his recovery he was listed under the March Replacement Battalion for *Germania*. He returned to the front in early April and was promoted to *SS-Obersturmführer* on the twentieth. In May, he moved to the role of adjutant for *SS-Panzergrenadier Regiment 24 "Danmark."* He remained in that role until early January 1944, when he was placed in command of *Danmark's 5. Kompanie*.

While in this role during late January, Seebach's activities during the defensive fighting prompted Regimental Commander *SS-Obersturmbannführer* Hermengild Graf von Westphalen to recommend him for the Knight's Cross in a document dated February 18:

> The proposed—who has been employed as a regimental adjutant since 1.5.43 and on the significant list of the regiment since 1.5.43—has since the early days of January taken over the *5./SS-Pz.Gren. Rgt. 24 "Danmark."* Following the heavy anti-partisan fighting in

A formal image of Walter Seebach taken to mark his award of the Knight's Cross.

Croatia (Hrastovica), this kompanie was unfit and no longer combat ready. *Obersturmführer* Seebach was supplied with forty recruits to supplement the group leaders and, in the shortest time (ten days), brought these men to a high standard, making them fresh and ensuring the unit was full and ready for use by 15.1.44 in the Oranienbaum Pocket.

His freshness and fighting spirit conveyed to his young kompanie, which was clearly evident during the fighting retreat below.

On 30.1.44, Seebach led the night groups of the regiment from the position at Opolje - Kerstowo into the new positions on the Luga. Through his leadership and energy he reached *5. Kompanie*, despite being continually pressed sharply by the enemy. They reached positions around 06:00 hours on 30.1.44 without great losses.

On 31.1.44, at about 16:30 hours, the enemy began their attacks against the sector of *5./SS-Pz.Gren.Rgt. 24 "Danmark"* (Danish No. 1). They were led by two Russian regiments in several waves and lasted until the morning hours of 1.2.44. Eight armed attacks were identified. The position was held until 1.2.44.

This was thanks to the frontline leadership and excellent attitude of the brave kompanie Leader *Obersturmführer* Seebach, who in bold attacks constantly threw back the enemy. At 20:30 hours, Seebach was wounded by shrapnel in the foot (his seventh wounding in this war!). Despite this wound, he personally led his kompanie further and, after detecting the enemy, led a kompanie squad to success. When his wound became aggravated by non-treatment and the initially only slightly battered foot bones broke, it took an order from the regiment to take him back and another kompanie leader replaced him.

This example shows the excellent bravery and strong will displayed to the kompanie, which fought with boldness and liveliness. The remaining kompanies of the battalion, in whose focal point Seebach fought, recognized his strength and the defensive resistance was strengthened considerably through Seebach's example and his strong *kompanie*.

This was the position until the early morning hours of February 1, and a breakthrough of the front of the regiment by the opponent was avoided. This tactical success, thanks in large part to Seebach, allowed the various elements of the division to plan their withdrawal to the bridgehead in the area of Jamburg and prevented the premature

> rupturing of the Luga front on the 31.1, which would have had a bad effect upon the overall situation.

This recommendation received approvals from Von Scholz and Steiner; it was approved officially on March 12, 1944. He added the award of the Gold Close Combat Clasp four days later.

Seebach is listed as still being with *Wiking* until the start of April 1944, the same date he received promotion to *SS-Hauptsturmführer*. He then moved to the *SS-Panzer Aufklarungs Replacement Battalion* until early June, followed by a stint with the *SS-Panzergrenadier Training and Replacement Battalion* until October 27. He then had a posting to the SS officer's school in Prague that lasted until February 1945. He was placed back with the *Wiking Division*, only this time in the role of regimental adjutant for *Germania*, which took him to the end of the war. He spent time as a prisoner of war and was one of the *Wiking* men able to keep their weapons but not ammunition for their planned use by the Americans in the anticipated advance by them against the Russians. He died on July 4, 2004.

Name: Hans-Heinrich Lohmann
Date of birth: 24.06.1911
SS Number: 29 097
Award: Knight's Cross

Born in Gutersloh, he was a very early member of the *Hitler-Jugend Bund*, the pre-cursor to the *Hitler Youth* movement, which he joined in 1923. He remained a member for two years; in 1929, he joined the *SA*, staying there until the end of January 1932. The following day he entered the *Allgemeine-SS* and was placed with the *19. SS-Standarte*. By the end of April 1933, he was holding the rank of *SS-Scharführer* (*SS-Unterscharführer*). *SS-Oberscharführer* (*SS-Scharführer*) followed in late March 1934, before a further move on April 20, 1934, to *SS-Untersturmführer*; Lohmann had moved to the *82. SS-Standarte* by then Towards the end of January 1935, he moved to *Deutschland's* III Battalion at Ellwangen, taking part in a leader's training course around the same time. At the start of April 1936, he was promoted to *SS-Obersturmführer* and at the same time moved to the Bad Tolz officer's school, being placed as the adjutant; he also attended various courses while there. On November 9, 1938, he moved to the rank of *SS-Hauptsturmführer*, having spent a one-month spell with the *Leibstandarte* prior. Lohmann remained at Bad Tolz until mid-June 1940, but did have a two-month stint at the Doberitz infantry school. Lohmann was selected to join the newly created *SS-Division Wiking*.

His service with *Wiking* began with the leadership of *2.* kompanie within *SS-Regiment Westland*; he would remain with this regiment until early 1942. His first front-line action took place with the advance into the Soviet Union in mid-1941. He quickly earned the Second Class Iron Cross on July 13, followed on September 14 with the First Class Iron Cross; the Infantry Assault Badge was approved on April 20, 1942. At that stage Lohmann was back in Germany recovering from an illness. He returned to the front in late 1942, and was given command of I Battalion of *SS-Regiment Nordland.* Lohmann was promoted to *SS-Sturmbannführer* at the end of January 1943, then on March 11 he was awarded the German Cross in Gold for his actions as battalion commander. When *Nordland* was expanded to a divisional level formation, Lohmann was given command of III Battalion within *SS-Regiment Norge*. The division was formed in the Balkans in the second half of 1943, but by the closing days of 1943, was sent to the northern sector of the eastern front.

Lohmann and his men entered a difficult situation almost immediately; during January, he proved his leadership abilities, warranting his regimental commander to ask for the award of the Knight's Cross for him:

> On 31.01.1944 *III. / Norge*, under the command of *SS-Sturmbannführer* Lohmann, was operating at the eastern perimeter of Jamburg, in the Luga bridgehead position. The ordered evacuation of the bridgehead took place during the night 31.01 to 01.02.1944, following defensive engagements that were fierce and successful for our troops.
>
> *SS-Sturmbannführer* Lohmann was assigned to move into new defensive positions on the western bank of the Luga after the evacuation of the bridgehead and, by placing his battalion between von Kramer's Battalion and *Kampfgruppe "Vogt,"* to reinforce the thinly manned defensive line *Kampfgrupper "Stoffers."*
>
> At the start of the retreat movement from out of the bridgehead, the following situation presented itself in the western bank's southern area.
>
> All day long, strong opposing forces had crossed onto the unoccupied western bank of the Luga River south of Saretschje. Several attacks against the flanks of *II. / Norge* in its positions at the paper mill and Saretschje had been successfully repelled by the battalion, sometimes by counterattack. In the evening hours of

Hans-Heinrich Lohmann shown in a signed and clear studio photograph.

31.01, it had become necessary to pull back *II. / Norge* to a blocking position between Luga and Pjatnitzkij Swamp due to the arrival of additional reinforcements for the opponent.

In the course of the retreat movements, at roughly 04:30 hours, out of Lohmann's Battalion, the first elements of *9.* kompanie and the *Heavy* kompanie were at the eastern perimeter of Nowo Pjatnitzkoje and the *10.* and *11.* kompanies were in the western part of Jamburg. Following the report that strong, superior opposing forces had overrun the blocking positions of *II. / Norge* in a wide swing to the west, and that some elements had already advanced as far as 300 meters [328 yards] south of the railway line, *Sturmbannführer* Lohmann acted on his own; he immediately deployed his battalion on a counterattack past the pushed-back elements of *II. / Norge*.

Through the surprisingly quick deployment of *III. / Norge*—with its *9.* kompanie moving from Nowo Pjatnitzkoje via Hill 25.2 to the southeast and its *10.* and *11.* kompanies moving from the railway line to the south—the enemy was thrown back in fierce nighttime hand-to-hand combat. During this, *Sturmbannführer* Lohmann distinguished himself through outstanding personal bravery and the enemy suffered extremely high, bloody losses; the former positions could be taken back.

The counterattack could yield these successes only through the outstanding personal bravery of *Sturmbannführer* Lohmann, who swept his men forward through example at the critical moment of the close-quarters fighting.

Extraordinary initiative and a willingness to make independent decisions on the part of the commander of *III. / Norge*, coupled with selfless personal effort, succeeded in keeping the troops still in the bridgehead and holding the west bank from being cut off. Furthermore, the enemy suffered high manpower losses and extraordinarily severe losses of materiel due to his light and heavy infantry weapons. The losses were such an extent that the enemy lost a large part of his attack forces, making it possible for the division to carry out its subsequent ordered withdrawal towards Dubrowka in a coordinated fashion and with only the most minor losses.

This recommendation was sanctioned by Divisional Commander von Scholz, who highlighted the importance of Lohmann's attack. It was further endorsed by *III. (Germanisches) SS-Panzer* korps Commander Felix Steiner. The main document was written by Regimental Commander Stoffers on February 13, and the award of the Knight's Cross was approved on March 12, 1944. Lohman had been heavily wounded back on February 2 and was in Germany recovering when news reached him. His capabilities and recognition of them were not complete with this award. We will continue the coverage of this *Waffen-SS* soldier in the final volume.

Name: Arnold Stoffers
Date of birth: 01.09.1910
SS Number: 61 313
Award: Knight's Cross

Born in Voorde, near Kiel, he joined the SA in April 1931, then moved to the *Allgemeine-SS* in August 1932. In early October 1933, Stoffers was selected to attend the inaugural SS officer's training course at the Bad Tolz school, which started in April 1934; he held the rank of *SS-Truppenführer (SS-Oberscharführer)* then. He moved to *SS-Standartenoberjunker* in December. After finishing his course at Bad Tolz, he was sent to a platoon leader's course at Dachau. When this training was completed he was then placed with *SS-Regiment Germania*, with promotion to *SS-Untersturmführer* taking place on April 20, 1935; he moved one rank further exactly a year later. Just prior to the outbreak of war, he was promoted to *SS-Hauptsturmführer* on August 25, 1939. He had been with *8.* kompanie since 1935 and led that unit into Poland.

He earned the Second Class Iron Cross during that campaign, with the medal awarded on October 14, 1939. He also moved west in 1940, adding the First Class Iron Cross on August 20 and the Infantry Assault Badge. With the forming of the new *SS-Division Wiking*, *SS-Regiment Germania* was used as the main foundation. Stoffers became a soldier in the new division, but moved to the role of battalion commander for the flak battalion. During July 1941, when they were advancing east, he was in command of II Battalion in *SS-Regiment Nordland*. He had also briefly commanded one of *Westland's* battalions. Despite commanding at battalion level for over six months, he did not receive a promotion to *SS-Sturmbannführer* until November 9, 1941. The award of the German Cross in Gold came the following month.

As part of the renewed *Wiking* advances in July 1942, Stoffers led the regiment when the existing commander was wounded. This lasted until

Arnold Stoffers earlier in the war with his *Germania* collar patches. His posthumous Knight's Cross was another of *Nordland's* March 12, 1944, awards.

November, when Stoffers was wounded, removing him from the front line for the time being. The award of the Black Wound Badge and the Russian Front Medal were approved in November. He spent time with the replacement battalion for *SS-Regiment Westland* after recovering from his wounds, then moved to the newly raised *SS-Division Nordland* during April 1943. He was promoted to *SS-Obersturmbannführer* on November 9, and then in December, he took command of *SS-Regiment Norge*.

Stoffers was leading that unit in the difficult fighting in northern Russia in the opening weeks of 1944. It was with them that he was killed in action on February 25, near Sirgula, in Estonia. Ten days prior to his death, his divisional commander and existing Knight's Cross holder Fritz von Scholz had written a recommendation for the Knight's Cross for Stoffers:

> *SS-Obersturmbannführer* Stoffers was assigned to cover our troops' retreat movements from out of the Jamburg bridgehead during the night of 31.01 – 01.02.1944; the opponent managed to break into the left neighbor's location, as well as at the combat group's right wing, and overran the blocking position. While it was possible to force back and stop the enemy at the right wing, strong enemy forces had managed to break in deeper at the left neighbor's location. Counterattacks undertaken by the left neighbor remained fruitless, so the opponent managed to swing around in a southeastern direction to push into Combat Group Stoffers' rear, taking possession of the route at the same time.
>
> Acting spontaneously, *SS-Obersturmbannführer* Stoffers gathered all elements of the regimental staff of "*Norge*" together with gathered stragglers and *8. Kompanie's* 1. Infantry Gun Platoon to stop the enemy's breakthrough.
>
> In cooperation with two assault guns *SS-Obersturmbannführer* Stoffers deployed against the intruding enemy's right flank on the road 500 metres [546 yards] west of the regimental command post, the ad-hoc combat group set out on a counterattack. The intruding enemy was attacked under the regimental commander's personal leadership. Those opposing forces that had already advanced to close quarters fighting were stopped through an energetic counterattack, and by direct short-range fire from the 1. Infantry Gun Platoon. The motorcycle platoon, operating at the stretch of forest east of the regimental command post, engaged the enemy at his flank so that, in short time, he could be thrown back and largely destroyed in a counterattack by our weak forces.

In the subsequent flank attack from the southwest undertaken by weak elements of the regiment's command section and two assault guns, *SS-Obersturmbannführer* Stoffers succeeded in completely throwing back or destroying, respectively, the enemy forces following from the depths. Those elements of the left neighbor that had pulled back in a northwestern direction were swept forward by the successful counterattack, until contact with the left wing of Combat Group "Stoffers" had been re-established.

Through the total employment of all available reserves under the energetic leadership of its resolute regimental commander, the weak elements of our combat group were rewarded with this success. This act made it possible for those elements of our troops that still stood to the east to keep on retreating in a coordinated fashion, and it was the reason the route to Narwa remained in our hands. This guaranteed an orderly occupation of the Narwa bridgehead by the *11. SS-Freiwilligen Panzergrenadier Division "Nordland"* and the *SS-Panzergrenadier Division "Nederland."*

This request was approved on March 12, 1944, making Stoffers the sixth *Nordland* Knight's Cross related award that day. Stoffers's death nearly a month earlier prevented him from enjoying this recognition of his abilities.

Name: Albrecht Krugel
Date of birth: 22.04.1913
SS Number: 11 433
Award: Knight's Cross

Born in Nordhorn, his attraction to the views of Adolf Hitler started at an early age, when he joined the SA in October 1930 at age seventeen. Four months later, he joined the fledgling SS and was a member of the *35. SS-Standarte*. He moved to the *Wachsturm Merkers* in April 1933, and remained there until September 1934. He then began an eighteen-month training stint to become an officer, including time at Ellwangen, then a move to Braunschweig, and finally Dachau. His promotion to *SS-Untersturmführer* was approved on April 20, 1936. Less than five days earlier, he began a short spell with the *SS-Oberabschnitt "Nord."* By the start of September, he was with *SS-Battalion "Nurnberg"* and remained there until March 1939, serving as platoon commander and battalion adjutant. While there, on April 20, 1938, he received a promotion to *SS-Obersturmführer*. He had the chance

Albrecht Krugel shown in a field-captured image wearing his Knight's Cross.

to take part in the annexation of Austria in March 1938, and the Sudetenland in October. He returned to the officer's school at Braunschweig from March 1939, remaining there as the war broke out in September.

He was promoted to *SS-Hauptsturmführer* on November 9, 1939, and then in May 1940, was sent to the front in France to serve with the *SS-VT Division* as they moved into southern France. He also commanded *Deutschland's 13.* kompanie during that summer. He was one of the men selected to help form the new *Wiking Division* towards the end of 1940. He held various staff posts—including divisional adjutant and regimental adjutant—for *Germania* before taking command of *6.* kompanie in *Nordland.* He went with *Wiking* into the Soviet Union in the second half of 1941, and began to earn the first of his awards: the Second Class Iron Cross was first on July 13, the Black Wound Badge followed on September 2, and the First Class Iron Cross was awarded on September 13. By the autumn of 1942, he had added the Infantry Assault Badge and the Russian Front Medal. Before the end of 1942, he had assumed command of *Nordland's* II Battalion. Krugel was awarded the German Cross in Gold on February 8, 1943, although the details of why are not known, as the recommendation does not survive in his file. He was promoted to *SS-Sturmbannführer* in April. In the first half of 1943, he moved the command of II Battalion, *SS-Regiment "Norge,"* which was part of the newly created *Nordland Division.* He was moved, with his men, to the northern sector of the eastern front at the start of 1944.

In mid-February, Krugel was put forward for the Knight's Cross by Divisional Commander *SS-Brigadeführer* von Scholz:

> *SS-Sturmbannführer* Krugel took over a combat group that had been assembled from three kompanies for the purpose of quick containment of an incursion that had taken place outside the divisional sector. With this combat group, he repelled two attacks undertaken from the area of the incursion (Vepskula-Vasa and the forest west of it) at the line from Puhklemae to the wooded area one kilometer [0.62 miles] north of Germansberg. When the combat group had been reinforced by an additional two kompanies and the enemy had been shaken by the effects of permanent artillery fire, he engaged the opponent, acting on his own decision and contrary to orders. In a daringly conducted night attack he threw the enemy back to the far bank of the Narwa.
>
> Thus, Krugel prevented infantry action against the Narwa-Reval route and the loss of the dominant bastion around Germansberg. The taking of that by the enemy would have made holding the

> Narwa bridgehead extraordinarily difficult, and they wiped out the bulk of the enemy's 131st Rifle Division during the attack and in defense against subsequent counterattacks.

The award was approved on March 12, 1944, during a short spell when Krugel was in command of the regiment. This award took *Nordland's* total awards to seven Knight's Crosses and one set of Oakleaves. The award would not end Krugel's connection to the grades of the Knight's Cross and we will return to his history in a later volume.

Name: Philipp Wild
Date of birth: 28.3.1921
SS Number: Not issued
Award: Knight's Cross

Born in Dornheim, near Darmstadt, his early-war career and date of joining the SS is not known, or if it is, it is well hidden.

His date of entry into the *Waffen-SS* is not listed, but on August 25, 1942, he was awarded the Second Class Iron Cross. He was in command of a tank by mid-April 1943. By the start of 1944, he was holding the rank of *SS-Oberscharführer* and serving in *Nordland's* panzer battalion. He was in the *1. Kompanie* commanding a Panther tank. On March 6, 1944, he was awarded the First Class Iron Cross; the same day he was part of the forces caught up in the battles around Narwa. His activities there resulted in him being put forward for the Knight's Cross by *SS-Nederlande Brigade* Commander Jurgen Wagner, who detailed the following on March 17, 1944:

> Strong enemy air units bombarded the bridgehead and city of Narwa during the nights of 6. / 7. and 7. / 8.3. in unremitting attacks, each lasting ten to eleven hours. On 8.3.44 at 07:00 hours, two and half hours of intense artillery barrage began, supporting an attack that was followed by the 63rd Guards Rifle Division. That attack was supported by fourteen tanks and conducted on a narrow front against the northeast pillar of the bridgehead.
>
> Twelve tanks broke through the main line of resistance and advanced as far as the positions of the heavy infantry weapons of *SS-Freiwilligen-Panzer-Grenadier-Regiment 48 "General Seyffard."*

A formal signed photograph of Philipp Wild, the last of *Nordland's* soldiers awarded the Knight's Cross on March 12, 1944.

> At that critical moment, *SS-Oberscharführer* Wild, *1./SS-Panzer-Abteilung 11,* joined the fight with his Panther and, in an extremely short time, destroyed all of the T-34s that had broken through.
>
> As a result of his decisive intervention, he substantially thwarted the enemy's plans to roll up the Narwa bridgehead.
>
> The destruction of the tanks was additionally decisive. Because of their loss, the ongoing infantry attacks, supported by isolated tanks, could be repulsed.

To this was added a short endorsement by *SS-Gruppenführer und Generalleutnant der Waffen-SS* Matthias Kleinheisterkamp:

> The engagement of *SS-Oberscharführer* Wild was decisive in the continued holding of the Narwa bridgehead.

This recommendation was approved on March 23, 1944. What Wild got up to after that is not listed. The only awards he is listed as having are these three grades of the Iron Cross; no Wound Badge, Tank Assault Badge, or other awards are listed. There are some very scant reports of him being wounded in the fighting near Arnswalde in the closing stages of the war. He did survive the war and died on July 29, 1999.

Name: Hinrich Schuldt
Date of birth: 14.06.1901
SS Number: 242 677
Award: Knight's Cross with Oakleaves and Swords

This *Waffen-SS* soldier is an existing, multi-level Knight's Cross related award holder. We first featured him in volume 1 of this work, when on April 5, 1942, he joined the ranks of the Knight's Cross holders. This continued in volume 2, when he was approved for the Oakleaves on April 2, 1943.

Straight on the back of his Oakleaves award, he was approved for the award of the German Cross in Gold on April 21. His battle group had been dissolved by then and Schuldt enjoyed some well-earned rest back in Germany. This came to an end in early September, when he then took over command of the *Latvian SS-Freiwiligen Brigade.* This unit was redesignated the *2. Lettisches SS-Freiwilligen Brigade* as part of the late October 1943 redesignation of the main SS units. Soon after this, on November 9, he was promoted to *SS-Oberführer*. He found himself back in the Leningrad area as 1944 opened. He led *Freiwilligen* during January, as his formation once again received a name change, this time to the *19. Waffen-Grenadier Division der* SS *(Lettisches Nr. 2)*. They were embroiled in the heavy defensive fighting in that area during the opening weeks of the year. Schuldt led them up to March 15, 1944, when he was killed at the front line by an enemy anti-tank round.

On March 16, 1944, Gen. Kurt Herzog, commander of the *XXXVIII. Army Korps*, wrote a recommendation for the posthumous award of the Knight's Cross with Oakleaves and Swords for Hinrich Schuldt:

> Oakleaves holder *SS-Oberführer* Schuldt has activated and trained the *2. Latvian Volunteer Brigade* in the Wolchow bridgehead under the most difficult conditions. The fact he managed to build a combat unit capable of the highest performance in mobile warfare from mostly untrained Latvian volunteers in a dangerous, swampy land in only a few months is due to his organizational talent, high military knowledge, and unequalled energy. The brigade is a result of his work.
>
> In mid-January, the Russians, with far superior forces, forced back the right adjacent division. The break-in from Podbereshje threatened to widen to a full break-through. *SS-Oberführer* Schuldt, recognizing clearly the extreme seriousness of the situation, decided to hit the enemy—which was moving west—with a severe blow in the flank. He inflicted heavy losses on the Russian assault divisions and gained at least forty-eight hours of decisive significance for the battle command of the korps and for the operations of the army. The road *Kampfgruppe Schuldt* kept open allowed an army korps with five subordinate divisions to pull back.
>
> To achieve the highest possible concentration of forces for the active defense, *SS-Oberführer* Schuldt removed men from his line not attacked initially by Spaskaja Powistj so that in every kompanie sector one NCO and two to four men simulated a complete garrison through noise and movement. This was done although the idea of a strong enemy thrust against this sector seemed completely possible.
>
> He gave the order for retreat of his south sector that was threatened in the deep flank. This was done only after he accomplished, with the minimal forces available and great difficulty, the recovery of the last stationary positioned weapons.
>
> When the advance of the newly committed Russian divisions on the road Raglizy-Sselo-Gorka towards the west was no longer preventable with diminishing forces, *SS-Oberführer* Schuldt proposed

Hinrich Schuldt earlier in the war, proudly wearing his Latvian arm patch and Oakleaves to his Knight's Cross. He was posthumously awarded the Swords and was the *SS-Latvian Brigade's* only such level award.

> letting himself become encircled with his battle group. He wanted to cause the highest possible harm to the enemy, which was attacking from all sides, and then break through.
>
> That this decisive success could be achieved—and *Battle Group Schuldt* in the ensuing bitter and heavy retreating battles with its left flank almost always open against strong Partisan troops in the rear was successful—is due to *SS-Oberführer* Schuldt. He reached his objective in strict order and must be thanked. Besides the bravery and hardness of the Latvian volunteers, his outstanding personal bravery, power of decision, superior calmness, and almost unique energy is to be credited.
>
> *SS-Oberführer* Schuldt, who was killed on 15.03.1944 amongst his grenadiers, whose name far beyond his unit served as a standard for the success of even the heaviest and seemingly meaningless undertakings, is considered especially worthy of being awarded the Swords to the Oakleaves of the Knight's Cross of the Iron Cross.

This recommendation was approved on March 25, 1944, and gave the *Latvian* SS their first and only set of Swords to the Knight's Cross with Oakleaves. It also gave the first posthumous approval for 1944 and the seventh of the war to date. It would be the highest-level posthumous recommendation of the war so far.

Within this project, we will define a "posthumous" award as one that was recommended after the recipient was killed. There are other posthumous approvals that were made after the initial recommendation was written, but the recipient was still alive when the proposal was put forward.

This soldier had moved through what became the *Waffen-SS* and served with some of the main units during his history, and was also there at some of the formative points in time. This started with the *Leibstandarte* in 1933, moved to *Germania*, and then *Deutschland* prewar (and Poland), the *Polizei Division, 4. SS-Totenkopf Standarte* (later named *Langemarck*), *Das Reich* in late 1942, his own named battle group by the end of that year, and then on to the *Latvian Brigade* in 1943, which became the *19. Waffen-Grenadier Division der* SS *(Lettisches Nr. 2)* in early 1944. It was leading his Latvian volunteers that brought his career and life to an end. He had received a posthumous promotion to *SS-Brigadeführer und Generalmajor der Waffen-SS* backdated to March 14, 1944.

His name lived on when *Waffen Grenadier Regiment 43* received the honor title "Hinrich Schuldt." His death left a deep void within the existing ranks of the *Waffen-SS* regarding experience, bravery, and capability.

CHAPTER FOUR

BREAK THE ENCIRCLEMENTS & HOLD THE LINES - APRIL 1944

The worsening situation that arose in March carried on into April, as the Soviets were keen to make as many gains as possible and annihilate any German forces they could, but also not allow their enemy any respite to gather themselves and withstand the Soviet onslaught.

The German command structure could ill afford any further losses at this stage in the war in the east with the expected western offensive expected at any time. They shifted further units eastward, while the soldiers on the ground played their part in averting another disaster. Those potential disasters loomed large for *Leibstandarte* and *SS-Kampfgruppe Weidinger* in the Kamenets-Podolsk Pocket. In the western extremes of the Ukraine, elements of *Wiking* were fighting for their lives around the Kovel encirclement. Farther north, Steiner's korps and the Latvians south of there fought to hold their lines and keep the enemy at bay.

We will start with *Wiking*, as the next Knight's Cross award was made to a soldier of that division, but during this month, the first of two exceptionally high-level forms of recognition was given to another one of the men in that formation.

5. SS-Panzer Division Wiking

In the last chapter we finished the coverage of *Wiking* as Karl Nicolussi-Leck had reached Gille's command post with some all-important Panther tanks. Although Nicolussi-Leck had reached Kovel, the Soviets had successfully "closed the door" behind him and their strong forces focused on stopping any further attempts by the Germans to get into Kovel. This placed great pressure on the mixed SS and Heer forces fighting fifteen miles outside the city. The defenders, now strengthened by the *Wiking* Panthers, were continuously attacked at the same time and their casualty list grew daily. To help shift the balance, further Heer divisions were moved into the sector between Kovel and Cholm in the first days of April. On April 4, the main push to decisively relieve Kovel began. This push was made to the northwest of the city and, despite strong enemy resistance, Heer units penetrated the Kovel ring on April 6. *SS-Obersturmbannführer* Muhlenkamp and his Panzers were part of this push. One of his men, *SS-Obersturmführer* Otto Schneider of *7. Kompanie*, led an assault near Dubowa and also pushed on towards Kovel on April 5. Those successes led to Schneider being awarded the Knight's Cross.

Once inside the city, the mixed force of Heer and *Waffen-SS* troops expanded their hold and pushed back or defeated enemy troops in the surrounding area. The fighting lasted for almost a further three weeks and the end result was a German-held area over six miles east of Kovel. Some of the fighting that took place included Franz Hack's battle at Hill .189.5 on April 17, which resulted in him becoming a Knight's Cross holder in early May. Hans Dorr's actions on the seventeenth within the Kovel area concluded his later Swords recommendation (covered in the next volume). On the Führer's fifty-fifth birthday, Hitler approved the recommendation for the award of *SS-Gruppenführer* Herbert Gille's Diamonds to his existing (and recently awarded) Swords and Oakleaves to the Knight's Cross. This was the first of two such awards for soldiers of the *Waffen-SS*. The basis of the award was Gille's successful defense of the city of Kovel.

Their ability to hold the enemy gave them much needed temporary respite from recent unrelenting enemy pressure. We will complete their story in the final chapter.

SS-Kavallerie Regiment 17. / SS-Kampfgruppe Ameiser

The men of this regiment were within Kovel as part of the overall forces that Herbert Gille had under his temporary command.

They played their part in fighting against the Soviets pushing to constrict the Kovel pocket as their comrades established their strong defensive ring west of the city to hold off the expected German relief effort. The fighting caused continuing casualties for the regiment, and it was not long before the remnants were being commanded by *SS-Hauptsturmführer* Anton Ameiser (it became known as *SS-Kampfgruppe Ameiser*). These SS soldiers

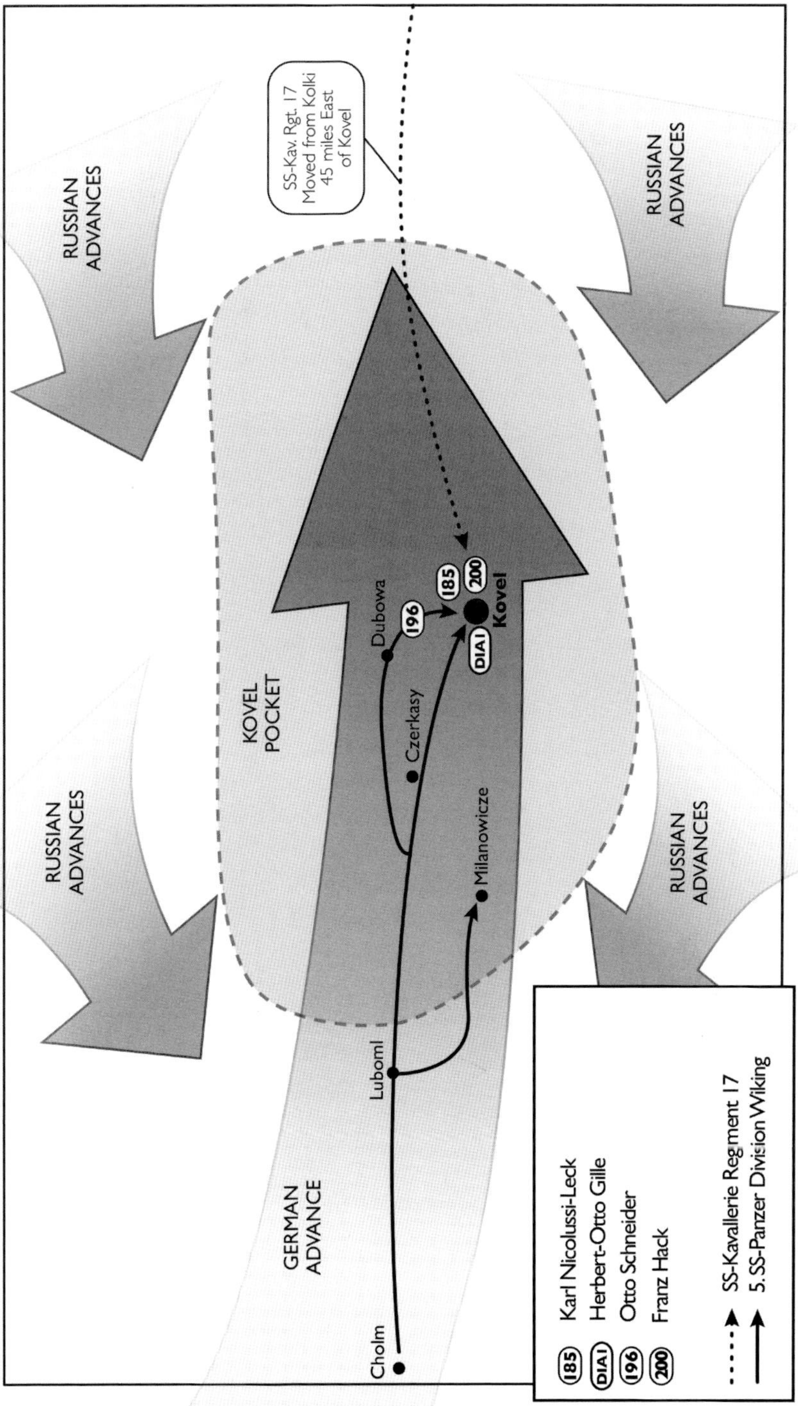

Map 13 – Kovel Encirclement: March and April 1944

held off the Russians until the relief forces broke the encirclement. Once relieved, they remained in the general Kovel area until the end of April.

What was left of that regiment was then earmarked to be the basis of a new *22. SS-Freiwilligen-Kavellerie Division "Maria Theresia."*

The halting of the enemy advances in northwest Ukraine was a success, but their kameraden to the south were not so lucky.

1. SS-Panzer Division Leibstandarte SS Adolf Hitler

As April 1944 began, the men of the *LSSAH* were fighting hard for Andrejewka. During the next week, they moved fifteen to twenty miles west to Losiacz and Dawidkowce, then fifteen miles farther west to Ulaskowcze. It was also at the end of this first week in April that elements of the relief force (*10. SS-Panzer Division Frundsberg*) made their initial link with the forces trapped inside the pocket. *SS-Hauptsturmführer* Werner Potschke completed the final actions that constituted his recommendation for the Knight's Cross on April 7 (detailed in volume 5).

The *Leibstandarte* continued in a northwesterly direction towards Buczacz, which was another thirty miles of advance through difficult terrain including many rivers and streams. On April 14, 1944, the *Leibstandarte* were relieved by Heer kameraden and moved into the Trybuchowce area. The rest of the forces inside this pocket managed to make it out and reach the relief forces, despite Soviet attacks and attempts to defeat them. That successful move westward ensured 200,000 men avoided destruction; the *LSSAH* were part of that group. Over the next few days they moved west of Buczacz and were then loaded onto trains; they were to leave the eastern front for the third time in their fighting history. Hundreds of their kameraden who had been killed over the past six months would remain in Russian soil forever. The survivors were sent to Belgium for a rest and refit.

We will complete their pre-Normandy story in the final chapter.

SS-Kampfgruppe Weidinger

Trapped in the Kamenets-Podolsky Pocket—or Hube's Pocket, as it is also referred to (named after the overall senior commander of the forces inside)—they focused on moving closer to their objective in the opening days of April: to link with the relief forces moving to the east. Part of that relief force was the *9.* and *10. SS-Panzer Divisions*. The battle group moved to Germakowka by April 4, then to Wokowze the following day. By the seventh, they had moved to Skypowce, then by the ninth they were in Chartanowze. The "wandering" Hube's Pocket was in full effect and helping to reduce the threat of annihilation at the hands of the Soviets. The ninth was the same

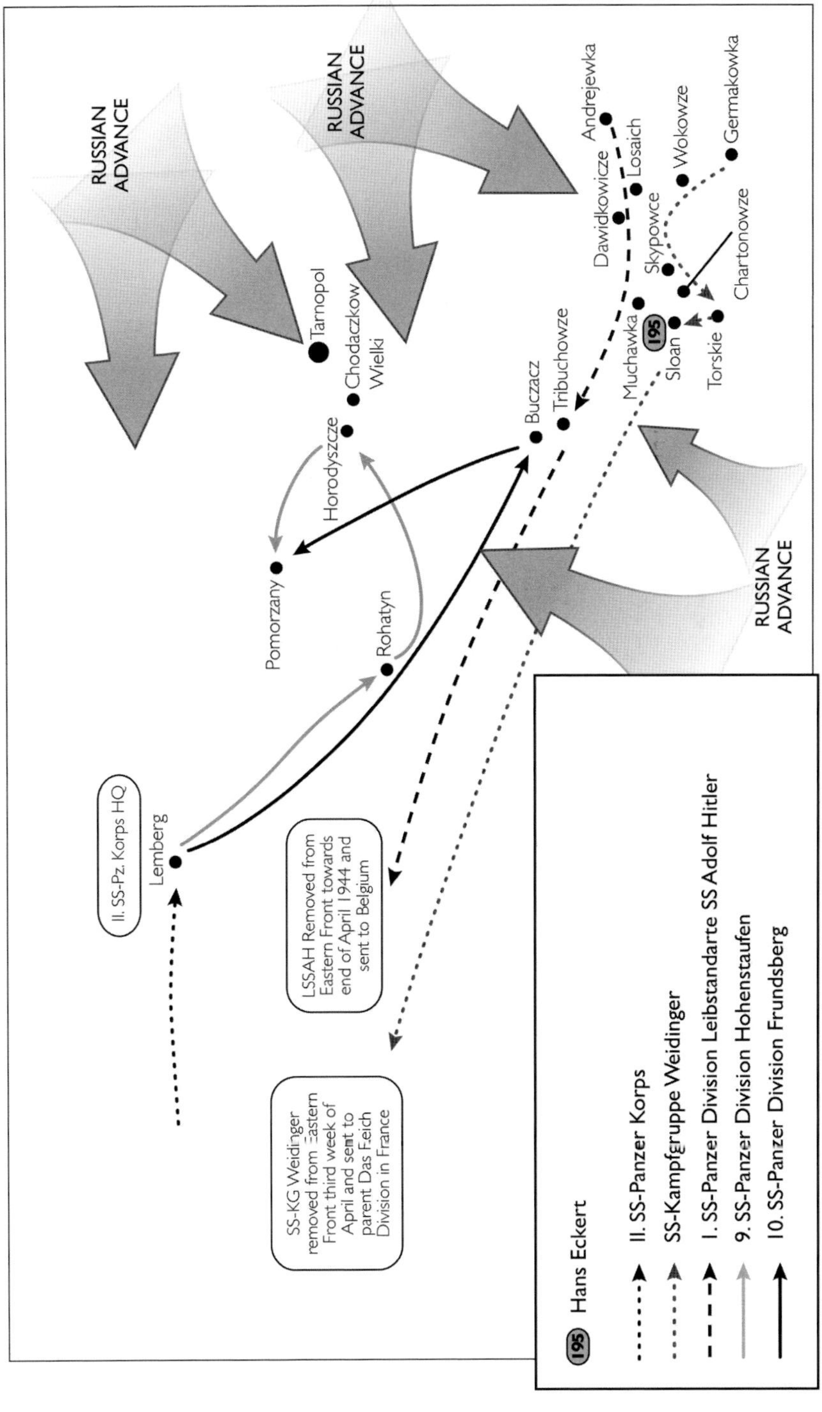

Map 14 – Kamenets-Podolsky Pocket Breakout: April 1944

day Hausser's *II. SS-Panzer* korps made their initial contact with the *1. Panzer Armee* inside the pocket. The Soviets were attacking the edges of the pocket and against the relief forces; this fight was far from over, although the linking of both elements made them much more capable of defending against the enemy.

The following day, the battle group was in Torskie, where they were tasked with securing an important height being controlled by the Russians. Although they had linked with friendly forces and the pocket had been "opened," the enemy was in a strong position to continue to wreak havoc on the exhausted troops still moving west. The significance of that action is directly relevant to this project. The hill was close to Worwolince, around six miles northeast of their current location. They moved into position and began their assault on April 13. This attack was successful, despite enemy counter-thrusts; assault leader *SS-Obersturmführer* Hans Eckert had this successful action as the final part of his subsequent Knight's Cross approval.

On the fourteenth, the battle group had some respite and began the task of cleaning everything, getting ready for the next orders / action. This turned out to be the same day they were ordered to move to France and join their *Das Reich* kameraden. They had a fifty-mile trek to reach their entraining station in Halicz to the north. They began their moves over the next few days and on April 20, 1944, their train took them away from the eastern front, thereby removing another SS unit from the east and moving it west in readiness for the fight with the western enemy. Their rail journey took them through Poland, Germany, and on to Toulouse, France, reaching there on April 27.

Outside the pocket, their SS kameraden relief force arrived . . .

II. SS-Panzer Korps

9. SS-Panzer Division Hohenstaufen

Moving east in the closing days of March, the *II. SS-Panzer* korps headquarters set themselves up in Lemberg. The men of *Hohenstaufen* were moved to the southeast, initially between Unterwalden and Rohatyn. Their first attack was made almost immediately on April 4. They were to move to the south and towards the Dnjester River, then advance on Buczacz. Destroyed bridges hampered their advance and slowed the pace considerably. Due to the slow pace the direction of *Hohenstaufen*'s advance was changed and they moved in behind *Frundsberg*.

After their kameraden successfully reached Buczacz, *Hohenstaufen* advanced eastward towards the Strypa River. Strong enemy forces were all along this sector and the success of the mission to rescue the "Hube Pocket" men was reliant on this area being controlled by the Germans. *Hohenstaufen* had a strong part to play in this; they reached the river on April 8.

Due to threats farther east and north, *Hohenstaufen's* objective was changed and the following day, they temporarily left the framework of the *II. SS-Panzer Korps*. They were to be used as part of the relief efforts for the encircled city of Tarnapol. Their advances began on April 10, but the Russians were waiting and had built up strong defensive forces. A heavy fight ensued around Horodyszcze that rattled on for days. This fighting would earn the *Hohenstaufen Division* its first Knight's Cross award, albeit a posthumous one, for *SS-Sturmbannführer* Robert Frank (see the next volume).

The smaller location of Slobodka to the north became a focus of the fighting from the thirteenth. Tarnapol was virtually wiped out on the fourteenth, but the SS men fought on. A bridge was erected at Horodyszcze and on the fourteenth, the *Waffen-SS* were at last able to move their armor east over the river. The following day witnessed heavy fighting at Chodaczkow Wielki, with *SS-Obersturmbannführer* Otto's tanks leading the fight. This fighting continued for another two days, while at the same time enemy attacks were launched along the length of the advance route. Meyer would become the second *Hohenstaufen* man to receive the Knight's Cross, and his actions will also be covered in the next volume.

The increasingly hopeless situation resulted in orders being issued for the abandonment of further advances east. The operation itself did not yield the desired outcome and only resulted in losses to the men of the *Waffen-SS*. The retreat back across the Wosuszka River at Horodyszcze was completed by the end of April 19, and the recently constructed bridge was blown up by the Germans. Just over fifty Germans made it west out of Tarnapol, but over 1,000 soldiers lost their lives trying to reach them. This brief operation was a resounding failure from the German perspective. For the men of the *Waffen SS*, their efforts yielded two more additions to the list of Knight's Cross holders.

Hohenstaufen moved back westward towards their former arrival positions and awaited new orders; these soon came, along with a move to Pomorzany. Elements fought partisans during early May, but overall this division remained in reserve in this area. We will return to them in volume 5.

10. SS-Panzer Division Frundsberg

Despite the difficult road conditions, it was men from *Frundsberg* that reached the Buczacz objective first on April 6. This allowed the lead elements of the men in the encircled "Hube Pocket" to link with friendly forces. The fight was not over yet, though; other elements of this division were positioned farther to the north and had to contend with strong enemy attacks. They consolidated their positions over the next two days with the help of further friendly forces.

The enemy switched their emphasis and amassed heavy forces northeast of Buczacz. The next objective for *Frundsberg* was to attack this threat, and the actions began on April 10. For the next week, these men fought seesaw battles in the area, focused on holding the Strypa River. This greatly assisted in holding the line, and the following week saw a reduction in enemy activity. *Frundsberg* was relieved on April 25, and moved back towards their former positions. They were able to take pride in the part they played in helping the almost 200,000 men of "Hube's Pocket" escape destruction or capture by the Soviets.

In the closing days of April, existing Knight's Cross with Oakleaves holder *SS-Standartenführer* Heinz Harmel assumed command of this division. He would take his new unit to the northwest of Tarnopol, around Pomorzany. They moved into reserve and remained in that role for the rest of May 1944. We will return to them in the next volume.

While in that southern sector, we will cover *Totenkopf*, much farther south and undergoing their own struggle.

3. SS-Panzer Division Totenkopf

The Soviet push towards the southwest forced the Germans in the same direction. That movement sent *Totenkopf* up to and over the Romanian border at the start of April, initially at Dubasari. The move across the Romanian border was significant, as *Totenkopf* became another *Waffen-SS* unit to be pushed out of the Soviet Union. *Totenkopf's* advance east across that border began thirty-two months earlier, in the extreme northern sector. Now they found themselves in the extreme south, around 800 miles from their starting point and closer to the Black Sea than their Baltic Sea origins in 1941!

Over the first week of April 1944, they moved a farther thirty-five miles southward to Kischinew. The *Totenkopf* troops were given additional vital supplies and had a few days respite, but relentless enemy thrusts forced them to move once more. In the third week of April, they were moved over one hundred miles to the northwest, to Stolniceni Prajescu. *Totenkopf's*

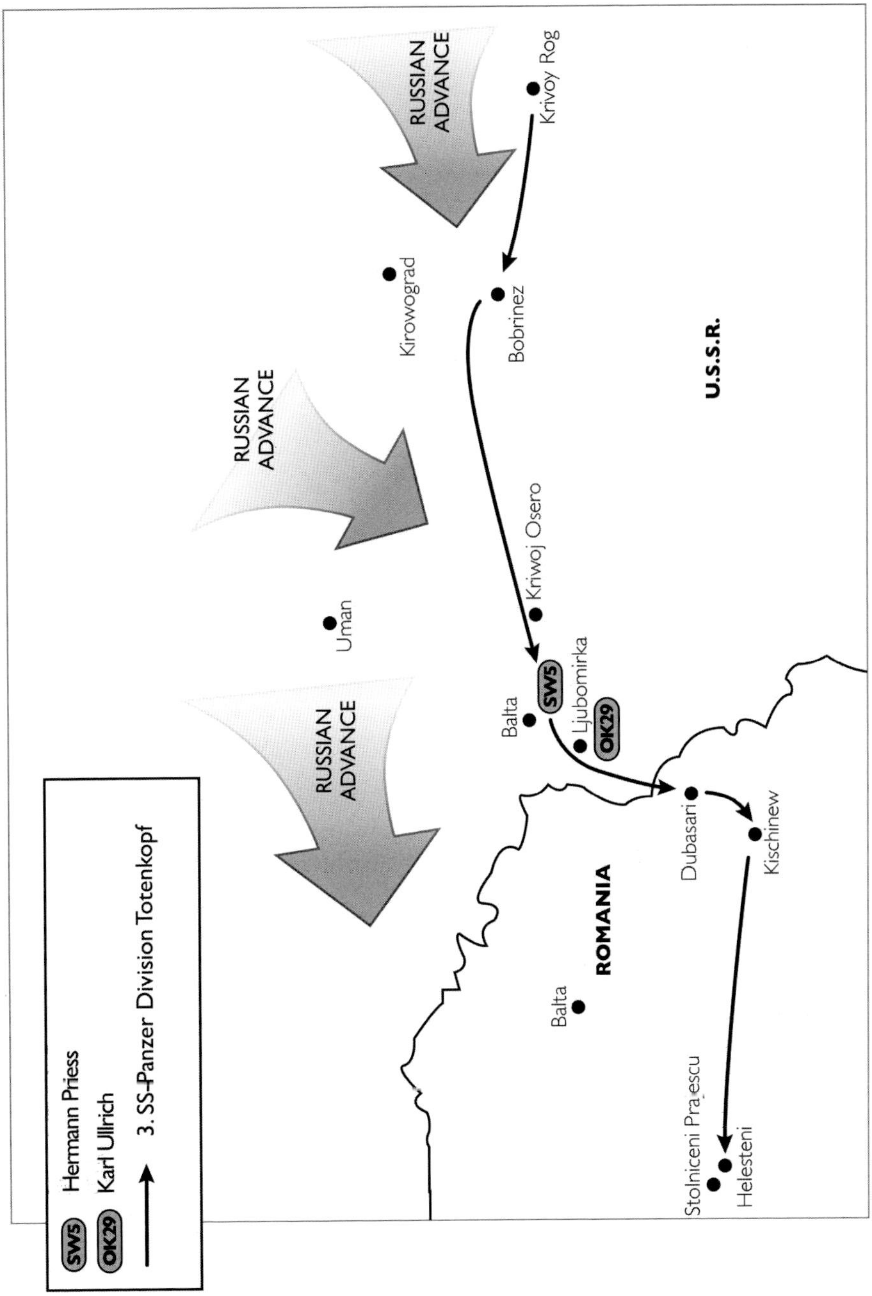

Map 15 – *SS-Totenkopf* Movements: January to May 1944

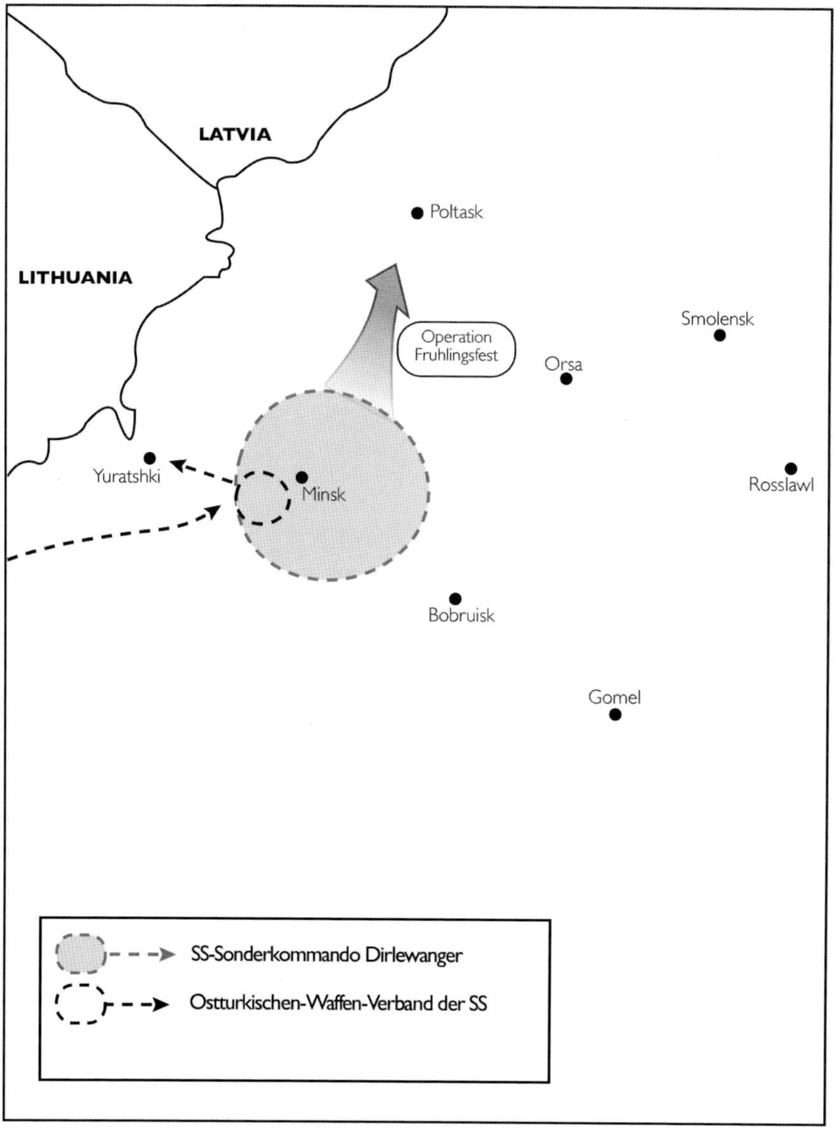

Map 16 – Army Group Center: January to May 1944

soldiers went on the attack against the enemy there and managed some localized victories, causing the enemy to pause for the moment; that fighting lasted up to the end of April. *SS-Unterscharführer* Johann Fiedler's actions around that area in the closing days of April 1944 would result in him becoming a Knight's Cross holder. *SS-Unterscharführer* Josef Rollecke would be awarded his Knight's Cross the same day, also presumably for actions around this time (detailed in volume 5).

In the central sector of the eastern front . . .

SS-Sonderkommando Dirlewanger

Their relatively quiet opening phase of 1944 came to an end the second week of April; prior to that, their only notable change was back on March 19, when Oskar Dirlewanger received a promotion to *SS-Standartenführer*.

They participated in an anti-partisan operation (Operation *Fruhlingfest*) between April 11 and May 10, in an area north of Minsk stretching from Czernizka to Hornowo-Sswatki, Hornowo-Wiercinski, and Krownica. They fought alongside various units from the *Police* and *Heer*. The operation was against sizeable partisan forces operating in this area and the end result was almost twenty dead SS men, with claims of sixty-five dead partisans and the destruction of some partisan camps.

They enjoyed a period of rest following this, and during the remainder of May 1944, they were sent additional men, which took them to just over 700 men by the end of May (read more in volume 5).

To the north . . .

VI. SS-Freiwilligen Korps (Lettisches)

15. Waffen-Grenadier Division der SS *(Lettische Nr. 1)*

The fighting in the "Panther" positions on the Velikaya River went on into April, and the Russians inflicted significant losses on the Latvians that forced some of the remnants to be removed from the front line; those moves began around the middle of April and carried on for the rest of the month. The enemy shifted their emphasis to the Latvian's sister division area.

The new location of the *15. SS-Division* was to be between Lavi and Bardovo, around thirty-five miles east of Opotschka. Once there in May, they focused on rebuilding themselves as best they could, as well as training

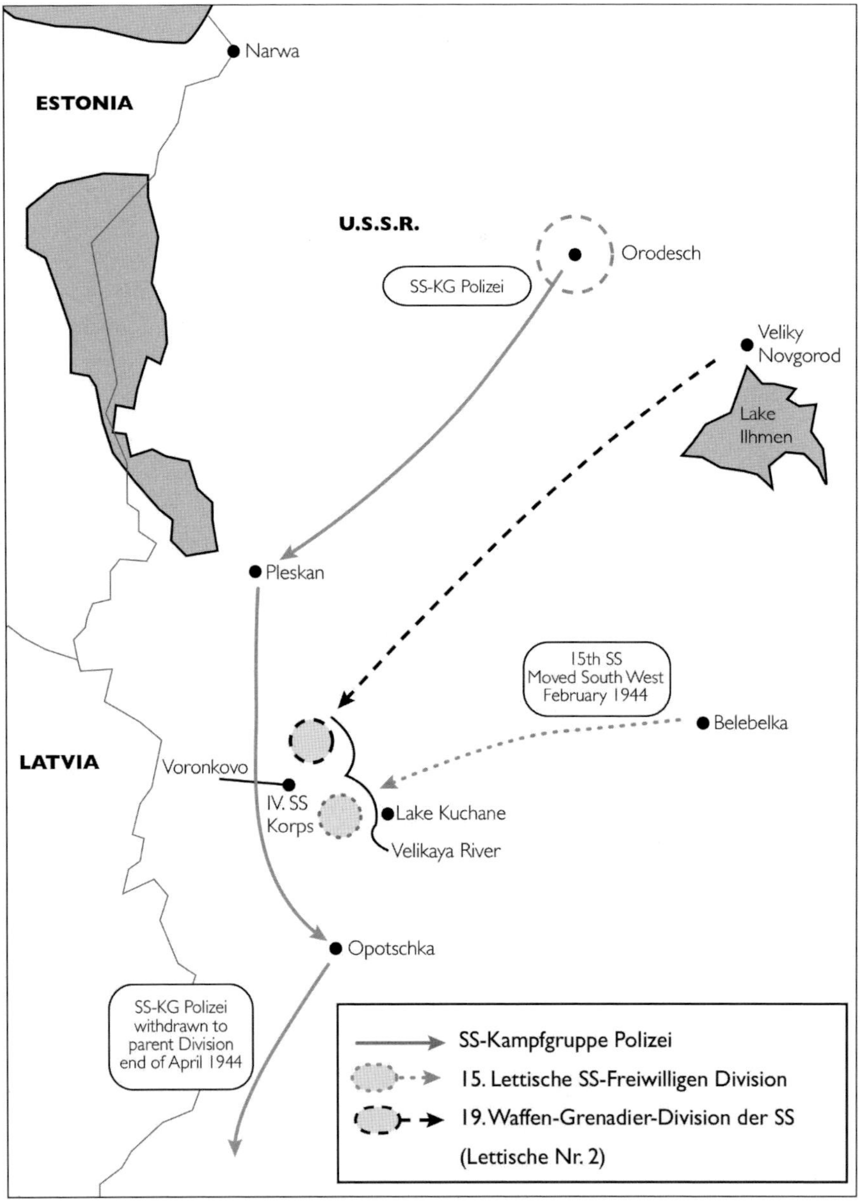

Map 17 – Southwest of Leningrad: February to May 1944

men. There were no further significant changes for these SS soldiers (see next volume).

19. Waffen-Grenadier Division der SS (Lettische Nr. 2)

After around a week of respite, the Russians renewed their efforts and successfully took the dominant heights at Sapronovo, while also establishing a firm bridgehead. The weight of that effort fell on the *15.* SS, but from early April, the Russians shifted emphasis north to the area under the control of the *19.* SS. That thrust began on April 4, with well-proven tactics of aerial and artillery softening-up quickly followed by an infantry assault. The enemy infantry focused on Grigorkino. It was on the following day that recent Knight's Cross awardee Voldemars Veiss was heavily wounded and moved to the rear. He succumbed to his wounds ten days later; the *Waffen-SS* had lost another brave and accomplished soldier who had been recognized at the highest level for his abilities.

The focus for the Soviets moved to Pechane, on the river itself. That location was fought for over the next few days, ending with the Latvian line in the north being moved slightly westward. The men from the *19. SS-Division* were also ordered to the Kudever area and their moves started on April 19, 1944. These moves were complete by month end and the soldiers took up their new locations centered on Kudever itself, with their *15.* SS kameraden located to the south. They had no further major incidents during May 1944, other than focusing on the raising of further elements to bolster their ranks.

Although 1944 to date had allowed these *19.* SS Latvian men to demonstrate their abilities and become recognized for them in the form of one Knight's Cross and one set of Swords to an existing Oakleaves holder, both of these men were killed during this period; a hefty cost, and one that would only mount. We will rejoin the story of these soldiers in the next volume.

Kampfgruppe SS-Polizei Division

Elements of this battle group fought north of Opotschka from the end of March through to the second week of April What was left of *Polizei Kampfgruppe* was withdrawn from this northern region as April 1944 closed. They were sent to Kurmark just over one month later and began a period of re-training and re-fitting. Their time in the Leningrad area had come to an end over two-and-a-half years after it had begun.

All other northern *Waffen-SS* units were in a quieter phase of their story (see chapter 3), so we will return to them in volume 5. Let us divert to the extreme southern front . . .

In Italy and the Balkans:

16. SS-Panzergrenadier Division Reichsführer-SS

In the second half of April, the *RF-SS* soldiers in Debrecen, Hungary, were joined by their kameraden who had been fighting in Anzio. (The Italian SS remained at the bridgehead and will be covered below.)

It was also in mid-April that they had to send over 4,000 men to the *3. SS-Panzer Division Totenkopf.* To counteract the drain on a much-needed resource, the *RF-SS* was sent a couple thousand Hungarians in the following weeks. In May, they would be moved again, and for some of the men it was a return to the Italian front.

The western Allies made a further landing, this time farther south of Anzio around Gaeta. The *Reichsführer-SS* was initially sent back to Livorno and they began to arrive the second half of May. We will continue with the coverage of this formation in volume 5.

Italianische SS-Freiwilligen Legion

They continued their defensive fighting at the Anzio bridgehead during the first half of April. One notable element was the Vendetta Battalion, under the command of *SS-Obersturmbannführer* Frederico degli Oddi. They fought so well they were issued a unique collar patch personally by Himmler; they were also permitted to wear the traditional black and silver colored collar patches instead of their previous red and silver patches.

One soldier who fought in Anzio as part of that battalion was *SS-Obersturmführer* Pio Filippani Ronconi. He earned the Second Class Iron Cross during the fighting and remembers the ferocity of their inaugural action in the uniform of the *Waffen-SS*. Ronconi had previously fought in north Africa as part of the elite Arditi formation. I was lucky enough to meet Ronconi in his home in 2007. He displayed the award documents for the Second Class Iron Cross and the Black Wound Badge, both signed by Karl Wolff. He also had a stunning blue enamel medal with Arabic writing on it. When asked what it was and why he earned it, his reply was, "I did something very special for the Shah of Iran."

East into Yugoslavia . . .

V. SS-Gebirgs Korps:

7. SS-Freiwilligen-Gebirgs Division Prinz Eugen

In late April, *Prinz Eugen* took part in a large operation to help clear the northeastern sector of Bosnia. They operated in an area south and southeast of Vlasenica, while their kameraden from the *13. SS-Gebirgs Division* operated farther to the northeast. The objective was to prevent multiple partisan divisions from escaping eastward across the Drina River into Serbia. For the men of *Prinz Eugen*, they continuously engaged the enemy into the third week of May, inflicting thousands of casualties.

13. SS-Freiwilligen Bosnien-Herzegowina-Gebirgs-Division (Kroatien)

They launched their next offensive on April 12, with a push to the south toward Mackovac and Priboj and west toward Gradacac; these were reached during the rest of April and the area was secured.

Their successes were to be built upon and not allow partisans to regain control, so it was not long before larger operations were planned and started. The next operation for the Croatian SS men started on April 23, with a push to the south and southeast. This overall operation also included the *7. SS-Gebirgs Division* and the *SS-Fallschirmjaeger Battalion 500*. As part of the operation, an intensive battle took place in Sekovici in the closing days of the month. Zvornik was also reached. The area in between that stretched to the Drina River / Serbian border was under German control. The operation concluded on May 6, 1944.

A smaller operation was launched in mid-May, during which the division defeated partisans in the Majevicas Mountains. The remainder of May saw no major activities for this unit (their history continues in volume 5).

Northwest into Hungary . . .

8. SS-Kavallerie Division Florian Geyer

The elements located in the southern Hungarian region remained there throughout April and May, and continued with their training; other elements were being trained at Debica.

Back at the start of April, *SS-Obersturmbannführer* Joachim Rumohr took over as divisional commander; before the end of the month he had been promoted to *SS-Standartenführer*. It was also during this period that recognition arrived for two additional men from this SS division: on April 21, *SS-Untersturmführer* Otto Kirchner was approved for the Knight's Cross

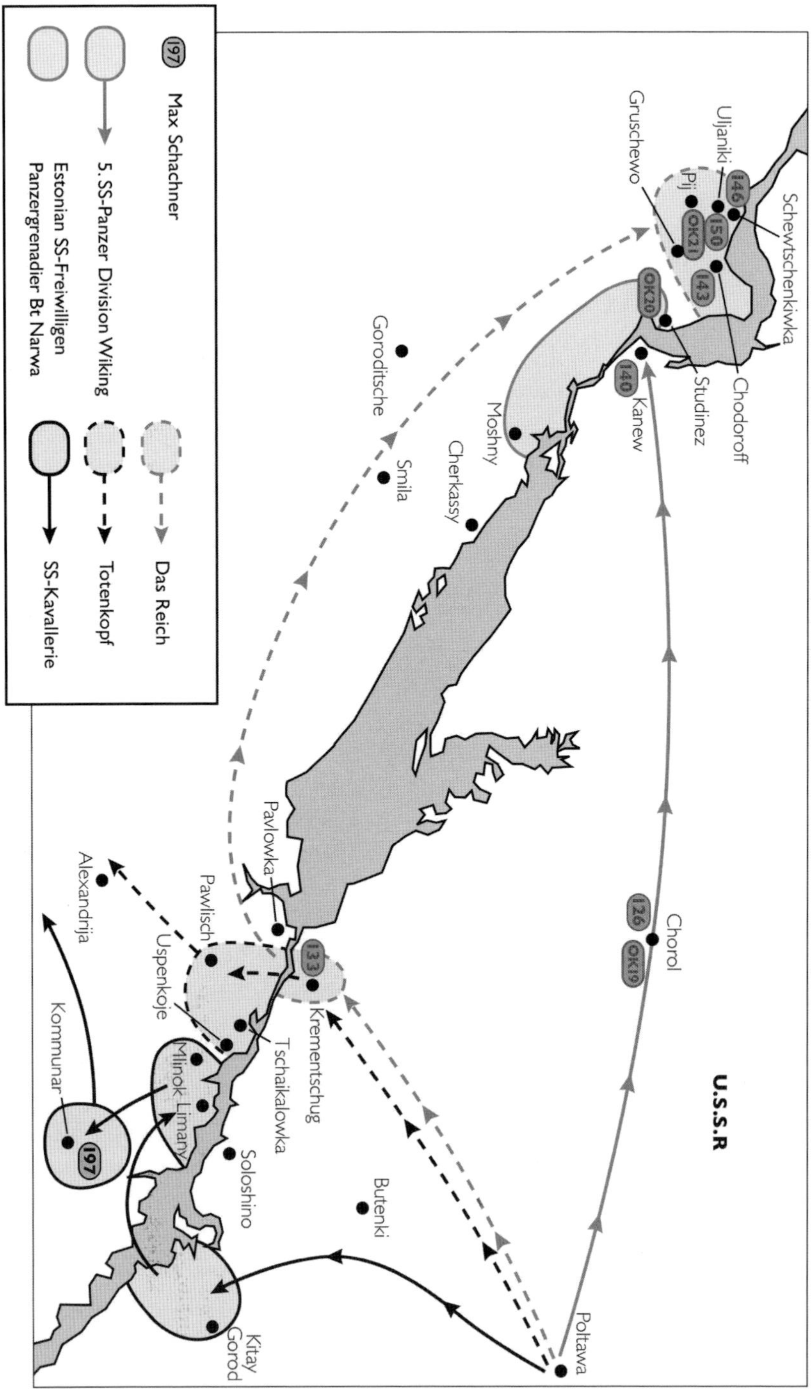

Map 18 – Dnjepr River North: Late September – October 1943

for his actions back in August 1943; then, on May 14, *SS-Obersturmführer* Max Schachner was also approved for his Knight's Cross for bravery displayed on October 16, 1943.

We will halt return to the SS cavalry in volume 5.

18. SS-Panzergrenadier Division Horst Wessel

In April, the division was relocated to Batschka, on the southern Hungarian border, as part of the overall occupation of Hungary; they were operating at just over 60% of their authorized strength. They continued with their training and formation during April and May 1944. We will return to their history in the next volume.

Before detailing the Knight's Cross-related awards approved in April, a quick overview for some of the training units that had seen notable changes during the month.

12. SS-Panzer Division Hitlerjugend

During February and March, focus on training and readiness remained the priority. In April, the men of the *12. SS-Division* were relocated to France, in the Normandy region. They took up locations stretching from Nogent to Louviers, Vimoutiers, and Mortagne. The long-anticipated western enemy landings were in the forefront of the German general staff and the relocating of the *12. SS-Division* was to fill an important strategic gap left behind by the *9. SS-Panzer Division Frundsberg*. They continued to gather strength and effectiveness during April and May, and this youthful SS division would be considered fully trained and ready for deployment on June 1, 1944 (see volume 5).

Schwere SS-Panzer Abteilung 101

In April, members of this formation were present in Brussels when the survivors of *SS-Sturmbrigade Wallonie* paraded, following their return from the Russian front. It was also during April that *101* moved to France and took up locations around Gournay-en-Bray.

Schwere SS-Panzer Abteilung 102

In April, they were relocated to Zwolle, in Holland. It was later that month they received their first half-dozen Tiger tanks.

With no other significant changes for the remaining soldiers of the *Waffen-SS* in April, here are the eight men who were recognized for their bravery, including the first set of *Waffen-SS* Diamonds and another set of Swords to existing award holders.

Name: Harald Nugiseks
Date of birth: 22.10.1921
SS Number: None assigned
Award: Knight's Cross

Born in Karjakula, Estonia, his military service began in early October 1941, when he volunteered for the newly raised East Battalion 185, made up of Estonians who wanted to free their homeland from the Soviet yoke. The battalion was under overall command by the Germans. He fought in the Volossovo area from early 1942 with this unit, staying there until September, when he then returned home. During his service at that time he was promoted to *Gefreiter* and was presented with the Russian Front Medal.

In May 1943, he volunteered for the *Estonian SS-Freiwilligen Brigade*. This unit was raised and trained in Heidelager, Poland.

Due to his front-line experience and his rank, he was one of the Estonians selected for the NCO training program. For Nugiseks, this started in August in Lauenburg, Hamburg, and lasted until November 1943. He was promoted to *SS-Unterscharführer* on November 9, 1943. He was placed with *1.* kompanie in *SS-Freiwilligen-Grenadier-Regiment 46*, which was part of the recently re-named *3. Estonian Freiwilligen Brigade*. They were sent to the Nevel area, south of Leningrad, so once again, Nugiseks was back in his old "home." Soon after arriving he received a grenade splinter wound, but remained at the front, earning the Black Wound Badge. In December 1943, the Infantry Assault Badge was added to his tunic.

In January 1944, this brigade was re-formed into the *20. Estonian Freiwilligen Division*. The men were initially returned to Estonia, but due to the worsening situation in this northern region of the eastern front they were committed to battle once more. Nugiseks was among the men placed near the Narwa River in the second half of February. This coincided with the Russians establishing their bridgeheads across that river. The enemy pressure was heavy and fell upon the Estonians hard. Nugiseks was involved in the fight for the Riigikula bridgehead in the closing days of February; the award of the Second Class Iron Cross followed on the twenty-seventh. Once that bridgehead had been destroyed, the emphasis shifted to the Vaasa-Vepskula-Siiverts bridgehead from February 29. The main attack that involved Nugiseks started on March 1; it was for his actions at that bridgehead that he would ultimately receive the Knight's Cross.

The actual recommendation does not appear to survive and is certainly not in his file. Before we cover the award of the Knight's Cross we need to detail a few instances that occurred in between. The battle for the bridgehead

A signed image of Haralt Nugiseks showing his Knight's Cross and distinctive Estonian collar patch. He was the *Estonian-SS'* first Knight's Cross awardee.

came to a successful conclusion on March 6; Nugiseks was awarded the First Class Iron Cross the following day. Five days later, he was given some home leave. It was during this home leave that he developed a serious illness, culminating in him slipping out of consciousness for many days. At one stage it was feared he would not survive this illness and its accompanying fever. A top-level medical professor was sent from Germany and this man's treatment started to put Nugiseks back on the road to recovery. On April 9, 1944, Harald Nugiseks was approved for the Knight's Cross to the Iron Cross. We can presume that Divisonal Commander *SS-Oberführer* Franz Augsberger wrote the recommendation. The award itself was made on April 20, while Nugiseks was still confined to his hospital bed. So what had he done to warrant this high award?

Back on March 1, the main attack was launched against the enemy positions. It started with artillery fire and under this the men pushed forward. They got to within a few hundred meters of the enemy trenches when the enemy artillery gave their own response. This coincided with some of the Estonian men hitting enemy mines. The enemy soldiers then moved in with grenades. Against this scenario, the men slowly slogged forward. The enemy defenses, combined with their attacks, inflicted injury and losses to the Estonians. Machine gun fire, barbed wire, and further mines all had to be contended with, but they managed to get within fifty meters [164 ft.] of the enemy. This last section of enemy trenches was among the strongest.

With his officers wounded and unable to carry on, Nugiseks took it upon himself to push the remaining men forward. The adjoining Estonian attack was reaching its culmination, but needed help to drive home the final defeat. He led a small group of twenty men into this remaining enemy trench and using countless hand grenades backed up with machine pistol fire, they closed the attack all the way to a successful outcome. Nugiseks received many close calls during this advance, but none of them hit their mark—a good thing for Nugiseks!

The successful attack by Nugiseks along his defined advance line did not end the ordeal. The enemy launched counterattacks over the next few days, but each of them was defeated. The fight for this particular bridgehead was concluded in the closing hours of March 6, 1944. For the time being, Nugisek's work was over.

The immediate recognition he received for his actions was the First Class Iron Cross, but in the following weeks, his actions were deemed worthy of the higher recognition he was approved for on April 9. This made him the first Estonian *Waffen-SS* soldier to receive this award. He was promoted on June 21 to *SS-Oberscharführer.* It was not until July that he left hospital, but he was then sent to Merano, in northern Italy. While there, he was involved in a disagreement with a Wehrmacht officer that resulted in him being demoted to *SS-Unterscharführer*. Towards the end of 1944, Nugiseks was sent to Neuhammer, Germany, to join the surviving Estonians. In January 1945, he found himself at officer's training school in Newklau, Czecheslovakia. In April, the training was halted, as the front line was getting near. Nugiseks was captured by Czech partisans on May 7, and one of them tore off his awards, including his Knight' Cross, throwing them to the ground. He was handed over to the Russians within days and remained a prisoner until 1958.

Nugiseks rebuilt his life back in Estonia and even received a reserve captain rank. When Estonia gained independence in the 1990s, Nugiseks took part in the memorial held for the fighters of WWII and his kameraden of the *Waffen-SS*. Harald Nugiseks died on January 2, 2014.

Name: Karl Nicolussi-Leck
Date of birth: 14.3.1917
SS Number: 423 876
Award: Knight's Cross

Born in Pfatten, Bozen—a region that used to be part of the Austro-Hungarian Empire—Nicolussi-Leck grew up in an area that had a predominantly German "feel" to it, but was also undergoing transformation under its new Italian rulers. He was active in local German sympathizer groups prewar and large parts of the population spoke German. He was studying sciences at university, but at the end of 1939, he opted to move to Germany. He quickly volunteered for the SS in April 1940.

He initially spent time with *SS-Regiment Deutschland* and took part in the Balkans campaign, holding *SS-Scharführer* rank by then. In the early stages of Operation Barbarossa he was with *SS-Regiment Der Führer*. Due to the capabilities he displayed in the field, he was selected to take part in an officer's preparatory course; he followed that by attending Bad Tolz between November 1941 and January 1942. His promotion to *SS-Untersturmführer* was approved on April 20; at that stage he was with the Panzer regiment in *SS-Division Wiking*, serving initially with *2. Kompanie*, which was equipped with Panzer IVs. This principal armored unit of the *Waffen-SS* was being trained in Germany in early 1942, but in June, they embarked for the southern reaches of the eastern front with Nicolussi-Leck in tank number 221.

The second half of 1942 was a "busy" time for *Wiking*, which in turn made it testing time for Nicolussi-Leck. The Second Class Iron Cross was awarded on July 25, 1942, for helping to push through to Rostov. This was quickly followed on August 9 with the First Class, awarded for his part in the capture of Krapotkin. The Black Wound Badge was approved on September 2, and the Tank Assault Badge on the eleventh; the first of four wounds for this *Waffen-SS* soldier. During October 1942, he was placed in command of *1. Kompanie*, commanding tank number 111. He was wounded by enemy machine gun fire four days later and it was serious enough to warrant a move back to Germany.

When Nicolussi-Leck was fit for duty again (May 1943), he remained in Germany and was sent to the newly raised II Battalion in *Wiking's* Panzer Regiment; they were being formed in Grafenwohr in the summer of 1943. He became the commander of *8.* kompanie and as their training neared its end, they were equipped with Panther tanks (January 1944). A promotion to *SS-Obersturmführer* came in November 1943. The relentless Soviet push evident at the start of 1944 found itself swallowing up the town of Kovel. *Wiking* Commander and recent Swords awardee Herbert Gille was sent to that location and found himself trapped within an enemy ring of defense with less than 5,000 assorted defenders to help him. There were initial attempts by *Wiking* to break through the enemy defensive ring and link with Gille and the mixed force inside, but the enemy resistance was strong. Into this situation arrived the II Battalion from Germany.

During the closing days of March, *SS-Obersturmführer* Nicolussi-Leck arrived at the positions of the *Wiking Division*, who were outside the besieged city. In conference with senior commanders, he was tasked with leading the push towards the encircled location. At the start of the push a radio message was sent through, ordering him not to advance and abandon the attempt. Nicolussi-Leck told his radio operator to relay a reply that he was unable to find him. By making this decision Nicolussi-Leck was disobeying a direct order, but also instructing one of his men to do the same. His rationale was that he felt the trapped soldiers and civilians' need was too great to ignore, so he pushed onwards toward Kovel. He started the push on March 27, and by the morning of the thirtieth had arrived at the command post of Herbert Gille. This feat earned him a multi-level request for the award of the Knight's Cross.

The initial document was composed by Johannes Muhlenkamp on April 1, 1944, but was added to by *SS-Standartenführer* Richter and Herbert Gille:

> *SS-Obersturmführer* Nicolussi-Leck has, on 29.3.1944—as the leader of *8./SS-Pz.Rgt. "Wiking"*—penetrated into Czerkasy with his Panther kompanie under the most difficult ground conditions. This was despite established and strong enemy positions occupying 8 km [5 miles] west of Kovel that destroyed numerous vehicles. On 30.3.1944, Nicolussi-Leck made the decision to advance from Czerkasy at 04:15 hours, along the road and then the railway line from Maciejow to Kovel. During fighting against enemy tanks Kovel was reached with seven Panthers.
>
> He has thus brought a decisive reinforcement to the position of Kovel and on the same day shot up seventeen enemy tanks in Kovel.

To this was added the thoughts of *SS-Standartenführer* Richter on April 2:

> This recommendation is warmly agreed with. *SS-Obersturmführer* Nicolussi-Leck has, through his surprise advance with seven Panthers under his own initiative, broken into Kovel. He thereby significantly strengthened the position of Kovel. He has distinguished himself through his exemplary personal bravery.

SS-Gruppenführer Gille added his thoughts on April 3:

> Through the successful independent and bold advance of *SS-Obersturmführer* Nicolussi-Leck, the strength of Fortress Kovel—trapped for three weeks—was decisively reinforced. I especially agree with this proposal for the brave SS leader.

This request was approved on April 9, 1944, and it made Nicolussi-Leck the first of a raft of Kovel-related Knight's Cross awardees. That approval also had echoes of the very first Knight's Cross award to Sepp Dietrich, where a soldier knowingly ignored orders in place of the "bigger picture"; so the *Waffen-SS* were indoctrinated to blindly follow orders no matter what?

He continued to lead *8.* kompanie through the battles of summer 1944, mainly around Warsaw. Nicolussi-Leck was wounded again in early October, necessitating another temporary removal from the front. He returned in December and just prior to that had been given command of II Battalion, *SS-Panzer Regiment 5*, in mid-November 1944; bear in mind he was still holding the rank of *SS-Obersturmführer*. In January 1945, he moved with

An autographed image of Karl Nicolussi-Leck shown after the award of the Knight's Cross and his Panther tank in the background. He was the first *Waffen-SS* soldier to endorse this overall book project.

his men into Hungary. A promotion to *SS-Hauptsturmführer* came on January 30, 1945. They fought within Hungary, including the outer area of Budapest, throughout January and February. Nicolussi-Leck added the German Cross in Gold on March 10, 1945, given for actions between July and October 1944.

At the end of March 1945, Nicolussi-Leck was selected to lead a group of 150 *Waffen-SS*. Their assigned task was to travel to Paederborn, in northern Germany, and collect a new batch of tanks, then return to the southern front. They arrived in the first few days of April, initially in the Gutersloh area, and elements almost immediately ran into parts of the British 6th Airborne Division. They initially had no vehicles, but soon acquired thirteen armored halftracks. They made their way towards Hannover, where their arrival coincided with the arrival of strong American forces in the shape of the US 84th Infantry Division and the 771st Armored Battalion. The *Wiking* men took up defensive positions in the city of Hannover in agreement with the city commandant. Then things started to get more "interesting."

On April 8, 1945, Nicolussi-Leck learned of potentially available tanks in a nearby factory, so he took a small detachment and went there. Their visit netted them seven brand new Jagdpanther tank destroyers. I have been lucky enough to "crew" a restored Jagdpanther and can testify to the prowess and imposing nature of this armored fighting vehicle, which included the firing of the impressive 88 mm main gun. In 1945, Nicolussi-Leck and his men were about to put that prowess into full effect! The addition of these mighty vehicles bolstered his small battle group and they were ready to halt the American advance in this area.

Over the next few days, this battle group operated around the Hannover and Celle areas. They destroyed dozens of American tanks and other armored vehicles, with the Americans under the impression they were up against a full German division. The reality was seven Jagdpanthers and thirteen halftracks under *SS-Hauptsturmführer* Nicolussi-Leck. He was captured in the course of this fighting on April 22, 1945, bringing his war to an end and starting three years as a prisoner of war. He was awarded the Silver Wound Badge during the war, but the date is not listed. Some sources state he was wounded five times; Nicolussi-Leck stated a total of four wounds: two light and two heavy.

During the fighting he had briefly taken prisoners, but released them within a day or so, as he could not be burdened with them. One of them was a young American, Lt. Albert Robbins. This former American soldier made contact with Nicolussi-Leck in 1980, to determine if he was the same *Waffen-SS* soldier he recalled in this fighting at the end of the war. He was indeed, and both men corresponded and met up many times over the intervening years. Why include this information? Well, we know of the long list of atrocities attributed to the *Waffen-SS*. The details of the correspondence between these two men show the true nature of soldierly values that combatants on both sides held one another in that area of the front in late 1945.

The reader may may recall that Karl Nicolussi-Leck wrote the foreword to volume 1. I was lucky enough to visit this former *Waffen-SS* soldier at his home near Bozen. He was the first former *Waffen-SS* Knight's Cross holder to endorse this project. I was very honored to receive this endorsement from a soldier with a combat record such as he, and of course to have had the chance to meet him. Unfortunately, Karl Nicolussi-Leck died at the end of August 2008, merely weeks prior to volume 1's release; he did not get to see the end result he helped "start," although his surviving family did.

Name: Heinz Lammerding
Date of birth: 27.08.1905
SS Number: 247 062
Award: Knight's Cross

Born in Dortmund, he was a qualified engineer and worked in that profession until late 1933. He joined the SA in 1931 as an *SS-Obertruppführer*, and remained with them until the end of March 1935. In that time, he worked through various posts and rose to adjutant to one of the high command's senior officers. He moved to the SS in April 1935, and was placed with the engineer battalion in the *SS-VT* as an *SS-Untersturmführer*; the following month, he was given the rank *SS-Obersturmführer*. He was with the *1. Sturm* and, by the start of 1936, had taken over command of that kompanie and held that post until October 1939; a promotion to *SS-Hauptsturmführer* took place in January 1937. He attended a range of training courses during the prewar years and was also an instructor. He is listed as holding the prewar Austrian and Sudetenland campaign medals.

Following the conclusion of the opening campaign of the war in Poland, Lammderding was one of the men selected to join the newly created *SS-Division Totenkopf*. He was given command of their engineer battalion during October 1939, and was promoted to *SS-Sturmbannführer* before the end of the same month. His first campaign was in the west during May and June 1940. He earned both classes of the Iron Cross there on May 23 and June 22, respectfully. He moved to first general staff officer for *Totenkopf*

SS-Kampfgruppe Lammerding Commander Heinz Lammerding, shown here with his Knight's Cross at his neck. He is wearing *SS-Brigadefuhrer* rank here; his award was made when he was an *SS-Oberfuhrer*.

in late December 1940. Lammerding attended a general staff officer's training course in February 1941. He advanced into northern Russia with *Totenkopf* in July 1941, and was then promoted to *SS-Obersturmbannführer* at the start of September. He was caught up in the Demjansk Pocket fighting in the first half of 1942, and was presented with the campaign shield for that. The Infantry Assault Badge was awarded on June 10, and the Russian Front Medal followed at the start of August; it was also in August that Lammerding was placed in command of *SS-Regiment "Thule."*

The year 1943 would be busy for Lammerding, starting on January 30, when he was promoted to *SS-Standartenführer*. The award of the German Cross in Gold came on April 24, for actions during February and March. From May through late July, Lammerding was chief of staff for the *II. SS-Panzer Korps*, which would have been during the critical Kursk fighting. In the second half of 1943, he was chief of staff for Erich von dem Bach and his anti-partisan units operating in central and northern Russia. By mid-November, he was in command of Battle Group von Gottberg and stayed with them for three weeks. Just following this, he was promoted further to *SS-Oberführer* on December 9. In the closing days of the year, Lammerding was placed in command of the Das Reich Battle Group, which remained on the eastern front as their kameraden were being refitted back west. He led this unit until early March 1944, and it was his leadership that resulted in him being recommended for the award of the Knight's Cross. The recommendation was composed by Commander of the *LIX. Army* korps *Generalleutnant* Schulz in mid-March:

> On 20.02.1944 *Battle Group "Das Reich"* was deployed to the west of Shepetowka and the command of *SS-Oberführer* Lammerding was ordered to secure a 60-km [37-mile] gap in our front line. Although the battle group contained no more than three battalions, *Oberführer* Lammerding was able to prevent the enemy advance southward with agile movement of his troops, despite the fact the enemy attacked daily and was constantly reinforced. Lammerding's skill and leadership placed the troops where danger was most imminent. He was always found at the main point of the fighting, where he led daily counterattacks. With his leadership, it was possible to prevent the enemy breakthrough in the korps area until he could launch his main attack. From 20.02 to 06.03.1944, Lammerding and his troops were responsible for the western flank of the *korps*. During that time they inflicted the following heavy losses:

52 Tanks
1 Assault gun
32 Anti-tank guns
42 Anti-tank rifles
85 Machine-guns
127 Machine-pistols
172 Prisoners

The success of the battle group was of critical importance, not only for the *LIX. Armee Korps*, but for the whole southern flank of the *4. Panzer Armee*.

I request the bestowal of the Knight's Cross of the Iron Cross for *Oberführer* Lammerding.

This request was approved on April 11, 1944. By that stage, Lammerding was in command of the full *2. SS-Panzer Division Das Reich* in France. On April 20, he was promoted to *SS-Brigadeführer und Generalmajor der Waffen-SS*. Lammerding led this division until late January 1945, taking him through the Normandy and Ardennes fighting, although he had a three-month stint away from the front line from July to October due to being wounded in Normandy.

In the closing months of the war, Lammerding was chief of staff for *Army Group "Weichsel"* (January to March), then left for further medical treatment before becoming divisional commander for the last SS Division raised: the *38. SS-Panzergrenadier Division "Nibelungen."* This was at the end of April, but he only held the position for a matter of days, as his unit went into captivity. According to Lammerding, he was held captive for a brief spell and then lived in southern Germany. He formed his own engineering business and led that until his death on January 13, 1971.

Name: Herbert-Otto Gille
Date of birth: 08.03.1897
SS Number: 39 854
Award: Knight's Cross with Oakleaves, Swords and Diamonds

We last covered Herbert Gille earlier on February 20, 1944, when he was approved for the award of the Knight's Cross with Oakleaves and Swords in recognition of his division's actions in the Cherkassy Pocket. No sooner was this battle concluded than his men were caught up in what became known as the Kovel Pocket battle. It did not take long for the successful outcome of that fighting to form the basis of another recommendation for Herbert Gille.

Since the second half of March 1944, Gille and a small group of men—including many civilians—had successfully held Kovel until relieved by friendly forces. The preceding pages have detailed the heroic actions of some of the soldiers of *Wiking* who were part of the relief force that rescued their charismatic commander, but we also need to give more detail to exactly what Gille's contribution was.

After arriving in the city, he assessed the situation and the "forces" at his disposal, ranging from elements of *SS-Division Florian Geyer*, small elements of artillery and anti-aircraft, and engineers, right through to railway workers. This combination would be no match for the strength of the Soviet troops bearing down on the city and Gille knew it. One of his first actions was to obtain supply support from the *Luftwaffe*, which air-dropped hundreds of tons of supplies, including weapons, to help strengthen the defender's ability to hold off any enemy attacks. He used the collection of men to build up the defenses in the east while ensuring all able-bodied men were trained how to defend against tank attacks. The engineers established mine fields and other defenses; measures all aimed at slowing the advance of the enemy in Kovel. Gille's personal front-line experience—fighting the Soviets for almost three years—made the difference between survival and annihilation for this ad-hoc collection of four thousand-odd men. The short recommendation below does not give insight into the significance of Gille's activities and decisions in those crucial days for Kovel, but the senior officers above Gille certainly knew he was the right man in the right place at the right time and that he deserved recognition for his activities.

On April 9, the commanding general of *LVI. Panzer* korps (Hossbach) sent a radio message:

> Proposal for the award of the Diamonds for *Lt. Gen.* Gille, Commander SS *Div. Wiking*.
>
> For weeks, the heroic defense of the completely encircled but fortified Kovel has been achieved, despite the greatest of supply difficulties and considerable losses against a far stronger enemy. This has only been possible through the determined leadership and greatest personal bravery of the general.
>
> Due to the particular combat situation, this telex has been sent ahead. Written request follows.
>
> Signed Hossbach
>
> Infantry General and Commanding General *LVI. Panzer Korps*

Herbert-Otto Gille once again in the field. This image was taken after he had become the very first *Waffen-SS* soldier to be presented with the Diamonds to the Knight's Cross with Oakleaves and Swords. He is the second and final person to be featured twice in this volume.

This recommendation was then endorsed by *Supreme General* Weiss, who added the following:

> *SS-Gruppenführer und Generalleutnant der Waffen-SS* Gille has once again, through his outstanding courageous leadership and personal effort, given the highest honor to our heroes. When the defense of the entirely isolated and fortified Kovel lasted several weeks, he was the soul of resistance there, standing with his very small group of troops against a far superior opponent. The enemy outnumbered them to a high ratio and continuously attacked them. His lively and admirable example enabled the battle for the city. He remained there through the highest determination and good, prudent, but hard decisions. This was shown in an instant during what seemed an almost hopeless struggle and earned him the highest appreciation.
>
> I therefore approve the award of the Oakleaves with Swords and Diamonds to the Knight's Cross of the Iron Cross for this outstanding divisional commander.
>
> Signed: Weiss
> Supreme General
> and Commander of the *2. Armee*

This dual-endorsed recommendation had even greater weight added to it by *General Field Marshal* Busch, who stated:

> *Generalleutnant der Waffen-SS* Gille is credited with successfully holding fortified Kovel through his superior achievements.
>
> I approve the award of the Oakleaves with Swords and Diamonds.
> Signed: Busch
> *General Field Marshal*

An even higher endorsement was added when *Reichsführer-SS* Heinrich Himmler added his approval from his field command location on April 18, 1944:

> I approve the proposal of the award of the Oakleaves with Swords and Diamonds to the Knight's Cross of the Iron Cross upon *SS-Gruppenführer* and *Gen.Lt.d.W-SS* Gille, Herbert.

This multi-level recommendation was approved on April 19, 1944, and made him the twelfth German soldier to be recognized with this exceptionally high award. It also made him the first of only two *Waffen-SS* soldiers who would be given this grade of the Knight's Cross during WWII. This level of recognition officially made Herbert-Otto Gille the highest combat-decorated *Waffen-SS* soldier of the entire conflict. This final award for Gille was testament to the endurance of Gille's *SS-Wiking* soldiers and what they had to contend with in the closing months of 1943 and the first few months of 1944. If you recount the range of dates, Herbert-Otto Gille was approved for the Oakleaves, then the Swords, followed by the Diamonds in a period of less than six months! Another aspect is he was still only at divisional command level when this award was presented to him.

He was given command of the *IV. SS-Panzer* korps from early August 1944; then, on November 9, he was promoted to *SS-Obergruppenführer and General der Waffen-SS*. He surrendered to American forces in Austria in May 1945 and was kept a prisoner of war until 1948.

Herbert Gille survived the war and worked for a newspaper. He also formed *Der Wiking Ruf*, a veteran's magazine for the *Waffen-SS* better known today as *Der Freiwillige*. He died December 26, 1966, near Hannover.

Name: Otto Kirchner
Date of birth: 05.09.1921
SS Number: 423 699
Award: Knight's Cross

Born in Braunschweig, he entered the *Waffen-SS* on September 30, 1940, having been a member of the *Hitler Youth* from mid-September 1934. Upon joining the *Waffen-SS*, he was placed with *SS-Kavallerie Regiment 1*.

From the start of November 1941 through to the end of April 1942, he attended officer training at the school of his hometown. This was immediately followed by a platoon leader's course, with promotion to *SS-Untersturmführer* on June 21, 1942. He returned to the *SS-Kavallerie Division* and began to add recognition to his tunic, with the Second Class Iron Cross coming on October 2, 1942, and the Infantry Assault Badge following in late December. He attended a short kompanie commander's training course at Duchowschtschina that started the last few days of December and lasted until January 18, 1943; while there (January 8) he was presented with the First Class Iron Cross. The Black Wound Badge followed on April 9.

Otto Kirchner shown wearing his Knight's Cross. He was the third *SS-Kavallerie* soldier to be awarded this medal in this opening phase of 1944.

In late August 1943, Kirchner conducted actions around the Sapadenka area that resulted in his later recommendation for the Knight's Cross. It would appear he was wounded again in the latter part of 1943, as he is listed with the training and replacement battalion from November 1943 through March 1944, when he then returned to the *8th SS-Kavallerie Division "Florian Geyer."*

On April 3, 1944, *SS-Obersturmbannführer* Joachim Rumohr penned the recommendation for Kirchner's actions over seven months earlier:

> 1. and 3. Squadron of *SS-Kav. Regiment 16* had the task to occupy and hold the forest line Sukhaia - Gomolscha - Bol. Gomolscha. On 28.8.1943, the enemy attacked the sparse line held by 1. and 3. Squadron with several battalions in three waves after artillery and repeated mortar fire. He managed to break through in several places deep into the forest with strong forces. The danger of a fast enemy thrust upon Verchne - Bischkin was certain.
>
> *SS-Untersturmführer* Kirchner was placed as regimental reserve with two motorcycle platoons. (The strength of these motorcycle platoons was sixty men.) He was placed close to Hill 168.4 and shielded Bol. Gomolscha and the valley south of there from the enemy. With his shock troops, he joined the enclosed 1. and 3. Squadrons, resulting in him holding a line stretching from the decisive heights of Hills 168.4 through to 177.7. Because of this decision, it was possible to repeatedly push forward with his troops during an eighteen-hour battle. Meantime, the enemy had become very strong. *Untersturmführer* Kirchner led a raiding party against the south end of the valley from Bol. Gomolscha and connected with the strong enemy, forcing them from Hill 188.6. He engaged these hostile forces in their flank and inflicted heavy losses of 120 men and twenty-one MGs, as well as a mortar group, with his use of unprecedented personal heroism. He managed to escape the threat of encirclement and the line from Hill 168.4 to Hill 177.7, all the way up to Hill 188.6. He exchanged places with the enemy and his own weak forces by repeatedly confusing him during surprise shock attacks. During the twilight hours the enemy managed to insert their own forces. *Ustuf.* Kirchner made an independent decision and repeatedly smashed into these men with the exceptional and audacious use of trapped troops. He was once again able to inflict sensitive losses upon the opponent so, in the melee of this forest battle, he had already destroyed, amongst other things, several vehicles from the enemy battle armada.

> By the prudent and skillful leadership of *Ustuf.* Kirchner, who on his own initiative and with the remaining parts of 1. and 3. Squadrons launched surprise attacks out of the forest, he frustrated the intentions of the enemy to take the line from Hills 168.4 through to 188.6. He also succeeded, without disturbing the bolt position (Anna position), to obtain an extension of this line west to Hill 203.3 with a field replacement battalion of the army.
>
> *Ustuf.* Kirchner, who has participated in all attacks of the *SS-Kavallerie Division* and has repeatedly distinguished himself through outstanding bravery, is worthy to be awarded the Knight's Cross of the Iron Cross.

This proposal was approved on April 21, 1944; the day before Kirchner was promoted to *SS-Obersturmführer*. What is not listed is why there was such a delay in the actions and subsequent recommendation being conducted. In October he was at the *SS-Kavallerie School* in Gottingen. His war came to an end on May 3, 1945, when he was killed by Czech partisans.

Name: Otto Weidinger
Date of birth: 27.05.1914
SS Number: 114 921
Award: Knight's Cross

Born in Wurzburg, he joined the SS on April 16, 1934. He was placed with the *Wachsturmbann Dachau* and by March 20, 1935, had reached the rank *SS-Sturmmann*. Although it had taken him almost a year to reach that rank, he clearly displayed qualities that were of higher regard, as at the start of May he was sent to the officer's school in Braunschweig. He was moved to *SS-Unterscharführer* one month later and then, on November 9, he was promoted to *SS-Standartenjunker*. A short platoon leader's course came in February 1936, and then, by mid-March, he was holding the rank *SS-Standartenoberjunker*. In early April, he joined IV Battalion of *SS-Regiment "Deutschland,"* based at Ellwangen; on the twentieth he moved to *SS-Untersturmführer*.

In mid-1937, he attended the pioneer school in Dresden. He was a participant in the Austrian Anschluss action. By September 1938, he was an *SS-Obersturmführer*; a stint with *Jaeger Regiment 14* also took place that month. He took part in the occupation of the Sudetenland in October 1938. The first days of January 1939 would see him as adjutant for the SS motorcycle battalion. He moved to the reconnaissance battalion in May, and it was with this unit that he advanced into Poland.

He was awarded the Second Class Iron Cross in mid-November 1939. He moved to the command of *1.* kompanie in the reconnaissance battalion of *SS-Division "Reich"* prior to the western campaign in 1940. At the start of July, he was promoted to *SS-Hauptsturmführer*; before the end of the month, he had added the First Class Iron Cross to his existing awards. Towards the end of the year he became divisional adjutant. His next action was the invasion of the Balkans in April 1941, soon followed by the move towards the Soviet Union in July. The Black Wound Badge was given on September 4, and the Infantry Assault Badge followed on October 21. The following day, he is listed as being an instructor at the Braunschweig officer's school, although he did not take up that position until the start of November. He added the War Merit Cross, Second Class, with Swords on April 20, 1942. He remained at Braunschweig until mid-1943, when he returned to the *Das Reich Division*.

Returning to front-line service soon added additional forms of recognition for this talented and capable *Waffen-SS* soldier: he was promoted to *SS-Sturmbannführer* on June 21. Further wounds inflicted resulted in the award of the Silver Wound Badge in August, and the German Cross in Gold was approved in late November for actions stretching back to July 1941. In late November 1943, Weidinger was engaged in defensive actions that resulted in him being proposed for the Knight's Cross. These actions were detailed as follows by his Divisional Commander Heinz Lammerding:

> In the heavy defensive battles east of Shitomir, a reconnaissance detachment patrol under the daring leadership of *Sturmbannführer* Weidinger proved itself repeatedly in outstanding performances. On 22.11.1943, the patrol was engaged in a heavy defensive battle in the area around Negrebowka. To the north of the patrol were two enemy regiments. To the west, a strong force of anti-tank weapons blocked off and defended an enemy breakthrough towards the south near Sabalotsche. When the enemy patrol breached the positions of the reconnaissance detachment in two places, it was Weidinger who, in personally conducted counterattacks, cleaned up the inroads of the enemy again and again.
>
> In the afternoon, the enemy was able to gain a wide breakthrough at the neighboring position to the right and continue pushing until the entire detachment was encircled. Even in this situation, Weidinger kept a clear head and ordered a counterattack with his weak reserves.

Otto Weidinger in a formal setting to commemorate the award of his Knight's Cross. The *SS-Kampfgruppe Weidinger* commander added that to his long list of existing combat and campaign awards; this would not be his last.

Although to the west a five-kilometer [three-mile] deep flank had to be defended, Weidinger pulled out his reserve. To halt the break in the counterattack he fought at night beside parts of *2.* and *3. Kompanies.*

With seventeen men, Weidinger personally threw himself against the enemy forces that had broken through the northern part of Negrebowka. He stopped the attack, pushing the enemy back of the main line in a counterattack that inflicted severe Russian losses. Although Weidinger had orders to avoid stronger enemy resistance, he held his positions until Armored Group Stadler brought relief. Due to his initiative, determination, bravery, and setting a superior example, the bridgehead at Negrebowka could be held. This was the basis for the successful attack of the *1. SS-Panzergrenadier Division "Leibstandarte"* and the *2nd Fallschirmjaeger Division.*

Personal bravery; prudent, agile leadership; and great decisiveness make *SS-Sturmbannführer* Weidinger worthy to wear this high award.

This proposal was approved on April 21, 1944, less than three weeks after it was written. Weidinger would add further grades of the Knight's Cross to his list of awards (see later volumes).

Name: Wolfgang Joerchel
Date of birth: 19.08.1907
SS Number: 272 820
Award: Knight's Cross

Born in Zaborze, near Hindenburg, he began his service at an early age, starting out with the border force in the Upper Silisien area; he also had a keen interest in cross-country sports and taught this to others. From September 1930 through the end of March 1934, he is listed as being with the Stalhelm organization. During that time he also had a stint with the *Hitler Youth* as a sports instructor and a *bann* leader. From April 1934 until June 1935, he was with the *SA,* where he earned the Sports Badge in Gold. There was then a two-month spell with Infantry Regiment 8, where he was listed as a reserve officer candidate. In October 1935, he was promoted to *SS-Obersturmführer* and moved to the SS officer's school at Bad Tolz as a replacement training officer. He was a machine gun instructor there and in March 1936, he moved to adjutant. He retained this adjutant role as he moved to *SS-Regiment*

Germania's 1. kompanie at the start of February 1937. By October, he was with *SS-Regiment Deutschland*, serving in III Battalion; he remained with *Deutschland* up to the outbreak of war. During 1938, he took part in the occupation of Austria and later the Sudetenland, and was awarded both campaign medals. On April 20, he was promoted to *SS-Hauptsturmführer*. While with *Deutschland* he served in the staff kompanie, took command of *12.* and *8. Kompanies*, and also attended a technical training course at the tank training school in Wunsdorf.

Joerchel went with *Deutschland's 8.* kompanie to Poland and was one of the SS soldiers awarded the Second Class Iron Cross for actions there (October 30). He remained in his role as the *Waffen-SS* went west in 1940, and in early June, moved to the staff of II Battalion. In July, he added the First Class Iron Cross to his tunic. It was also in July that he assumed the role of Ib (second general staff officer) for the *SS-VT Division*. In November, he attended a battalion commander's training course and at the start of December, assumed command of *Germania's* II Battalion, which was now with *SS-Division Wiking*.

He took his battalion into Russia in July 1941, and soon after, in September, was promoted to *SS-Sturmbannführer*. His bravery was further recognized in March 1942, when he was awarded the German Cross in Gold. In September, he was presented with the Russian Front Medal. Promotion to *SS-Obersturmbannführer* followed at the end of January 1943. He was given command of *SS-Regiment 48 "General Seyffard"* in early January 1944, just in time for the major Soviet offensive in the Narwa area. His actions there would result in him being recommended for the Knight's Cross.

The recommendation itself was penned by *SS-Brigade Nederland* Commander *SS-Oberführer* Jurgen Wagner on March 18, 1944:

> After the heaviest bombardment of the city and bridgehead at Narwa through strong enemy bomber attacks that followed the full destruction of the city, and after unusually heavy artillery fire, the enemy attacked the Narwa bridgehead on a broad front on the 8.3.44, with numerous and superior infantry and tank forces. The main enemy attack was directed against the sector held by *SS-Obersturmbannführer* Joerchel and *Frw.Pz.Gren.Rgt. "General Seyffardt."*
>
> Although the regiment had been in heavy fighting during the disengagement from the Oranienbaum front, where the best part of his leaders and junior leaders were lost, the attack was halted with unusually high bloody losses for the enemy and the destruction of

Wolfgang Joerchel seen wearing his Knight's Cross. He was the second and last *Nederland* Knight's Cross holder awarded within the time of this volume.

twenty-seven enemy tanks. This great success was due in significant part to the considered and clear leadership, plus exemplary personal assertiveness of the regimental commander. Since all of the new communication links had been substantially destroyed due to heavy bombing and violent artillery fire, he took himself to the most dangerous places and his men, fired by his example, resisted to the utmost. Smaller incursions were dealt with quickly when he gathered together alarm groups and under his personal leadership went immediately against these attacks.

For five days running, the enemy tried again and again to force a breakthrough of the regiment's positions. This effectively led to substantial losses for the enemy, who was far superior in number and weapons. That the positions of the regiment were still held without substantial reinforcement, and the opponent thwarted in all of their breakthrough attempts, is accredited to the high personal ability of *SS-Obersturmbannführer* Joerchel.

He and his regiment were praised in the OKW daily report on 15.3.44.

(Signed) Wagner

SS-Oberführer and Brigade Commander

Four days later, *SS-Gruppenführer* Kleinheisterkamp added his warmest approval for this award and the actions of Joerchel. The Knight's Cross to the Iron Cross was approved for Joerchel April 21, 1944.

In May 1944, he is listed with the SS main office, then from July, he moved to the role of commander of the SS officer's school in Prague—a role he retained until the end of the war. At the start of September 1944, he was promoted to *SS-Standartenführer*. Joerchel was still in Prague in May 1945 when Czech partisans captured him. They killed him on May 12, although a few reports state he committed suicide before the partisans got to him.

Name: Hermann Priess
Date of birth: 24.05.1901
SS Number: 113 258
Award: Swords to the Oakleaves to the Knight's Cross

This is the seventh person in this volume that has appeared in preceding volumes (2 and 3). For Priess, this additional coverage of his history completes his hat trick.

We left his coverage in volume 3, after the then-*SS-Brigadeführer* added Oakleaves to his existing Knight's Cross on September 9, 1943. One month later he was officially named the *Totenkopf* divisional commander (he had been the temporary commander since April). Staying in that role, he was put forward for the award of the Swords to his existing Knight's Cross with Oakleaves, which was initiated on April 6, 1944, by Gen. von Knobelsdorff:

> *SS-Brigadeführer* Priess, Commander of *3. SS-Panzer Division "Totenkopf,"* has been known to me a long time as an especially proven and resolute officer. In the last action he especially distinguished himself in the Balta-Birsula area. His division scattered, partially encircled to the right and left, and his rear guard connections were cut off. Through his clear leadership and independent decision making, he contributed considerably to holding the Balta-Odessa railway line for a longer time, enabling the disengagement of the elements of the korps and neighboring army situated farther to the east. Always remaining in the front line, he stood firm with his division under the heaviest challenges to their security, firmly and securely guiding them and providing a great role model to his people.

To this was added the views of Gen. Woehler:

> *SS-Brigadeführer* Priess always leads his division with decisiveness and firm hands. Through his personal bravery and endurance he always pulls his men forward, despite the bloody battles. His excellent performance and leadership feats make *SS-Brigadeführer* Priess especially worthy of being awarded the Swords to the Oakleaves.

Generaloberst Schorner added his warmest approval and then Heinrich Himmler added his approval for this suggested award on April 20, 1944. This was the same day Priess received a promotion to *SS-Gruppenführer und Generalleutnant der Waffen-SS*. The official award of the Swords to his Knight's Cross with Oakleaves was made on April 24, 1944. This was *Totenkopf's* first and only award of the Swords to the Knight's Cross with Oakleaves and made Priess the fifth *Waffen-SS* soldier to hold this level of recognition.

Priess led *Totenkopf* until July 1944, when he had a short spell on the reserve officer list. In early August, he assumed the role of commander for the *XIII. SS-Army Korps,* which was fighting in the west in Autumn 1944.

Another signed image in my collection, this one showing Hermann Priess wearing his Swords to the Knight's Cross with Oakleaves. That award made him *Totenkopf's* only Swords-level awardee of the entire war.

Then, in late October, he was moved to command of *I. SS-Panzer* korps and led that formation until the end of WWII. His leadership of that korps oversaw their involvement in the Ardennes Offensive during December 1944 and into the last advance east into Hungary in early 1945. He led his men westward in the opening days of May 1945, where they surrendered to American troops along the Enns River.

Due to his position as *I. SS-Panzer* korps commander during the Ardennes Offensive he was tried as part of the American "Malmedy Trial" postwar, receiving a lengthy prison term as a result. He was released in late 1954 and died on February 2, 1985, in Ahrensburg, northern Germany.

CHAPTER FIVE

TITO'S THE TARGET! - MAY 1944

There were some notable activities that occurred in May 1944. Although the eastern front had adapted a quieter "feel," plans were underway for one of the most ambitious operations of the war: to remove the Yugoslavian partisan leader Tito. This month would also see much-needed new formations added. Alongside was an overall focus on preparing for the expected western offensive, with more units being located in that region, but also knowing that the current "quiet" spell in the east would not last.

Let us take a look at the units who saw significant changes in this final month covered in volume 4. The next approval for a Knight's Cross related award was to a soldier from *Wiking*, so we'll start there.

5. SS-Panzer Division Wiking

The men of *Wiking's* Panzer regiment remained in the Kovel area throughout May and June 1944. The rest of their kameraden were being reconstituted as an effective fighting force at the Heidelager training grounds in Poland during those two months, rebuilding themselves from their recent mauling at Korsun and Kovel. The supply of fresh equipment helped greatly here. We will return to the *5. SS-Panzer Division* in volume 5.

To the south of there . . .

3. SS-Panzer Division Totenkopf

The temporary enemy pause that took place in northern Romania came to an abrupt halt on May 2, when they exerted pressure east of their positions.

Totenkopf was put back into the fight, and over the next few days they fought against strong enemy forces at Facuti and west of there, toward Helestieni. *Totenkopf* fought alongside Heer and Romanian kameraden to halt this major offensive. There was significant enemy tank support used for the push, but the Soviets suffered the loss of over 300 tanks; *Totenkopf* contributed to that destruction.

Helestieni was the location for the Knight's Cross related actions of *SS-Obersturmbannführer* Josef Swientek (see volume 5). The remainder of May 1944 saw them enjoying a period of relative rest, made even better by the arrival of new tanks and replacement troops.

In the Balkans . . .

7. SS-Freiwilligen-Gebirgs Division Prinz Eugen

No time for respite; their next operation started on May 25, and was bold in its objective: the capture of the partisan leader Tito. It was determined Tito and many of his main command structures were in Drvar, in the extreme west of Bosnia. *Prinz Eugen* was selected to be part of the forces that were to move against that objective. Within the context of this project, they would be joined by their SS kameraden from *SS-Fallschirmjaeger Battalion 500*, taking part in their first combat action. *Prinz Eugen's* start point was Vijenac, and their moves were westward towards Drvar; Krcevina, Kadina Voda, and Sipovo were also all advanced upon in the opening stages. Enemy resistance was heavy and difficult to break through. Ribnik became a focus of the fighting on May 27, with Berici and Mihailcici reached two days later. By the end of May 1944, *Prinz Eugen* had reached Uvala—only twenty miles from Drvar—and were busy counting the dead and the large supply dumps found there. The operation itself was not concluded, but we will continue with coverage of it in volume 5.

SS-Fallschirmjaeger Battalion / SS-Fallschirmjaeger Battalion 500

Their next employment was actually their first true combat operation: the operation to block the large concentration of Tito's partisans in southeast Bosnia. This unit took part in the fighting around Vlasenica, working with elements of the *13. SS-Gebirgs Division*. Fighting ended on May 10, 1944, and the *SS-Fallschirmjaeger* could count their involvement a success. They temporarily moved back into Serbia to await their next deployment.

That deployment has been touched on: the action to capture the headquarters of the partisan leader Tito at Drvar. This operation would be the first use of the *SS-Fallschirmjaeger* in the role they were trained for: a direct parachute drop into enemy-held territory. The action began on May 25, and involved 850 of these SS soldiers. They dropped in more than one wave, but the rocky, mountainous terrain resulted in many dead and wounded, not to mention losses from fighting with the enemy! Their limited survivors came under heavy pressure from the partisans and it was not until day two that they received help from friendly forces; most of them thought they had seen their last day. The objective of the operation was not possible during this attempt. Following this action, the *SS-Fallschirmaeger* moved to Petrovic, north of Drvar (continued in volume 5).

While still in the active front of the Balkans, we will cover the initial creation of a new *Waffen-SS* formation, the first of two raised at this stage of 1944.

21. Waffen-Gebirgs Division der SS Skanderberg (Albanische Nr. 1)

This new *Waffen-SS* division was created on April 17, 1944, but the men did not start assembling until the start of May in the Pristina area, southern Serbia. The men were existing Albanian soldiers who had been part of the *13. SS-Freiwilligen Bosnien-Herzegowina-Gebirgs-Division (Kroatien)*. Their commander was *SS-Standartenführer* August Schmidhuber. They busied themselves with formation and initial training during May 1944 (see next volume).

Farther to the south . . .

4. SS-Polizei-Panzergrenadier Division

Members of the division were killed by partisans near Klissoura Pass in early May, the scene of Kurt Meyer's successful Knight's Cross action back in 1941. Elements of *Polizei* that had been refitting in Neuhammer were relocated to Greece in mid-May (see volume 5).

Before leaving this southern area of the active front, we will cover the initial creation of the second and final new *Waffen-SS* unit, which was transformed from a recently battle-tested group of soldiers.

22. SS-Freiwilligen Kavallerie Division "Maria Theresa"

This second raised *Waffen-SS* cavalry division began life at the start of May 1944. The existing *SS-Kavallerie Regiment 17*, from the *8. SS-Kavallerie Division Florian Geyer*, was removed to form the basis of this new division. Ethnic German Hungarians joined them to bulk out their numbers.

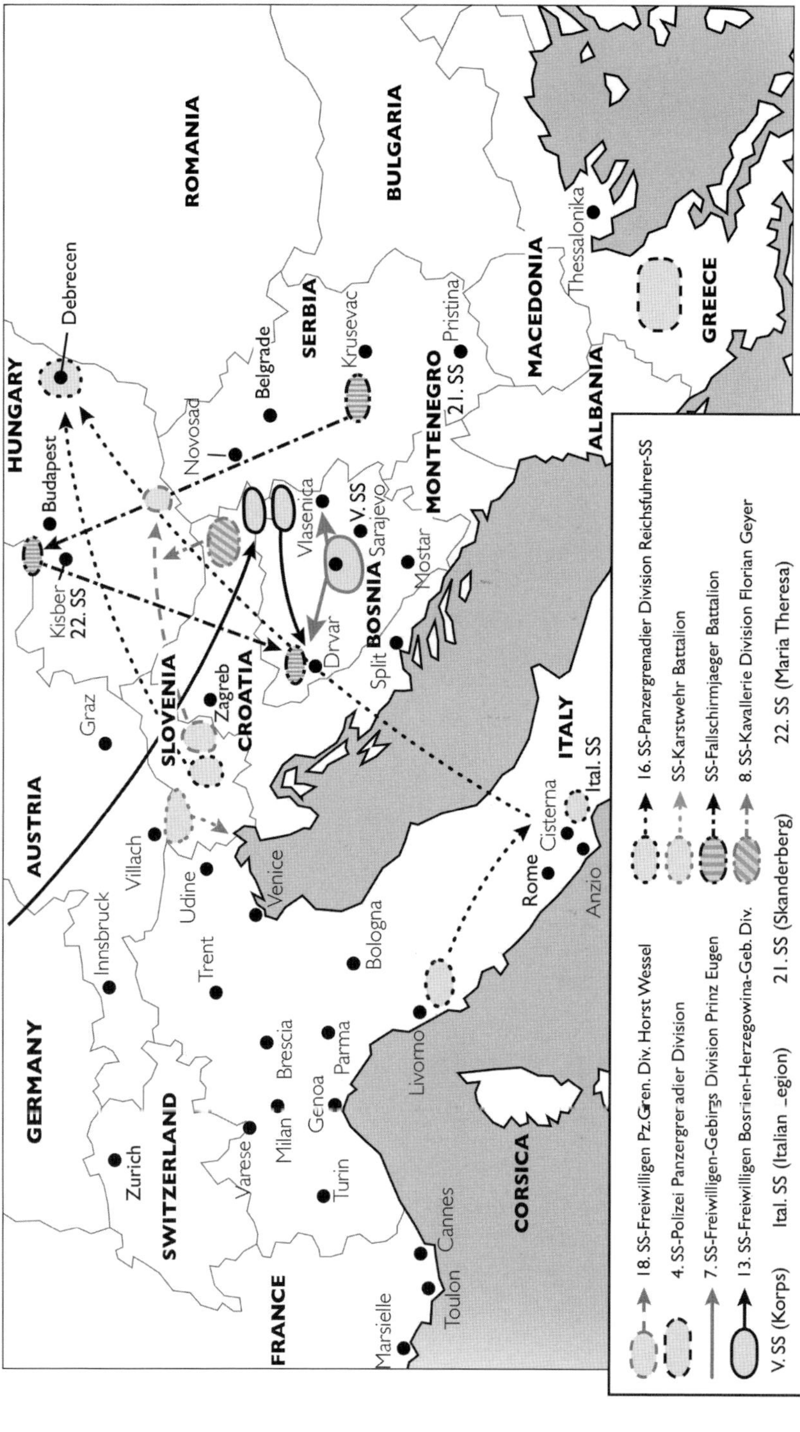

Map 19 – Italy / Slovenia / Yugoslavia / Greece / Hungary: January to May 1944

They were between Gyor, Kisber, and out toward Budapest. Their commander was existing Knight's Cross holder *SS-Standartenführer* August Zehender. Their activities for May were initially set up in this area and the arrival of the first recruits. *SS-Kavallerie Regiment 17* required an almost full rebuild after their recent mauling at Kovel. We will continue with their history in the next volume.

Now to the units in western Europe . .

1. SS-Panzer Division Leibstandarte SS Adolf Hitler

When they arrived in Belgium following heavy fighting in the Kamenets-Podolsky Pocket, they were positioned in an area northeast of Brussels. The focus was on receiving new equipment, replacing men, and getting ready for the expected western enemy invasion. When back in the west, the *Leibstandarte* were under the overall command of *I. SS-Panzer* korps and their former commander, *SS-Obergruppenführer* "Sepp" Dietrich. His old unit was a shadow of its former self by April 1944.

While there, *SS-Hauptsturmführer* Gratz was approved for and awarded his Knight's Cross for actions in early March. That approval came on May 14, 1944, the same day a second *LSSAH* Knight's Cross was approved. That second approval was for *SS-Untersturmführer* Heinz Nowotnik, and it was given for his successful fighting at Bulyschety in late November 1943. This was the final Knight's Cross award for a soldier from the *Leibstandarte* for this volume and it was one of six awarded to *Waffen-SS* soldiers the same day. We will leave the exhausted men of the *LSSAH* for now and return to them in volume 5, when they will be put to the test once more, this time from an enemy they last faced in early 1941 in Greece.

SS-Kampfgruppe Weidinger

This *SS-Kampfgruppe* arrived in France in the closing days of April and was then officially disbanded on May 2, 1944.

On April 21, Otto Weidinger had been approved for the Knight's Cross for his actions in November 1943; he received news of the award when he arrived in France. On May 4, Hans Eckert was also approved for this award for his recent actions in the final battle of the Kamenets-Podolsky Pocket for the battle group. When they arrived in France in late April, they joined their *Das Reich* divisional kameraden who had been rebuilding and refitting. The focus for the next four weeks was to complete training and incorporate the new additions in men and materiel. We will return to 2. *SS-Panzer Division Das Reich* in the next volume.

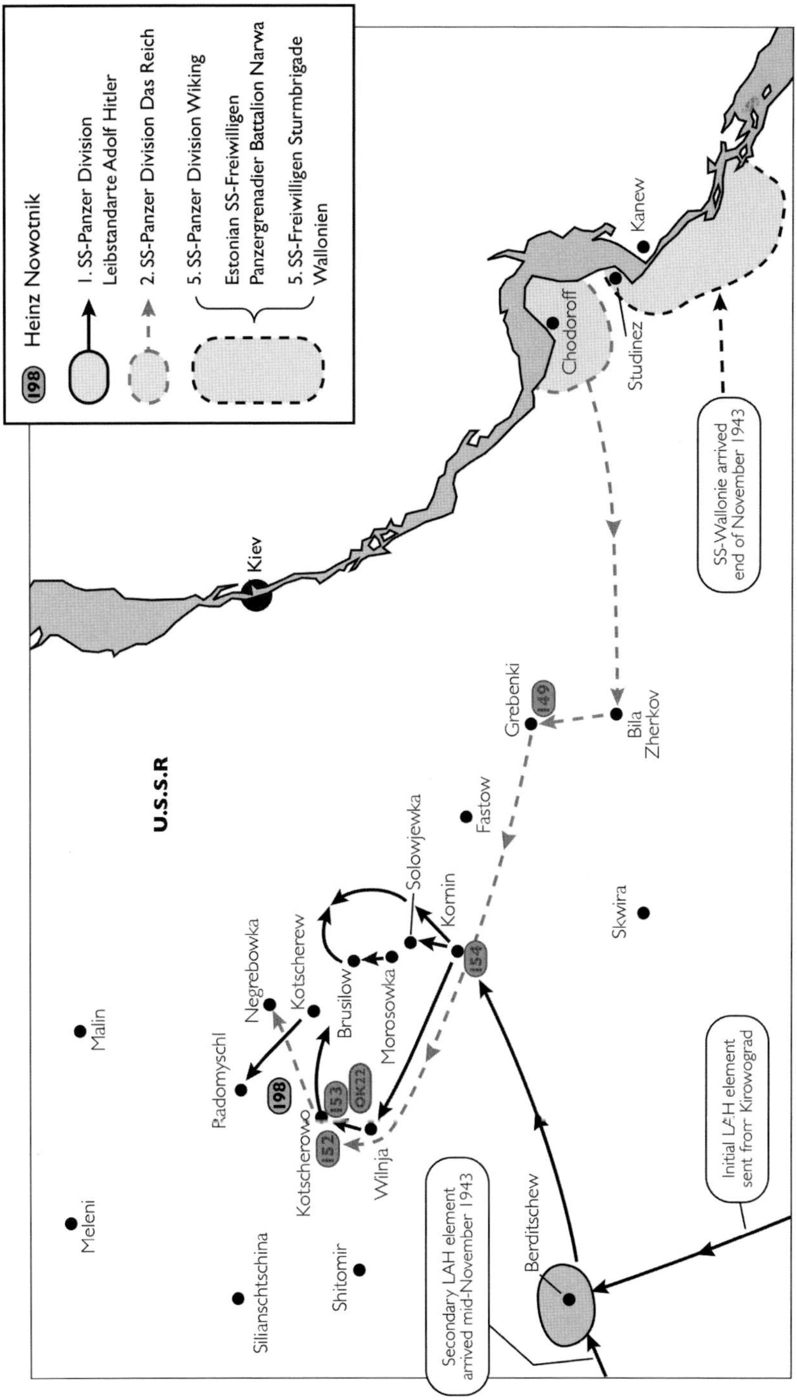

Map 20 – Dnjepr River North: November 1943

17. SS-Panzergrenadier Division "Gotz von Berlichingen"

In the weeks leading up to the Allied invasion partisan activity increased, resulting in counter-security measures from the men of *GvB*; they were increasingly vigilant in the areas they controlled. Enemy aerial activity also intensified, and in the closing days of May, the *17.* SS suffered their first (albeit light) deaths to enemy action—the absence of enemy troops on the ground made these losses bitter. The losses were through preparatory bombing in readiness for the imminent landings.

Other losses had been suffered as training intensified. One of the most significant training exercise losses was the death of *SS-Sturmbannführer* Walter Kniep, who was killed on April 22, 1944. He had been commanding *SS-Panzer Battalion 17* and was awarded the Knight's Cross in August 1943. His replacement was another existing Knight's Cross holder, *SS-Sturmbannführer* Ludwig Kepplinger; one of the very first *Waffen-SS* soldiers to be awarded the medal back in 1940.

The ongoing history of this division will continue in volume 5, when their situation would change significantly.

Schwere SS-Panzer Abteilung 101

Further exercises took place and by the end of May, *Schwere SS-Panzer Abteilung 101* was fully equipped with forty-five Tiger Is.

At that time, the formation contained the following battle-tested *Waffen-SS* Knight's Cross holders (besides Wittmann): *SS-Untersturmführer* Alfred Gunther, *SS-Standartenoberjunker* Franz Staudegger, and *SS-Unterscharführer* Balthasar Woll. These men were about to put their lengthy experience to good use.

Schwere SS-Panzer Abteilung 102

Their remaining complement of thirty-nine arrived in the final days of May 1944. In the middle of May, just over 250 men were transferred to this unit from *Schwere SS-Panzer Abteilung 103.* At the end of May, existing Knight's Cross holder *SS-Sturmbannführer* Hans Weiss was ready with his Tiger tank crews for the much-awaited enemy landings from the west.

Schwere SS-Panzer Abteilung 103

In May, over 250 of their rank were sent to *Schwere SS-Panzer Abteilung 102*, greatly reducing their capabilities. As May came to a close, further tanks arrived for the remaining men of this SS heavy tank unit.

We will return to the coverage of the three *SS-Panzer Abteilungen* in the next volume.

This not only completes the coverage of all of the *Waffen-SS* units up to the end of May 1944, but almost completes this current volume. Before bringing it to a close, we will cover the remaining thirteen men who were awarded the Knight's Cross—or higher grades—in May; *Wiking* would have the lion's share of those awards.

Name: Willi Hein
Date of birth: 26.04.1917
SS Number: 280 189
Award: Knight's Cross

Born in Hohenwestedt, he was an early member of the *Hitler Youth*, being with them from the start of September 1930 through the end of March 1936. As he was an early member, he held the Golden HJ Award and the Old Fighters Chevron. At the start of April 1936, he joined the *Allgemeine-SS* and before the end of the month was with the *SD*. He had a stint with the *RAD* in mid-1939, then moved to the armed SS from the start of October 1939, being placed with *SS-Regiment Germania*.

In mid-May 1940, he moved to the Nordland Regiment. On April 20, 1941, he was promoted to *SS-Unterscharführer*. His front-line abilities were recognized by a posting to Bad Tolz for officer training from the start of November 1941 to the end of January 1942; he received a promotion to *SS-Oberscharführer* five days earlier. His promotion to *SS-Untersturmführer* came on April 20; by then, he was with the motorcycle platoon in *Wiking's* Panzer regiment. The Second Class Iron Cross was awarded on July 26.

The year 1943 would be busy for Hein, starting off with the award of the First Class Iron Cross at the end of January; the Tank Assault Badge followed at the start of March. A placement to commander of *4.* kompanie *(Sturmgeschutze)* took place in 1943 (exact dates are not listed). He then moved to *2.* kompanie in September, with promotion to *SS-Obersturmführer* on November 9. He was awarded the Honor Roll Clasp in mid-November and the German Cross in Gold on December 30. Certainly a memorable year for all the right reasons.

As 1944 opened, he found himself caught up in the intensive fighting in northern Russia. He was involved in actions (January 29–30) that would result in him being recommended for the Knight's Cross. Before that took place, he was awarded the Black Wound Badge on February 21. It was on March 23 that his Battalion Commander *SS-Sturmbannführer* Paul Kummel had the time to write the proposal for the award of the Knight's Cross:

As a result of the merging of the two Soviet-Ukrainian fronts in the Schpola – Zwenigorodka area, the enemy undertook a surprise attack on 29.1.44 with tank support upon the supply units of *SS-Panzer Division "Wiking"* near Olschany. After a futile attack along the road to the north of Olschana—essentially due to the four assault guns under the command of *SS-Ostuf.* Hein—they shot up seven self-propelled anti-aircraft guns and brought this to a standstill. The enemy responded on 30.1.44 with an attack from two strong battalions supported by an anti-tank regiment. One attack went against the unsecured southern part of Olschana, where the enemy occupied the only supply road for the encircled Division. The other was in the north and was used to separate us into two parts.

Ostuf. Hein received three assault guns to assist, then moved toward the south with an infantry kompanie providing security. The enemy had now reached the outskirts and was advancing unhindered along the open road in a wide front. *Ostuf.* Hein, who on the way had lost one vehicle to mechanical damage and another to enemy fire, decided to immediately attack the enemy, despite not having infantry support yet and into what seemed a hopeless situation. With shrapnel grenades, machine guns, and shooting from his hatch with his machine pistol, he forced the Russian infantry in the lead to flee, then drove them farther, taking advantage of the resulting panic. He reversed their plans and the Russians suffered significant losses. Despite strong anti-tank fire from a well-camouflaged position on a ridge, Hein pushed farther and took these troublesome anti-tank positions under fire. He skillfully used the lay of the land to drive into their right flank, where he destroyed two 4.5 cm anti-tank guns, four 7.62 cm anti-tank guns, and a light assault gun. Hein scattered the enemy and shot up another self-propelled anti-aircraft gun.

Through this surprising shock attack the Russians fled, leaving behind their infantry weapons and retreating two km [1.24 miles] to the south of their original field positions.

Through the decisiveness and extremely adventurous behavior of *SS-Ostuf.* Hein, the loss of Olschana and our only supply road was prevented. It was possible to move the main supply units of the division, as well as Battalion "*Narwa*," at a later date from Olschana.

A signed image of Willi Hein, one of *SS-Wiking's* armor-related Knight's Cross awardees. His Honor Roll Clasp can be clearly seen too.

There was an additional short document from *SS-Gruppenführer* Gille that summarizes Hein's actions at Olschana, points out his repeated bravery and his recent award of the Honor Roll Clasp, and then goes on to warmly approve the proposal.

This dual recommendation was approved on May 4, 1944. Due to the wounding of his former commander Hein took over command of I Battalion in *Wiking's* Panzer regiment during September 1944. He held this command until January 1945, when he was heavily wounded fighting in Budapest; this was the same month he was promoted to *SS-Hauptsturmführer*. In November 1944, he was awarded the Tank Assault Badge "75" for taking part in at least seve nty-five separate tank engagements. He spent the remainder of the war in hospital. He survived the war and died on October 25, 2000.

Name: Gerhard Fischer
Date of birth: 12.11.1922
SS Number: 219 573
Award: Knight's Cross

Born in Wildbuch, he joined the *Waffen-SS* in mid-November 1940, and was placed with *3. Kompanie*, *Panzerjaeger Abteilung*, *SS-Division Wiking*, one month later. They were positioned in Pottmes at the time and he remained there until March 1941. On March 10, he moved to the Neuberg training ground and received training on 3.7 cm and 5 cm anti-tank guns. In June, he moved to Liegnitz with the rest of *Wiking Division* and prepared to advance into Russia.

While in Russia, where he spent the rest of the war, he was awarded the Second Class Iron Cross on May 16, 1942. (Fischer states the Russian Front Medal came the same day, but his file states this did not come until the following year—see below.) The First Class Iron Cross was awarded on March 18, 1943, following the destruction of his tenth enemy tank. The Tank Assault Badge was approved on May 9, with the Russian Front Medal coming on September 13 (see above). In mid-1943, Fischer had moved to command one of the 7.5 cm self-propelled guns mounted on the 38T chassis. The Wound Badge in Black was given in February 1944. In early February 1944, Fischer was caught up in the Cherkassy Pocket battle and he displayed courage that would lead to his recommendation for further recognition of his bravery.

A nicely autographed photograph of Gerhard Fischer showing his Knight's Cross adorning his assault gunner's uniform.

He personally stated he was near Burty and that the enemy had many anti-tank gun, anti-aircraft gun, and machine gun positions along the wide main street that led into this place. He moved overnight and stopped in the middle of this town; by daybreak, there began a short fire-fight in which enemy guns were firing at distances of between ten and twenty meters [32 and 65 ft] from his vehicle. He moved back to the ground west of this location and there then ensued a three-hour mobile fire-fight, in which Burty was taken back. Fischer stated this attack took place on February 2, although official documents list the fourteenth.

At the start of April, *SS-Sturmbannführer* Herbert Oeck, commander of *SS-Panzer-Sturmgeschutze Abteilung 5*, penned a recommendation for the award of the Knight's Cross to Fischer:

> In the early morning hours of 2.2.1944, around 04:30 hours, the Russians stormed our positions on the security line west of Burty with an infantry battalion reinforced with anti-aircraft and infantry guns. They succeeded in breaking through this position around 05:00 with a sudden attack and moved 1,200 m [1,312 yards] west of Burty. The enemy set up a position in houses just west of Burty.
>
> *SS-Unterscharführer* Fischer, deputy platoon leader in *3./SS-Panzer Jaeger Battalion 5*, was deployed in the northwestern part of Burty with two self-propelled anti-tank guns. At 04:45 hours, he received the order from the battalion to secure the western part of Burty. From the march to his intended position he could see the enemy had secured the train station and their house positions. Another strong vehicle-led company of enemy were protruding from the northwest of Burty, blocking the road to Wjasowog.
>
> Making his own decision, he attacked the latter group with the two self-propelled Pak and destroyed them in a dashing attack, despite enemy fire coming from his western flank during the race towards this enemy group. In the standing fire fight at the western edge of Burty in which Fischer moved back and forth, he prevented further help of stronger enemy forces moving from the forest northwest of Burty until 07:00 hours, when our own infantry took it in a rapid attack.
>
> Despite anti-tank gun and anti-tank rifle fire, he knew a rapid advance was essential, for Fischer, without direct orders, drove forward and attacked the enemy positions at houses and the railway embankment, throwing them out of there.
>
> Despite anti-tank gun and anti-tank rifle fire, and without regard

for risk to himself, he proceeded ahead with the infantry, personally leading them and thus prevented the strong enemy from advancing along the railway embankment. A surprise group of enemy vehicles (1.5 km [0.93 miles] southwest of Burty) that tried to take back Hill .205.0 were destroyed by well-aimed fire from his self-propelled guns.

The holding of Burty was crucial for the execution of the advance to the city of Gorodischtsche.

Through his own decision making, the advances of *SS-Unterscharführer* Fischer ensured the failure of the enemy's intentions:

1. Reopen Burty and west of there,
2. Move through Burty and block the road to Wjasowog, and
3. Prevent the moving of stronger forces positioned in the forest northwest of Burty.

SS-Unterscharführer Fischer captured the following during the course of the battle:

2 Infantry Guns and vehicles
1 4.7 cm anti-tank gun with vehicles

and destroyed:

1 7.62 cm heavy anti-tank gun
6 Anti-tank rifles and a large number of infantry weapons.

SS-Unterscharführer Fischer has distinguished himself during the eastern front battles with outstanding bravery. So far he has destroyed fourteen enemy tanks.

Awards:	
Second Class Iron Cross	awarded. 16.5.1942
First Class Iron Cross	awarded: 18.3.1943
Tank Assault Badge	awarded: 9.5.1943
Russian Front medal	awarded: 13.9.1943

The Battalion holds that *SS-Unterscharführer* Fischer is worthy to wear the Knight's Cross of the Iron Cross.

This recommendation was approved on May 4, 1944. Fischer had been sent to a training course at the assault gun training school in Beneschau, near Prague, at the start of May. A telegram was sent to the commander of that school on May 7, and Fischer was presented with his Knight's Cross the following day.

He received a promotion to *SS-Oberscharführer* on September 1. On May 7, 1945, *SS-Oberscharführer* Fischer was awarded the Tank Assault Badge "50" for having taken part in more than fifty separate tank battles. After fighting through Hungary and eastern Austria, he surrendered to American forces in Graz. He was placed in a prisoner of war camp in Leoben and remained there until mid-1947, when he was released. Gerhard Fischer survived the war and, as far as can be determined, was alive at the time of the writing of this volume.

Name: Werner Meyer
Date of birth: 18.09.1919
SS Number: 423 803
Award: Knight's Cross

Born in Pasewalk, he was an early member of the *Hitler Youth*, joining in mid-April 1931. He remained there until the end of March 1938. He immediately spent a six-month spell with the *RAD*, then moved to the SS at the start of November 1938. Meyer was placed in I Battalion of *SS-Regiment Germania* and he advanced into the Sudetenland with them, receiving the medal for that. He was with them as war broke out.

He served in Poland and then the west, and during that latter campaign earned the Second Class Iron Cross on June 20, 1940, and then the First Class Iron Cross exactly one month later. Remaining with *Germania*, he would have been moved to the *Wiking Division* as it was being formed after the western campaign. He would have also went with this division as it moved into the Soviet Union in mid-1941, although his file lists him with *Wiking* only from August 1942. He is listed as holding the Russian Front Medal, which could be due to the fact he was sent to Bad Tolz from the start of November; he had been promoted to *SS-Unterscharführer* two months earlier and it was time to test his leadership abilities. He remained at Bad Tolz until the end of April 1942. Promotion to *SS-Untersturmführer* was approved on June 21.

Meyer was back with *Wiking* by then, initially serving with III Battalion in *Germania*; he performed as a platoon leader and then adjutant for them.

He was wounded in July and once recovered, was placed in *1.* kompanie in his old I Battalion. The award of the Infantry Assault Badge came on April 2, 1943, and the Close Combat Clasp in Bronze followed at the start of May. He was wounded again on July 22. He was given the German Cross in Gold on November 21 for actions between October 1942 and July 1943; the Silver Wound Badge was awarded three days after that. The first of his Close Combat Clasps was awarded at the start of August (bronze grade).

On January 30, 1944, Meyer was promoted to *SS-Obersturmführer*; he was commanding *1.* kompanie at that time. He received the Close Combat Clasp in Silver the same day. During the first part of February he conducted actions that his commander, Hans Dorr (the same person that recommended him for the German Cross in Gold), considered worthy of official recognition. He compiled a document on April 7:

> In the continuation of the attack against Schanderowka—stubbornly defended by the Soviets—the night of 12. – 13.2.44, *SS-Ostuf.* Meyer, as kompanie leader of *1./SS Pz.Gren.Rgt. Germania*, has particularly distinguished himself by outstanding bravery in front of the enemy through rapid and independent decisions. The suppression of Shanderovka was of crucial importance for the breakout from the Cherkassy pocket. This had been recognized by the opponent and they defended the location with dogged tenacity and well developed positions with built in flamethrowers.
>
> In the first night attack on the 11. – 12.2.44, the battalion was successful in penetrating the enemy positions in the south and on 12.2., surprised them and rolled up this southern part of Schanderowka, taking possession of it. A continuation of the attack during 12.2. and full possession of Schanderowka was not possible due to tenacious enemy resistance. Thus, the start of the attack was set for 22:15 hours.
>
> Meyer received the order, along with his kompanie, to advance along the narrow road following *2. Kompanie*. After 03:00 hours, the attack of *2. Kompanie* halted against strong enemy heavy machine gun and anti-tank fire.
>
> Correctly recognizing this difficult situation, and clearly aware of the importance of the suppression of this place, Meyer made the decision to immediately attack this point with his kompanie.
>
> Using the protection of a ditch, he came in from the west and managed to surprise the enemy, engaging them in their flank. With only a few men, Meyer broke into the positions of the Soviets with

A very clear studio (signed) image of Werner Meyer showing his various combat awards, including his Knight's Cross, German Cross in Gold, and Close Combat Clasp.

reckless regard to himself and, in that position, put an anti-tank gun out of action with two hand grenades. By this spirited example he dashed with his men and under a loud "hurra" the kompanie stormed ahead, led by their brave kompanie leader. Moving along the road from house to house they conducted hard and dogged close combat, where Meyer was always found providing the most decisions, and they were able to throw the Soviets out and provide relief for *2.* kompanie from the enemy fire.

Meyer continued the attack and captured with his Kompanie

7 4.7 cm Anti-tank guns
3 7.62 cm Anti-tank guns
2 Infantry guns
6 Heavy machine guns
4 Light machine guns

as well as numerous hand guns; forty-eight prisoners were brought in.

From a house that later proved to be the enemy's regimental command post resistance was particularly obstinate. With his kompanie troops and some men from 1st Platoon, Meyer penetrated this house and took three officers prisoner. The regimental commander escaped capture through suicide.

The resolute and reckless grasp of Meyer brought the battalion through this significant performance and contributed significantly to the taking of possession of this closest place. From here occurred (on 16.2.) the escape from the Cherkassy Pocket of the combined trapped forces of the *XI.* and *XXXXII. Armee Korps*.

In this war Meyer is a repeatedly excellent SS leader. As one of the first men of the regiment, he was already awarded the Iron Cross First Class in the western campaign. He is a holder of the German Cross in Gold, the Close Combat Clasp in Silver, and has been wounded four times.

SS-Ostuf. Meyer is worthy to be awarded the Knight's Cross of the Iron Cross.

This recommendation is pre-dated by another shorter version written by the regimental commander. Five days after Dorr's full recommendation, Divisional Comander Gille signed an endorsement to this proposal for Meyer to receive the Knight's Cross. This multi-level recommendation was approved on May 4, 1944.

He was awarded the Close Combat Clasp in Gold on April 12, 1944, and also held the Gold Wound Badge for a further, severe wound that removed him from the front line until February 1945. Meyer is listed as being with *SS-Replacement Battalion Ellwangen* from May 20, 1944. He returned to the front in the role of regimental adjutant. A survivor of the war, he died on August 17, 1996, in Kirchbarkau, near Kiel, in northern Germany.

Name: Kurt Schumacher
Date of birth: 08.03.1923
SS Number: 359 222
Award: Knight's Cross

Born in Hannover, he was a member of the *Hitler Youth* from March 1933 through November 1939, when he joined the SS. He was placed with the *SS*-Artillery Replacement Battalion. From November 1941 until the end of March 1942, he attended officer training at Bad Tolz. His promotion to *SS-Untersturmführer* followed on June 21. He is listed as serving with *SS-Division Wiking* from this point, and their actions in the Caucausus in the second half of 1942 resulted in a series of awards for Schumacher. The first of these was the Tank Assault Badge, awarded on September 15. The Second Class Iron Cross came at the start of October, with the First Class Iron Cross being approved on December 21.

By early-1943, he was with *3.* kompanie in *Wiking's* Panzer regiment, although the date when he moved to serve in Panzers is not confirmed. The addition of the Black Wound Badge was made July 21, the Silver Wound Badge on October 22, and the Tank Assault Badge II Grade on November 9. His bravery and abilities were recognized further right at the end of the year, when on December 30, he added the German Cross in Gold to his tunic.

Continuing with *3. Kompanie*, Battalion Commander *SS-Sturmbannführer* Rudolf Saumenicht put forward a proposal for the Knight's Cross for Schumacher on March 23, 1944:

> To allow a link up between the elements enclosed within Tscherkassy and the relief group—planned from the outside at Lysyanka—a line from Steblew and the nearest location (Novo - Buda) was taken in the night attack. This was to allow the later flow of the enclosed korps out of the Shanderovka area. Due to only having limited

This very poor quality image shows the illusive Kurt Schumacher wearing his Knight's Cross. He added to the increasingly long list of *Wiking's* Panzer Knight's Crosses.

forces available, it was not possible to screen the resulting approximately 10 km [6.2 mile] long flank. Because of this, the enemy was able to attack Nowo-Buda from the west, but at the same time from the east.

The Russians attacked on 13.2.44 with two battalions toward the southeast part of Nowo-Buda and succeeded, through the establishment of strongpoints, to breach the line and obtain their own positions in several locations. Schumacher launched a counterattack with two vehicles against the Russians and threw them back from the eastern sector. The enemy also attacked the southwest sector of Nowo-Buda with fifteen tanks.

Ustuf. Schumacher decided to stop this. With his two vehicles, he moved against the invading enemy to destroy this armored breakthrough, and there were already eight tanks (T-34s) close to him. After the enemy tanks were shot up in that location, Schumacher could reach the southwest outskirts of Nowo-Buda, and proceeded to shoot up two more enemy tanks (T-34s).

The following day, the Russians attacked with eleven tanks. Schumacher decided to attack the enemy occupying the southern part with his two tanks and to advance against the enemy from their flank. The second vehicle was damaged by anti-tank fire, meaning Schumacher was the only operational vehicle. After he successfully shot up seven enemy tanks, he still possessed three explosive shells, with which he forced the crews of three remaining enemy tanks that tried to attack Schumacher to flee.

Only now was it possible to send another tank to support Schumacher. The three enemy tanks were hit and set on fire, and another, firing on Schumacher from the southern sector, was shot up.

Through this, Schumacher managed to keep control of the bridgehead of Nowo-Buda, allowing the enclosed korps to flow out of the area of Korssun and Shanderowka.

Through the independent decisions of Schumacher, the tanks of the enemy breakthrough were initially halted with two vehicles. The Russians managed another penetration of Nowo-Buda and nearby Shanderowka, but thirty-two T-34s were shot up, of which Schumacher carried the most significant share.

The destruction was managed by Panzer IIIs and Panzer IVs.

Divisional Commander Gille once again took the time to write his thoughts on one of his men. He mentioned Schumacher's excellent operational readiness, bravery, and the significance of his actions, recognizing the essential need to hold Nowo-Buda, which was crucial for the breakout attempts of the entrapped men at Tscherkassy.

While this was being considered at the highest level, *SS-Untersturmführer* Schumacher received a promotion to *SS-Obersturmführer* on April 20; the Knight's Cross was approved soon after, on May 5, 1944. Schumacher is listed as leading *3.* kompanie up to March 20, 1945, when he went missing in action near Stuhlweissenburg, Hungary.

Name: Heinrich Debus
Date of birth: 30.06.1921
SS Number: 316 063
Award: Knight's Cross

Born in Eckelshausen, near Biedenkopf, he became a member of the *Hitler Youth* in April 1933. Staying there for over three years, he then entered the *Allgemeine-SS* on November 9, 1937, at age sixteen. In April and May 1939, he spent time with the *RAD*. On September 12, 1939, he joined the armed SS.

He was posted to the artillery and served with the *SS*-Artillery Regiment in the western campaign in 1940. At the start of June he was promoted to *SS-Sturmmann*. After this campaign he was sent to NCO school and became an *SS-Unterscharführer* at the end of January 1941. In November 1941, he was sent to Bad Tolz, staying there until April 1942. Two months later, he was commissioned as an *SS-Untersturmführer*, by then with the *SS-Division Wiking*.

Fighting with them as they moved into the Caucausus in the second half of 1942, he earned the Second Class Iron Cross on August 17, followed by the Tank Assault Badge on September 28. The First Class Iron Cross was awarded on February 18, 1943, the Black Wound Badge on April 17, and the Bronze Close Combat Clasp followed at the start of June. A promotion to *SS-Obersturmführer* was approved on November 9, and around this time he was serving with the reconnaissance battalion, leading *1. Kompanie*. Later that same month he was the acting battalion commander. The award of the German Cross in Gold was given on January 23, 1944, for actions during the second half of 1943.

Another signed image from the Justin Horgan collection showing Heinrich Debus wearing his Knight's Cross in a formal studio setting.

On April 7, 1944, Debus's commander, Herbert Gille, penned a document asking for the award of the Knight's Cross. This document centered on Debus's actions during the recent Cherkassy fighting:

> *SS-Ostuf* Debus, since November 1943, has been commissioned as the acting commander of *SS-Aufkl Abt 5*. He displayed outstanding troop leadership and personal bravery during the heavy fighting in the cauldron west of Cherkassy, warranting a special award.
>
> During the night of 16. – 17.2.44, *SS-Ostuf* Debus led a breakout from the cauldron in the direction of Lysyanka with his alarm units from SS *Pz.Jg. Abt. 5* and two batteries of "*Wespen*" reinforcing the reconnaissance battalion, using this as the attack point "shock wedge" of the division.
>
> He had the mission to break through the area west of Chilki via Hill 213.1 and, by 23:00 hours, to speed over the lake south of Chilki—the forest west and southeast to Dshurshenzy—and Hill 239.0 to connect with our own armored forces.
>
> In proceeding forward, his attack was broken by three strong anti-tank hedgehog positions. In the middle of these were numerous anti-tank guns and heavy mortars. Here the battalion suffered high losses from heavy fire and the success of the breakthrough seemed hopeless. Support from "*Wespen*" was ordered during this phase of the battle, but was not possible because the vehicles could not advance over the difficult ground. *SS-Ostuf.* Debus gathered his infantry as close as he could and followed behind. He succeeded in throwing the enemy from that position by charging with a "hurrah" and destroying the self-propelled anti-tank guns and mortars.
>
> In this fighting, without support from the heavy weapons and surprising the enemy, *SS-Ostuf.* Debus led with his personal energy and extraordinary and audacious courage. His speed, selfless decisiveness, and determination guaranteed success in this difficult situation and decided the fate of those that were trapped.
>
> Just in front of Hill 239.0, the battalion came across a strong enemy tank force of eight to ten T-34s, plus well prepared infantry positions on the road from Dshurshenzy – Pochapintsy. Due to the absence of any anti-tank weapons, intense and constant heavy enemy fire rained down on the positions of this small, brave combat team. Flank attacks by the opponent from the north could only be defeated with the weakest of forces. Recognizing that a run against this position would fail and the success of the outbreak would be

> in question, *SS-Ostuf.* Debus made an independent decision to take his remaining men and move southward, through the woods east of Oktjabr. Despite further tanks rolling from Pochapintsy, the group stormed over the main road and reached the Tikich River (4 km [2.49 miles] east of Lysyanka), which was crossed by swimming. Thus, *SS-Ostuf.* Debus had meanwhile accumulated other battle groups from the division and paved the way that led to the unification of our own tank forces stationed at Lysyanka.
>
> I believe that *SS-Obersturmführer* Debus is worthy to be awarded the Knight's Cross to the Iron Cross.

This high level recognition was approved on May 4, 1944. Details of what Heinrich Debus did following this are very limited. He is listed as holding the rank *SS-Hauptsturmführer*, although the promotion date is not known. He survived the war and died on March 5, 1996.

Name: Hans Eckert
Date of birth: 01.06.1916
SS Number: 257 452
Award: Knight's Cross

Born in Zailach, Mittelfranken, he was a very early member of the *Hitler Youth*, joining in July 1929; he became a leader in that organization. He entered the SS in October 1934. He took part in the Austrian and Sudetenland campaigns and had the relevant campaign medals, although which unit he served with then is not listed. By mid-July 1939, he was holding the rank *SS-Unterscharführer* and was placed with *SS-Regiment Deutschland* in *5. Kompanie*.

He fought with *Deutschland* in Poland and then the west in 1940. Following this, he was sent to Bad Tolz from October 1940 through the end of January 1941; he was promoted to *SS-Untersturmführer* at the end of his time there. He returned to *Deutschland* and advanced with them into the Balkans, then soon after into Russia. The award of the Second Class Iron Cross came quickly on July 25, 1941. The First Class came exactly two months later, the same day he received the Infantry Assault Badge. The Russian Front medal was given to him on October 1, 1942; promotion to *SS-Oberstrumführer* came on November 9.

Presumably he was in the Kharkov area in late January 1943, as he received the Silver Wound Badge on the twenty-eighth. He was involved in heavy fighting in this area around mid-February, forming part of his subsequent proposal for the German Cross in Gold, as did actions during the Kursk Offensive in July, actions farther south in August 1943, and finally further combat activity in January 1944; he added the German Cross in Gold to his tunic on February 13, 1944. In September 1943, he was promoted to *SS-Hauptsturmführer*. He added the Gold Wound Badge to his list in mid-March 1944, and the Close Combat Clasp in Gold on April 20. This made him one of a select group of *Waffen-SS* soldiers to hold gold variants of the German Cross, Wound, and Close Combat awards.

On April 14, 1944, *SS-Sturmbannführer* Otto Weidinger put Eckert forward for the Knight's Cross, related to very recent actions:

> *SS-Obersturmführer* Hans Eckert, took over command of the grenadier battalion of *SS-Kampfgruppe "Das Reich"* on 28.3.44, after the wounding of the former commander.
>
> The kampfgruppe was ordered to replace the *101. Jaeger Divison* in the area northwest of Minkowzy. The enemy attacked their positions as they arrived with strong forces on both sides of the main road and succeeded in breaching their line for a 2 km [1.24 mile] wide gap.
>
> As a countermeasure *SS-Ostuf.* Eckert decided to gather all the SS men close by and turned the infantry around. Together, he led them from the front and dashed against this attack. Holding the front at this point was of crucial importance. He threw his opponent back far beyond his start positions. Through this, he held the positions throughout the whole day, up to the time of being ordered onward.
>
> On 29.3.44, *SS-Ostuf.* Eckert was in position with his battalion at the southern end of Ruda Gortschitschanskaja. His right border ran along the northern edge of Sszibory.
>
> During the course of the morning, the enemy succeeded in penetrating the right hand neighbors along the road in Sszibory, again creating a dangerous crisis. Hardly had he recognized this situation than Eckert gave the order to attack the neighboring area. This was his own decision, and it was led by *SS-Ostuf.* Eckert. After a short time he was leading a vigorous attack against the closest Russians and threw them back, thus eliminating a major risk. Even more important than the security of this road was the security of the field replacement battalion.
>
> Again, it was the determination and exemplary daring of *SS-Ostuf.* Eckert that had mastered a serious crisis.

Hans Eckert captured in a studio pose showing his Knight's Cross and other awards. He was *Das Reich's* final Knight's Cross level awardee for this volume.

On 05.04.1944, the kampfgruppe had the mission to take new positions eastward from Wolkowce and link with the *208. Infantry Division*. When the kampfgruppe was advancing up to the railway line toward its sector there came a message from the front: the Russians were marching in a column with infantry and anti-tank guns west, along the east to west road on the left border of their sector. Immediately *SS-Ostuf.* Eckert seized the initiative and decided to attack the enemy on the main road. He set about gathering as many forces as possible, moving west to engage the enemy while he also set the entire SS grenadier battalion in an attack on a broad front against the marching columns.

He stormed at the head of his battalion before this road. Instantly, the entire enemy traffic was interrupted and the march columns were shattered in the shortest time. One kompanie moved over the road and advanced to the east from the rear, then stormed back into the Russians, who were taken under withering machine gun fire from two sides.

The result was eighty enemy dead on the road alone, eighty guns, five SMG, three Anti-tank rifles, and two 4.7 cm anti-tank guns captured.

The important success achieved within the overall situation was all the more significant because for the entire day, the whole left flank was completely open. For the rest of the day, the grenadier battalion was engaged in further heavy defensive fighting. Several attacks were necessary to hold the front up to the required time.

The great success of the day was due to the exemplary fighting spirit of *SS-Ostuf. Eckert.*

On 12.4.1944 , the kampfgruppe was attached to the *XXXXVI. Panzer* korps in Amilowka. Around 16:00 hours, the kampfgruppe received orders to immediately march to Slone to help clear up a breach by the Russians on a broad front against the positions of the *75. Infantry Division*. Above all, it was to seize Hill .347 from the enemy—the dominant high ground for the entire sector. The kampfgruppe started their attack at 06:00 hours and unusually were met with a strong barrage attack by all of the enemy weapons as the enemy moved strong forces into the ring. It was initially unclear if the attack would succeed or falter. *SS-Ostuf.* Eckert attacked once again and moved through as an example to all of his men. Following the toughest struggle and suffering significant losses, the entire sector and the important hill were partially taken and held until nightfall.

> In the first hours of the night after midnight, after receiving more ammunition, the battalion leaders were ordered to storm part of the hill once more. This part of the dominant position remained in our hands for almost the whole next day. This attack was crucial to keeping control of the front of the left section of the *75. Infantry Division.*
>
> The performance is all the more remarkable given that in this attack, for the most part, were newly formed specialists as gunners, and flak men, tank crews, mechanics, and messengers were all first in the line of this infantry attack.
>
> Towering over all of this was the extraordinary personal leadership abilities of *SS-Ostuf.* Eckert, who led this heavy attack to a successful conclusion.
>
> *SS-Obersturmführer* Eckert has repeatedly demonstrated his excellent fighting spirit, selfless willingness, instant decision making skills and bravado, and unparalleled bravery. He is *the* shining role model for his men of an excellent frontline officer.
>
> *SS-Obersturmführer* Eckert has, up to now, been wounded six times. Since 13.2.1944, he is the holder of the German Cross in Gold and Gold Close Combat Clasp.
>
> *SS-Obersturmführer* Eckert is particularly worthy to bear the high award of the Knight's Cross of the Iron Cross.

This recommendation was endorsed by commanding general of the *XXXXVI. Panzer Korps* Arning, who added:

> *SS-Kampfgruppe "Das Reich,"* under the leadership of *SS-Sturmbannführer* Weidinger, was within the framework of the mauled *korps*. The battalion of *SS-Obersturmführer* Eckert had an outstanding share of the successful storming of Hill .347 on 12.4.44. This was crucial for the further holding of the main battle line of the *75. Inf. Div*. An enemy breakthrough at this point had endangered the entire korps front.
>
> The application is approved.

This dual recommendation was approved on May 4, 1944.

He is listed as being wounded for the seventh time on August 9, 1944. By early February 1945, he had moved from *Das Reich* and was at the SS Panzer grenadier school at Kienschlag. He survived the war and died on July 11, 1974.

Name: Otto Schneider
Date of birth: 28.09.1921
SS Number: 400 130
Award: Knight's Cross

Born in Schasslowitz, Sudetenland, he joined the SS on November 9, 1938, and was placed with *15. Kompanie*, *Deutschland.* He fought with them in Poland with the rank of *SS-Sturmmann*, and also started the campaign in the west with them. On May 16, he was sent to the officer school at Braunschweig and stayed there until the end of February 1941. It would appear that by early April 1941, he was fighting in the Balkans campaign, presumably with *Deutschland* once again. On April 20, he received a promotion to *SS-Untersturmführer* and a posting to *SS-Division Wiking's 2.* kompanie in their reconnaissance battalion. He was awarded the following medals: the Second Class Iron Cross on June 7, the First Class Iron Cross on June 18, and the Black Wound Badge on June 26, all presumably for actions during the recent Balkans Campaign. He advanced into the Soviet Union with *Wiking* at this time and in the opening months received further medals. He received the Tank Assault Badge on October 28, and just prior, he is listed as being with the *SS-Kradschutzen Replacement Battalion*, remaining there until February 1942. This would indicate a further wounding, one that resulted in months away from the front line. This wound could also have been the one that resulted in his Silver Wound Badge, but that actual award date is not confirmed.

When recovered, he had a short stint with the Panzer battalion of *SS-Division Reich*, but later in 1942, moved to *Wiking's* Panzer battalion. From mid-September 1942 through March 1943, he was with the SS Panzer replacement battalion. For the remainder of 1943, he was helping train recruits at Debica in the overall *III. (Germanisches) SS-Panzer* korps setup. His next promotion came on November 9, 1943, when he moved to *SS-Obersturmführer*.

By April 1944, he was back in *Wiking's* Panzer regiment in command of *7. Kompanie*, which had very recently been given Panther tanks. He was fighting near Kovel and his actions there prompted Regimental Commander Muhlenkamp to recommend Schneider for the award of the Knight's Cross on April 11:

> For the relief of the *LVI. Panzer Korps*, who for three weeks solid have been trapped in Kovel, elements of *SS-Panzer Regiment 5* and *5. SS-Panzer Division Wiking* were assigned.

Otto Schneider wearing his Knight's Cross in shirt sleeve order. He was another of *Wiking's* Panther tank / Kovel related Knight's Cross level awardees.

In the early morning hours of 5.4.44, *7.* kompanie of *SS-Panzer Regiment 5.* moved east from Moszczona and on to the breakthrough at Kovel. kompanie leader *SS-Obersturmführer* Schneider did not wait for the support of our own artillery and Panzer grenadiers. He made an independent decision, took advantage of a favorable battle situation and, in doing so, surprised the enemy. He successfully destroyed a strong anti-tank position that the enemy had built up close to Dubova and thereby opened access to Kovel for the following troops. With his kompanie he advanced into the northern sector and met strong enemy infantry. They destroyed them and at 14:00 hours, provided the first clear path through the encirclement at Kovel.

Schneider was exceedingly hard and tough, and led at the head of his kompanie during the fighting. He showed a dogged determination in finding a way through and was a role model of bravery and operational readiness for his subordinates.

During the course of the fighting his tank was shot up; nevertheless, he immediately got up again, used a different tank, and continued to lead his *kompanie*.

During the course of the battle kompanie *Schneider* destroyed or captured:

1 Anti-aircraft battery 8.5 cm (4 *geschutze*)
27 Heavy anti-tank guns 7.62 cm
1 Assault Gun
4 Heavy mortars
5 Light anti-tank guns
4 Light anti-aircraft vehicles
and numerous infantry weapons.

Four days later, Divisional Commander Gille added a short endorsement to this recommendation:

> The surprise and stand-alone advance by his Panzer kompanie was decisive for the breaking of the containment ring around Kovel.
>
> The proposal for the award of the Knight's Cross of the Iron Cross for *SS-Obersturmführer* Schneider is warranted, who in all of his battles has proven an excellent kompanie leader.

This recommendation was approved on May 4, 1944. Schneider remained with *Wiking's* Panzer regiment until the end of the war. In the closing weeks of the conflict he was listed as staff kompanie commander in I Battalion. He ended the war with the rank *SS-Hauptsturmführer*, but the exact promotion date is not listed. When attempting to surrender to American troops at the end of the war near Steiermark, Austria, he became involved in a fire-fight and was officially listed as missing. He was captured by the Russians after this fire-fight and spent four years in one of their prisoner of war camps. After being released, he made his way to America and died on November 6, 2001, in Rhode Island.

Name: Max Schachner
Date of birth: 01.05.1914
SS Number: 135 749
Award: Knight's Cross

Born in Haag, southeast of Linz in Austria, he was an early supporter of the German cause and joined the *Allgemeine-SS* at the start of September 1932. In 1933, he was in Germany and was a member of the *Austrian Legion*, but by November, he was serving in *SS-Regiment Deutschland*. At the start of April 1936, he was sent to Braunschweig for NCO training. In the prewar years he took part in the Austrian and Sudetenland actions, earning the relevant awards for them.

He returned to *Deutschland* and fought in the west with them during 1940, where he was awarded the Second Class Iron Cross. He fought in Russia too, adding the First Class Iron Cross in September 1941, the Infantry Assault Badge the following month, and then in February 1942, the Black Wound Badge. This wound may have removed him from the front line temporarily, as in late October 1942, he joined the *SS-Kavallerie Division* and served as a *batterie* leader in their *Panzerjaeger Abteilung*. On April 20, 1943, he was promoted to *SS-Untersturmführer*, which may have been a field promotion. At the start of October 1943, he moved to *SS-Obersturmführer*.

In mid-October 1943, he was fighting near Komunar; his actions there resulted in the battalion commander recommending him for the Knight's Cross on March 25, 1944:

> In the night of 16.10.1943, Cavalry Regiment 15 was released from the previous main battle line. They were ordered to take up positions in the Komunar area. The enemy identified the withdrawal very early on and, despite the bad weather, immediately moved strong tank and infantry forces during the night. The leading enemy hit

Another poor quality image showing a *Waffen-SS* Knight's Cross holder. This soldier is Max Schachner, who was another posthumous award, having been killed in October 1943.

the security position of *SS-Ostuf.* Schachner as he was disengaging. After a short fire fight, he was able to report that the enemy tanks had been shot up and the enemy infantry had been destroyed. This won time for our units to move to the new line of defense before first light.

At dawn, the enemy arrived in front of our positions with 150 tanks and strong infantry forces and went immediately to the attack.

The movement to the new positions during the night proved extremely unfavorable at the beginning of the attack, since the few remaining armor-piercing weapons could only take the oncoming enemy tanks under fire after they had rolled over our own infantry.

In this crisis, *SS-Ostuf.* Schachner took the decision to attack the tanks that had got as far as our main battle line. He took the fight to them, despite the huge numerical superiority of the enemy. Because the opponent had also broken through the neighboring unit to the right, this endangered the open flank of the regiment. During this crisis fifty enemy tanks, of which *SS-Ostuf.* Schachner shot up twenty-four (T-34s) with his two vehicles (he shot up twelve on his own), were shot up. The regiment, which was already partially rolled over deep into their flank by enemy infantry forces, was able to avoid being eliminated. The increasing pressure mounted after bitter, close combat at Ustimowka and halted at Berestki.

The decision by *SS-Ostuf.* Schachner to take up the fight despite the overwhelming enemy, the personal example shown to the younger commanders during the destruction of the enemy armor, and the inspired high achievements of his men during the resulting mobile tank weapon-led battle during this surprise attack that smashed into the regiment prevented further advances of the enemy.

On 19.10.1943, *SS-Ostuf.* Schachner was in his *Sturmgeschutz* and shot up during a reconnaissance foray into Piatichatki, dying a heroic death.

The recommendation was endorsed by Divisional Commander *SS-Oberführer* Bruno Streckenbach and was officially approved on May 14, 1944.

It is not known why his battalion commander waited six months before writing the recommendation, but it may have been due to heavy combat they were engaged in during the intervening months. You will also notice that Schachner was killed on October 19, 1943, resulting in him being approved for the posthumous award of the Knight's Cross. This approval added another posthumous Knight's Cross holder to the growing list and it was eight Knight's Cross related posthumous awards (seven Knight's Crosses and one set of Swords to the Knight's Cross) for the *Waffen-SS* to date.

Name: Heinz Nowotnik
Date of birth: 29.03.1920
SS Number: 363 650
Award: Knight's Cross

Born in Schmarse, he joined the *Hitler Youth* just prior to his thirteenth birthday on March 1, 1933. He remained a member until mid-October 1937, when he then joined the SS. He was posted to the *Leibstandarte* and trained as a gun leader, entering the war in this role and with that formation. Prior to the outbreak of war, he earned the Sudetenland campaign medal and the Memel medal; the German Reich Sports Badge was also on his tunic prewar.

He fought in Poland and then the west. Promotion to *SS-Unterscharführer* was made at the start of September 1940. His next campaign was in the Balkans, and he earned the Second Class Iron Cross on April 18, 1941; he was with *4.* kompanie then. Moving east into the Soviet Union soon after this, he was promoted to the rank of *SS-Oberscharführer* at the start of September. One new recruit who had recently joined the *Leibstandarte's 4.* kompanie was Erwin Bartmann. When speaking to this veteran over sixty years later, he recalled serving under Heinz Nowotnik at that time and how Nowotnik's experience shone during the heat of battle as they reached the Dnjepr River. For Nowotnik, the award of the First Class Iron Cross followed on December 3. Attending a training course at Bad Tolz from January to March 1942, then another at Dachau between February and May 1943, he received promotion to *SS-Untersturmführer* at the start of September. He was placed with the *Leibstandarte* and was in *14. Kompanie*, *SS-Panzergrenadier Regiment 1*. He is also known to have been awarded the Black Wound Badge and the Infantry Assault Badge, but the award dates are not listed. The Russian Front Medal was presented to him in 1942.

In the closing days of November 1943, Nowotnik was involved in heavy fighting on the Russian Front. Commanding *14.* kompanie at that stage, Regimental Commander Albert Frey later penned a recommendation for the award of the Knight's Cross on March 18, 1944:

> Justification of the Knight's Cross proposal for the SS *Untersturmführer* Nowotnik.

Heinz Nowotnik in a clear, signed image showing off his Knight's Cross.
Once again part of the Justin Horgan collection.

On 27.11.43, the reinforced *III. /SS-Panz.-Gren.-Rgt. 1 "LSSAH"* had the order to attack the enemy and remove him from Forst Bulyschety. To begin with, two rifle kompanies started out from the northeast part of the forest 1,500 m [1,640 yards] south of Bulyschety, with support from the *Sturmgeschutze* moving from the northeast of the forest south of Bulyschety. *14. (MG) / SS-Panz. Gren. Rgt.1 "LSSAH"* had the order to take a route north from the southeast and drive into Bulyschety, acting as a supporting position for the attack of the battalion. The kompanie went into position about 500-600 m [546-656 yards] southeast of Bulyschety.

Through the loss of multiple *Sturmgeshutze* from mines, through the fire from heavy weapons and artillery, and the sudden onset of a heavy snowdrift causing the loss of radio links all threatened to halt the attack of the battalion. Through this fire the enemy, who was no longer tied down, took to attacking the battalion with more artillery batteries, several rocket launchers, and numerous MGs. At 6 a.m., the closest positions on the southern part of this location were found to be under heavy fire from 7.62 cm guns.

SS-Untersturmführer Nowotnik recognized the difficulty of the situation and decided to use a platoon from *14.* kompanie to relieve the battalion, starting against the enemy's eastern positions. Consider that *SS-Untersturmführer* Nowotnik preceded his grenadiers while the enemy directed the mass of his fire against this platoon, especially the fire of their six 7.62 cm guns; the enemy gunners aimed at individual men. Through this fierce defense the attack of Platoon Nowotnik almost faltered. In this difficult situation, *SS-Untersturmführer* Nowotnik succeeded by his own individual heroic bravery—his platoon far ahead of his kompanie storming against the enemy position—and by his example roused his men to penetrate the opponent's position. Through this flowed the attack of *III. / SS-Panz.-Gren.-Rgt. 1 "LSSAH,"* so that the location could be taken into our possession once more.

The elevated position of the enemy near Bulyschety dominated the terrain far on all sides. By his overall individual attack, Nowotnik overthrew the enemy and seized from them approximately 1,200 m [1,312 yards] to the south of Bulyschety, up to the River Belka. The control of the key position Bulyschety was the prerequisite for the continuation of further determined attacks of the 1st Regiment, and beyond that, the *"LSSAH."* That the attack on Bulyschety led to an early success is only due to the excellence of *SS-Untersturmführer* Nowotnik.

> *SS-Untersturmführer* Nowotnik was severely wounded on 8.12.1943. Nowotnik is a deserving soldier in every sense, and is of high moral worth and character; he is worthy of the proposed high award.

This proposal was supported by "Teddi" Wisch, who highlighted Nowotnik's outstanding bravery, and also Sepp Dietrich; it was approved on May 14, 1944.

By July 1944, Nowotnik was in command of the *LSSAH's 10. Kompanie*. It is also known that he moved to the rank *SS-Obersturmführer*, although an exact promotion date is not listed. Heinz Nowotnik survived the war and died at the end of May 1999 in Wolfenbuttel.

Name: Erich Gratz
Date of birth: 14.08.1909
SS Number: 247 833
Award: Knight's Cross

Born in Neusalz on the Oder, Erich Gratz served with the police from April 1929 until June 1934 (from the end of 1930 until 1933, he had also been a member of the *SA*.) He started his career with the SS in July 1934, being placed with the *Leibstandarte,* where he retained his former police rank of *Wachtmeister*, which translated to *SS-Scharführer*.

Remaining with the *Leibstandarte*, he took part in the advance into Poland in 1939 and earned the Second Class Iron Cross for actions there, which was awarded in November. He also advanced west in 1940, adding the First Class Iron Cross on June 14. He was serving with *11.* kompanie then, but in September, he was holding the rank *SS-Hauptscharführer* and was moved to the reconnaissance battalion, serving in the anti-tank gun platoon. He is also listed as being promoted to *SS-Untersturmführer* at the start of September 1940; this would appear to be a field promotion, as there are no dates listed for him having attended any of the officer schools. His next campaign was in the Balkans and then, just prior to advancing into Russia, he moved to the rank *SS-Obersturmführer*. The award of the Infantry Assault Badge came at the start of October. On April 20, 1942, he was promoted to *SS-Hauptsturmführer.* Then, in mid-June, he was presented with the Bulgarian Bravery Medal IV Class, 2 Grade, presumably relating to his actions the previous year. On September 3, 1943, he was awarded the Close Combat in Bronze; then, on the twentieth, he added the German

Another sub-standard quality image, this time showing Erich Gratz from the *LSSAH*. The image is obscuring most of his Knight's Cross; he is the final *LSSAH* awardee for this volume.

Cross in Gold, recognizing his bravery at a high level. The details of the actions that drove this decision are not known, as the recommendation does not survive in his file.

By early 1944, he was commanding the *18. (Panzerjaeger)* kompanie and during the difficult fighting in March, Gratz demonstrated his bravery even further, prompting Divisional Commander "Teddi" Wisch to pen a proposal for the award of the Knight's Cross on March 18:

> On 6.3.1944, at 08:30 hours, strong Russian infantry forces with tanks broke into the area north of the town of Manatschin and Dg. IV between Tarnapol and Proskuroff. In this place was *SS-Wirtschafts Battalion 1* of the division, as well as elements of *SS-Pz.Gr.Rgt. 1* under the leadership of *SS-Hauptsturmführer* Gratz.
>
> During the break-in and forming up of the Russian tanks, *SS-Hauptsturmführer* Gratz truly exploited the confusion. He raced around to the northern part of the town and assembled all available elements there. He committed all combat capable elements into the fight, including trainees from the bakery kompanie and construction engineers. He added combat elements of *SS-Panz.Gr.Rgt. 1* to each of these *kompanies*, positioning them at key locations.
>
> With this collection of forces, and equipped with only a few machine guns, he moved into defensive positions south of the town of Manatschin. He advanced to the point of the enemy breach and led then to the area south of Dg IV reached on 11.3.44. Thus, it allowed the withdrawal from Proskuroff and the halting of the fighting by the division in Woitowzy and in the area north of there, keeping the left flank free of the enemy. Despite the Russians using strong infantry forces and a tank brigade, they failed to cut the supply road for the division or prevent the division from moving west.
>
> *SS-Hauptsturmführer* Gratz, combining his existing forces into a battle group and under personal outstanding bravery, destroyed the enemy who infiltrated their position. This was during the morning and evening of 6.3.44 and the morning of 7.3.44. The enemy was destroyed in place or at the penetration points and contained by his decision. A crucial part of the successful defense of the division was due to the determined, personal bravery of Gratz and excellent attitude of the men fighting under him.
>
> I consider *SS-Hauptsturmführer* Gratz, because of his independent decision, personal bravery, excellence, overall leadership, and

> because of the wider degree of success for this extraordinary defense worthy of the award of the Knight's Cross of the Iron Cross, and I propose the award of this high medal.

This proposal was approved on May 14, 1944. Gratz remained with the *Leibstandarte*, but in the latter part of 1944, spent time at various training schools, including the *SS-Panzerjaeger* school at Janowitz; this ended in mid-January 1945. Some sources list him as being promoted to *SS-Sturmbannführer*, although his file does not confirm this. It is unclear what he did in the closing months of the war. He survived the war and was alive at the time of the writing of this book.

Name: Franz Hack
Date of birth: 03.02.1915
SS Number: 227 129
Award: Knight's Cross

Born in Mannheim, he joined the *Allgemeine-SS* at the start of November 1933, serving with the *32. SS-Standarte*. Just under one year later, he was with *Germania* and was sent to NCO school. From there, he was sent to Bad Tolz from April 1935 through January 1936. This was immediately followed by a platoon leader's course that lasted to the end of February. From the beginning of April 1936, he was back with *Germania*, receiving promotion to *SS-Untersturmführer* on the twentieth. He was initially with I Battalion, but by the start of May 1938, he was sent to *III Battalion Der Führer*. His promotion to *SS-Obersturmführer* was made on January 30, 1939. He remained with *DF* as the war began.

In April 1940, he was back with *Germania* and fought with them in the west. He earned the Second Class Iron Cross there on July 20; there is also mention of him being wounded. A promotion to *SS-Hauptsturmführer* followed on April 20, 1941. The award of the First Class Iron Cross was made on July 10, 1941, with the Wound Badge and Infantry Assault Badge following the same year (exact dates are not listed). At the start of September 1942, he was awarded the Russian Front Medal. He was then awarded the German Cross in Gold in early January 1943, although the recommendation does not survive. He had a short stint on the staff of the *Germanisches SS-Pz.* korps in May before returning to *Germania*. He was promoted on June 21 to *SS-Sturmbannführer* and by then was III Battalion commander.

He remained in this post throughout the remainder of 1943 and the opening months of 1944. He was with them when they were caught in the fighting at Kovel. The bravery he displayed there earned him a proposal for the award of the Knight's Cross by Regimental Commander Hans Dorr on April 24, 1944:

> Corroboration of the proposal for the Knight's Cross for *SS-Sturmbannführer* Hack
>
> In the night attack on 17.4.44 against Hill 189.5 and the high ground south of there (1.5 km [0.93 miles] southwest of Kovel), *SS-Sturmbannführer* Hack, commander of *III./SS-Pz.Gren.Rgt. Germania*, distinguished himself excellently through outstanding bravery against the enemy.
>
> The enemy was on the important Hill 189.5, upon which he had a superb view of the full defensive perimeter of "fortress place" Kovel. They could observe the only supply road, the city itself, and all of the terrain north and northwest. We were clearly aware that this hill was defended tenaciously by the Soviets and also greatly expanded by them.
>
> The control of this dominant position enemy was expected and necessary for the relief of "fortress place" Kovel. A flanking night attack from the east and west was the only possibility due to the effects of strong enemy fire.
>
> Battalion Hack got orders to deploy to the railway triangle west of Kovel and, during the night, attack along the railway line Kovel – Wlodzimorz. From there, they were to push south and destroy the fixed enemy positions on both sides of the railway line, then push onward and in a surprise attack take the enemy positions on Hill 189.5 and hold it.
>
> The surprise attack against the first enemy position at the railway bridge executed by two shock squads got caught up in Soviet wire obstacles. Fire support from heavy weapons was not possible due to how close our troops were to the enemy. Hack rushed to the head of the shock troops and urged them not to delay because everything depended on the success of this first phase of the attack. He set about the enemy positions that had been built between the bridge pillars with five armored rounds and a hand grenade volley, allowing

Part of my collection, it is a nice shot of Franz Hack where his Knight's Cross is clearly visible alongside his German Cross in Gold and Close Combat Clasp. That Knight's Cross award made Franz Hack the 200th *Waffen-SS* Knight's Cross holder.

the two shock squad leaders to get into the first enemy position.

Through this exemplary and ruthless use of himself Hack fought through the smoke ahead of the two shock squads, using machine pistols and hand grenades, and threw the enemy out of the positions.

He was wounded in the face and on the right hand by hand grenade splinters. Hack remained in the attack despite his injuries and rapidly led his battalion through the second position. After a short stop for provisions they advanced against Hill 189.5, where the Soviets continued a dogged defense.

The enemy could not withstand the assault momentum of the battalion led from the front by the commander. After a short, hard, close-action fight, the enemy was thrown from their positions on Hill 189.5 and they retreated to the south. In the immediate aftermath, Hack recognized the importance of the need to continue the attack. He made the independent decision to attack along the railway line to the south and snatched one position after another from the Soviets. By first light, the battalion had taken and occupied the enemy's positions on Hill 189.5 and the road bridge 400 m [437 yards] to the southwest. Shortly thereafter, a surprise attack by the enemy from the southwest was repulsed, with the positions being held for the rest of the day against further enemy attacks.

Only then did Hack, after organizing the defense, go to a doctor for treatment for his hand. Through his shrewd leadership and thanks to his fearless, personal actions, he has a significant share of the success of this substantial undertaking for the relief of "fortress location" Kovel.

Hack has been wounded six times during this war, is a holder of the German Cross in Gold, the Close Combat Clasp I Class, and the Gold Wound Badge.

Hack is worthy to be awarded the Knight's Cross of the Iron Cross.

(Signed) Dorr
SS-Sturmbannführer und Rgt. Commander

Just under a week later (April 30), this recommendation received an endorsement from Herbert Gille (himself a Diamonds holder by then), who highlighted Hack's speed and energy during the hard fighting in Kovel around Hill 189.5.

Hack was approved for this award on May 14, but that would not end his association with the various grades of the Knight's Cross. We will return to Franz Hack's personal history in a later volume.

Name: Walter Schmidt
Date of birth: 28.01.1917
SS Number: 311 100
Award: Oakleaves to the Knight's Cross

Walter Schmidt is our penultimate soldier within this volume; he is also the eighth person in this volume who has been featured in previous volumes: in volume 3 he was recognized for his abilities on August 4, 1943.

He retained his position as commander of II Battalion in *SS-Regiment Westland*. He led them during the challenging battles in the closing months of 1943, and it was fighting at the end of November that would result in him being recommended for the Oakleaves to his existing Knight's Cross. On April 30, 1944, *Wiking* Divisional Commander Gille penned a recommendation for Schmidt:

> I. In the period from 24. to 30.11.1943, *II. / SS-Pz.Gren.Rgt. Westland*, as part of the *72. Jaeger Division*, was employed southeast of Tscherkassy to seal off the breach there. The battalion had the order on 28.11 to attack from Smogailowka and take the brickyard area on the southeast of Tscherkassy. The northwestern part of Smogailowka was ordered as the forming up location, but in the morning hours of 28.11. was surprisingly busy with strong Russian infantry forces. In the brickyard area a group of more than twenty enemy tanks was visible. Even the far-flung cornfield north of the brickyard contained strong enemy infantry forces.
>
> The danger of the enemy renewing an attack and expanding their breach area was recognized by *SS-Hstuf.* Schmidt. Without waiting for the arrival of supporting elements (a single heavy infantry gun platoon), he cleared the enemy from the northwest part of Smogailowka and penetrated into the northeastern part of the brickyard; the enemy was completely surprised. The battalion added a yield of:
>
> 2 Guns, 7.62 cm
> 3 Anti-tank guns, 4.7 cm
> 21 Anti-tank rifles
> 18 Machine-guns
> 60 Machine-pistols
> 83 Guns:

1 officer and 13 men were captured, and approximately 300 enemy dead were counted.

The battalion consisted of a fighting strength of 130 NCOs and men at the start of the attack. From the last transport of replacements seven Transylvanian recruits were added, and they experienced their first combat action. Thanks for this performance is therefore due in great part to the excellent dynamism and personal bravery of *SS-Hstuf.* Schmidt. The danger of Russian renewed attack after identifying the arrival of their heavy weapons, was strong. He even fought in the front line with his men and as a consequence was a high example of courage and bravery.

II. On 30.11.1943, the enemy moved over the road from Tscherkassy-Smela with strong forces. Battalion Schmidt was in the framework of the *42. Jaeger Division*, and was due to move from the east and take some widely dispersed farmsteads. The enemy had taken these farms and surrounding cornfields and set up defenses with stronger forces. Due to the previous heavy fighting, the battalion only had a small amount of firepower with which to defend themselves against the tenacious enemy. Since the terrain was uneven and closed-in, direct leadership of the men was not possible. In this situation, *SS-Hstuf.* Schmidt sprang into action and standing on a shot-up tank in the cornfield, incited his men with a loud voice, regardless of enemy fire, to proceed farther on. Inspired by this, his battalion managed to not only achieve the ordered attack objective, but also pushed 3 km [1.86 miles] deep into the enemy, up to the river.

Thus, once reached, this achieved the halting of the Russian attacks against this main road for three days, so during this time a new security line was established west of the main road.

III. In the southwest area of the Tscherkassy Cauldron, *SS-Hstuf.* Schmidt maintained himself to the highest degree during the very tough daily defensive fighting. His capabilities, luck, personal momentum, and outstanding bravery are appreciated in the first line. Although his battalion was exhausted, the enemy's failure in the battles at Buda 'Orlowezkaja, Mlejew, Skiti, Tscherepin, Derenkowez, Arbusino, and west of Korsun was due to his persistent ceaseless efforts and was a complete success for the defense of the regiment. Also, the inexperienced infantry and attached elements

A signed image of Walter Schmidt from my collection, showing him in a studio setting to capture his Oakleaves award. I have also been lucky enough to read through Schmidt's second (and final) issue *soldbuch* that has an Oakleaves-wearing image in there, too! He was *Wiking's* only Oakleaves-level awardee in this time frame.

> of the *Panzerjaeger* battalion and the anti-aircraft battalion were directed so they withstood the enemy onslaught as experienced infantrymen, each guided by the commander through his energy and exhilarating personality.
>
> At the breakout of the pocket itself, *SS-Hstuf.* Schmidt has gained a special distinction. His battalion marched at the start of the second meeting with the division, about 800 m [875 yards] northwest of Hill 193.3, first establishing a blocking position to the east with strong security. On the north edge of the forest to the southeast of Dshurshenzy, they captured one anti-tank and two machine gun positions, but were attacked by the enemy coming from Dshurshenzy. They defended against this attack and pushed it back to the church. These measures, mainly due to *SS-Hstuf.* Schmidt, were the basis for them first reaching the main road southeast of Hill 239.0 and later achieving the link-up that was made with our own forces outside of the pocket through the woods west of Pochapintsy.
>
> In the intervening time, he had joined up with a large group of army kameraden who increased their own group of weak defenders. Singly carried by the thought "We must get through!," Schmidt stormed forward at the head of his 300 assembled men to the forest northeast of Lysyanka. Following his example, the newly formed attack group always followed Schmidt. Therefore, *SS-Hstuf.* Schmidt has contributed significantly to the impending breakthrough into our own lines and did not falter.
>
> *SS-Hstuf.* Schmidt was awarded the Knight's Cross of the Iron Cross on 2.8.1943. I hold that, on account of his extraordinary virtues as a troop leader and on account of his frequently proven excellence and bravery he is worthy to be awarded the Oakleaves to the Knight's Cross of the Iron Cross.

This detailed recommendation was approved only two weeks later (May 14, 1944), resulting in Walter Schmidt becoming the twenty-eighth *Waffen-SS* soldier to be awarded the Oakleaves to the Knight's Cross.

Despite this even higher level of recognition and the fact he had been in command of II Battalion for some time, it was not until November 9, 1944, that he was promoted to *SS-Sturmbannführer*. By that time he was away from the front line, recovering from a combat wound. He was moved to the SS officer's school at Bad Tolz from the beginning of January 1945, taking him back to where he had been taught how to be an SS officer in 1937–38. In March 1945, he was given command of *SS-Regiment 96* in the last SS division to be created (*38. SS-Division Nibelungen*). This unit surrendered to the Americans on May 8, 1945. His final rank is listed as *SS-Obersturmbannführer*, but the actual promotion date is unconfirmed. Being one of the survivors of the war, he died on July 28, 2000. If you refer to volume 3, you will get a short insight into probably the final conversation he held before dying, plus an overview of his postwar activities with what became HIAG, the self-help organization set up by veterans of the *Waffen-SS*.

Name: Karl Ullrich
Date of birth: 01.12.1910
SS Number: 31 438
Award: Oakleaves to the Knight's Cross

The last *Waffen-SS* soldier to be covered in this volume is our ninth man to have graced the pages of preceding volumes. For Ullrich, he last appeared in our first volume when, on February 19, 1942, he was approved for the Knight's Cross.

From July 1942 through March 1943, he held the role of pioneer commander for the *I. SS-Panzer Korps*. He was then back with *Totenkopf*, and led their II Battalion during the Charkov fighting in early 1943; he led that unit through the Kursk campaign too. By November, he was in command of *SS-Regiment "Theodore Eicke,"* and on the ninth he was promoted to *SS-Obersturmbannführer*.

On April 28, 1944, *SS-Gruppenführer* Hermann Priess put Ullrich forward for the Oakleaves to his existing Knight's Cross:

> 1) On 19.03.1943, *SS-Regiment "Totenkopf"* had the task of attacking from the area of Murow to reach the Donez River from both sides of Iwanowka and to close the crossing areas over the river. Due to the stubborn resistance of the enemy, which displayed a tough defense from well-built positions, the attack faltered. In this situation *SS-Obersturmbannführer* Ullrich, as commander of *III./"Totenkopf,"* distinguished himself through his model personal bravery. Constantly staying with the forward elements of his battalion, he was the first to penetrate with them into the Russian positions and rallied his men to continue with the full-tempered led attack to a complete success. Through his personal action he managed early in the night of 19.03.1943 to take the villages Orguzewo, Botkino, and Iwanowka,

cutting off the crossings located there. With it, the escape route for the strong Russian forces still standing on the west bank of the Donez was closed and the conditions for their destruction in the course of the ensuing battle were accomplished.

2) On 10.07.1943, the Division started an attack to build a bridgehead over the Pssel River. From well-built positions ruling the terrain, the Russians shelled with heavy artillery and grenade launcher fire on our attacking elements. Our attack came to a standstill. In spite of severe casualties, *SS-Obersturmbannführer* Ullrich, through his exemplary personal bravery, pushed his battalion forward again. By 19:00 hours, the town Krassnyj-Oktjabar was occupied and a small bridgehead had been built over the Pssel. Then, the ensuing attacks carried out by the opponent with strong infantry and tank forces were contained by *SS-Obersturmbannführer* Ullrich with his weak forces for an entire week. *SS-Obersturmbannführer* Ullrich was the sole of the resistance in this sector, hammered day and night by heavy artillery fire. Every time the enemy, exploiting his massive superiority, succeeded to break in, he was beaten back by the counterattacks put into action by Ullrich, gathering his last men. Thanks to this remarkable feat, *SS-Obersturmbannführer* Ullrich set the conditions for the ensuing successful advance in the direction of Kursk. On 17.07.1943, following superior orders, the bridgehead had to be evacuated.

3) In the first hours of 14.11.1943, the Russians managed to break through the positions of one of our infantry divisions. *SS-Panzergrenadier Regiment "Theodore Eicke,"* under the command of *SS-Obersturmbannführer* Ullrich, was deployed near that sector. With a daring counterattack, he snatched back the ground gained by the vastly superior enemy forces. Ullrich and his unit then repelled several counterattacks the same day. On the 15.11.1943, with the deployment of newly brought-up units and the support of a strong artillery barrage, rolling air attacks, and the escort of forty-eight tanks, the Russians launched an attack. While the main fighting line could be held in the sector of II Battalion, the enemy managed to push back III Battalion to the eastern edge of Bairak, despite courageous and demanding resistance. In this critical situation, *SS-Obersturmbannführer* Ullrich gathered together his last men and with a bold counter attack relieved the heavily engaged III

A nice signed image of Karl Ullrich, showing his Oakleaves award and other combat and campaign medals. He was *Totenkopf's* only Oakleaves-level awardee in these opening months of 1944.

Battalion. By the evening of 15.11.1943, the old main fighting line was again firmly in our hands. *SS-Obersturmbannführer* Ullrich hindered a Russian breakthrough thanks to his excellent brave and personal action, and his flexible leadership.

4) The battle elements of *Regiment "Eicke"*—with II Battalion transported by air and III Battalion and regimental units by railway from Now-Ukrainka to the area of Balta—reached the deployment area on foot under difficult weather conditions. They were able to annihilate a recent widening enemy bridgehead by Olgopol and built a bridgehead over the Ssawarankabach River near Tschetschelnik. In the following days the regiment remained engaged in hard defensive battles, where the excellent personal action of the regimental commander—always located in decisive points—strengthened the will of his men to resist.

The break-through of the enemy on 19.03.1944 to the right and the advance of the Russians south to Ljubomirka and west to the main road Olgopol-Ssawranka seriously threatened the entire sector. At the personal decision of the regimental commander, the enemy force (600–800 men) was first stopped by a replacement unit on the western edge of Ljubomirka and to the east of the main road. A counterattack was carried out on 20.03.1944 in two directions that afterwards were gathered together for an assault towards the north. *SS-Obersturmbannführer* Ullrich, personally standing in the focal point of the attack, especially distinguished himself through his prudent leadership and personal bravery. This allowed the destruction of the enemy break-in, and with it the requirements were met for:

1) The further holding of the Ssawranka sector
2) The later orderly disengagement movements owing to the general situation

SS-Obersturmbannführer Ullrich is a model, brave, SS leader who has been in the battlefield since the first days. He has proven himself in an exemplary fashion at all the fronts. His never-diminishing readiness for action, superior leadership abilities, and his personal behavior designate him as an officer whose character grows in the face of every situation. I ask that *SS-Obersturmbannführer* Ullrich, in recognition of his extraordinary bravery and the great successes he has accomplished, be awarded the Oakleaves to the Knight's Cross of the Iron Cross.

This recommendation received approval on May 14, 1944, and added the twenty-ninth award of the Oakleaves to the ranks of the *Waffen-SS*. Ullrich received a promotion to *SS-Standartenführer* on July 29. He attended a divisional commander's training course between October and November, then moved to *SS-Division Wiking* as their divisional commander, retaining that post until the end of the war; his final rank was *SS-Oberführer*, being promoted on April 20. He surrendered to American forces on May 12, 1945, and spent over three years as a prisoner of war. He died in Bad Reichenhall on May 10, 1996.

SUMMARY

The completion of this volume has covered some of the most difficult and "legendary" battles the men of the *Waffen-SS* took part in during WWII. This volume opened with the men of the *Waffen-SS* still clinging to the Dnjepr River while continuing to contain the wider Leningrad area; we finish with a drastically changed situation. The fighting that ensued within these pages has shown how the Soviets managed to move the Germans farther west and, at the extremities of the front, succeeded in pushing them across the borders of Estonia and Romania. In the midst of this, the battles Shitomir / Berditschew, Tscherkassy, the first Narwa fighting, Kovel, and Kamenets-Podolsky unfolded and carved themselves into the fighting history of the soldiers of the *Waffen-SS*, helping to enhance their reputation.

The significant occurrences of being removed from Soviet soil would only continue to repeat themselves as the war ran its final year. The attempted annihilation of the men of the *Waffen-SS* did not materialize and in almost all cases, the units involved evaded the enemy and lived to fight again, albeit in a temporarily depleted form. The Balkans continued in a general stalemate situation, whereas in Italy, the Allies made their next significant landing, a portent of increasing overall enemy pressure on all fronts.

The fighting that occurred in the first five months of 1944 allowed these men to prove their expertise and bravery even further, producing an additional fifty-six Knight's Cross related awards: seven of these were adding Oakleaves to existing Knight's Crosses, three were adding Swords, and one of the awards gave the *Waffen-SS* their first set of Diamonds. Another key milestone was also reached: the 200th *Waffen-SS* soldier being approved for the Knight's Cross. Of note is the higher proportion of "second level," or higher awards; evidence of what these soldiers had to endure and how they dealt with the threat to themselves and their kameraden.

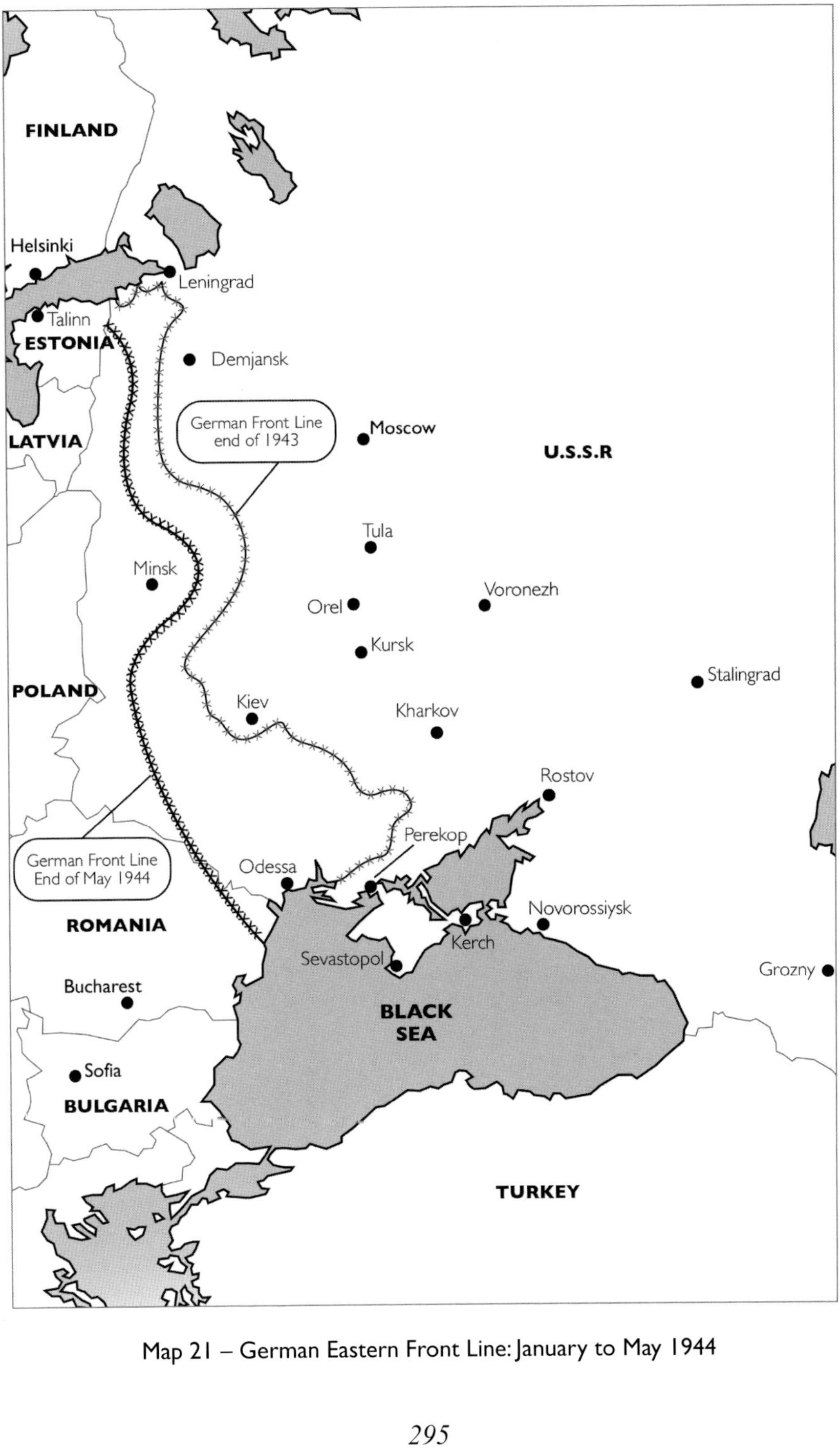

Map 21 – German Eastern Front Line: January to May 1944

Away from the front, training of various units moved closer to completion. The addition of newly created formations was welcome, but six out of the nine "new" units were upgraded versions of existing formations and the brand new ones would only add to the overall equipment shortages being felt at that time by the Germans. The imminently expected arrival of the main western offensive loomed large in the minds of Hitler and his generals; part of the reason for moving some of the premier *Waffen-SS* formations west as spring unfolded. As they moved westward, it was all too clear that the eastern threat was far from defeated, nor was it even contained; instead, it was increasing in effectiveness and strength and the impact was being felt by all who remained there.

We hope that you, the reader, continue to enjoy this series and that this particular volume has helped to clarify an often confusing situation and time for the men of the *Waffen-SS*, within their overall history.

APPENDICIES

Appendix 1: List Of *Waffen-SS* Units Raised to the End of May 1944

18. SS-Freiwilligen Panzergrenadier Division Horst Wessel (replaced the *1. SS-Inf. Brig.)*
19. Waffen-Grenadier-Division der SS (Lettische Nr. 2) (replaced the *2. Lettisches Brig.)*
20. Waffen-Grenadier-Division der SS (Estnische Nr. 1) (replaced the *3. Estnische Brig.)*
21. Waffen-Gebirgs-Division der SS Skanderberg (Albanische Nr. 1)
22. SS-Freiwilligen Kavallerie Division Maria Theresa (incorporated *SS-Kav. Reg. 17)*
Italienische SS-Freiwilligen Legion
Ostturkischen-Waffen-Verband der SS
SS-Jaeger Battalion 502 (replaced the *SS-Sonderverband z.b.v. Friedenthal*)
SS-Fallschirmjaeger Battalion 500 (replaced the *SS-Fallschirmjaeger Battalion*)

Appendix 2: Overview of Awards of the *Waffen-SS* Knight's Crosses (and Variants)

1944 (January to May)

The total (56) breakdown of all awards made during the above period is as follows:

1. SS-Pz. Div. Leibstandarte SS Adolf Hitler .... 11 Knight's Crosses, 4 sets of Oakleaves
SS-Kampfgruppe Lammerding / Weidinger .... 4 Knight's Crosses
3. SS-Panzer Division Totenkopf .... 1 set of Oakleaves, 1 set of Swords
Kampfgruppe SS-Polizei Division .... 1 Knight's Cross
5. SS-Panzer Division Wiking .... 11 Knight's Crosses, 1 set of Oakleaves, 1 set of Swords, 1 set of Diamonds
8. SS-Kavallerie Division Florian Geyer .... 4 Knight's Crosses
11. SS-Panzergrenadier Division Nordland .... 8 Knight's Crosses, 1 set of Oakleaves
1. SS-Infantry Brigade (mot.) .... 1 Knight's Cross
4. SS-Freiwilligen Pz.Gr. Brig. Nederland .... 2 Knight's Crosses
5. SS-Freiwilligen Sturmbrigade Wallonien .... 1 Knight's Cross
19. Waf.-Gren.-Div. der SS (Lettische Nr. 2) .... 1 Knight's Cross, 1 set of Swords
20. Waf.-Gren.-Div. der SS (Estnische Nr. 1) .... 1 Knight's Cross

1940–1944 (until the end of May)

The total (234) breakdown of all awards given from the start of the war is as follows:

II SS-Panzer Korps .... 1 set of Oakleaves
1. SS-Pz.Div Leibstandarte SS Adolf Hitler .... 39 Knight's Crosses, 8 sets of Oakleaves, 1 set of Swords
2. SS-Panzer Division Das Reich .... 43 Knight's Crosses, 5 sets of Oakleaves
SS-Kampfgruppe Lammerding / Weidinger .... 4 Knight's Crosses
3. SS-Panzer Division Totenkopf .... 33 Knight's Crosses, 6 sets of Oakleaves. 1 set of Swords
4. SS-Panzergrenadier Division Polizei .... 9 Knight's Crosses, 1 set of Oakleaves
Kampfgruppe SS-Polizei Division .... 1 Knight's Cross
5. SS-Panzer Division Wiking .... 35 Knight's Crosses, 5 sets of Oakleaves, 2 sets of Swords, 1 set of Diamonds
7. SS-Gebirgs Division Prinz Eugen .... 3 Knight's Crosses
8. SS-Kavallerie Division Florian Geyer .... 11 Knight's Crosses

SS-Kampfgruppe Fegelein .... 1 Knight's Cross
11. SS-Panzergrenadier Division Nordland 8 Knight's Crosses, ... 1 set of Oakleaves
19. Waf.-Gren.-Div. der SS (Lettische Nr. 2) .... 1 Knight's Cross, 1 set of Swords
20. Waf.-Gren.-Div. der SS (Estnische Nr. 1) .... 1 Knight's Cross
1. SS-Infantry Brigade (mot.) .... 5 Knight's Crosses
4. SS-Frei. Pz.Gr. Brigade Nederland .... 2 Knight's Crosses
5. SS-Frei. Sturmbrigade Wallonien .... 1 Knight's Cross
4. SS-Totenkopf Standarte .... 1 Knight's Cross
SS-Legion Niederlande .... 1 Knight's Cross
Sonderkommando Friedenthal .... 1 Knight's Cross
SS-Kampfgruppe Schuldt .... 1 set of Oakleaves

Appendix 3: Ranks of *Waffen-SS* Knight's Cross (and Variants) Holders

1944 (January to May)

Knight's Cross:

SS-Oberführer - 1 (2%)
SS-Standartenführer - 3 (7%)
SS-Obersturmbannführer - 6 (13%)
SS-Sturmbannführer - 8 (18%)
SS-Hauptsturmführer - 7 (16%)
SS-Obersturmführer - 8 (18%)
SS-Untersturmführer - 6 (13%)
SS-Hauptscharführer - 1 (2%)
SS-Oberscharführer - 2 (4.5%)
SS-Unterscharführer - 2 (4.5%)
SS-Rottenführer - 1 (2%)

Knight's Cross with Oakleaves:

SS-Brigadeführer - 2 (27.5%)
SS-Obersturmbannführer - 2 (27.5%)
SS-Sturmbannführer - 1 (15%)
SS-Hauptsturmführer - 1 (15%)
SS-Untersturmführer - 1 (15%)

Knight's Cross with Oakleaves and Swords:

SS-Gruppenführer - 1 (33%)
SS-Brigadeführer - 1 (33%)
SS-Oberführer - 1 (33%)

Knight's Cross with Oakleaves, Swords and Diamonds:

SS-Gruppenführer - 1 (100%)

1940 – 1944 (until the end of May)

Knight's Cross:

SS-Obergruppenführer -..........2 (1%)
SS-Gruppenführer -..........2 (1%)
SS-Brigadeführer -..........2 (1%)
SS-Oberführer -..........9 (4%)
SS-Standartenführer -..........10 (5%)
SS-Obersturmbannführer -..........15 (8%)
SS-Sturmbannführer -..........49 (25%)
SS-Hauptsturmführer -..........34 (17%)
SS-Obersturmführer -..........26 (13%)
SS-Untersturmführer -..........12 (6%)
SS-Hauptscharführer -..........10 (5%)
SS-Oberscharführer -..........13 (7%)
SS-Unterscharführer -..........9 (4%)
SS-Rottenführer -..........4 (2%)
SS-Sturmmann -..........2 (1%)

Knight's Cross with Oakleaves:

SS-Obergruppenführer -..........2 (7%)
SS-Gruppenführer –..........2 (7%)
SS-Brigadeführer –..........6 (21%)
SS-Oberführer -..........1 (3%)
SS-Standartenführer -..........3 (10%)
SS-Obersturmbannführer -..........7 (24%)
SS-Sturmbannführer -..........4 (14%)
SS-Hauptsturmführer -..........3 (10%)
SS-Untersturmführer -..........1 (4%)

Knight's Cross with Oakleaves and Swords

SS-Obergruppenführer -..........1 (20%)
SS-Gruppenführer -..........1 (20%)
SS-Brigadeführer -..........1 (20%)
SS-Oberführer -..........1 (20%)
SS-Obersturmbannführer -..........1 (20%)

Knight's Cross with Oakleaves, Swords and Diamonds

SS-Gruppenführer -..........1 (100%)

Appendix 4: Skills of *Waffen-SS* Knight's Cross (and Variants) Holders

1944 (January to May)

Knight's Crosses:

Infantry..........21 (46%)
Tank..........9 (20%)
Reconnaissance..........3 (7%)

Anti-Tank 3 (7%)
Cavalry 3 (7%)
Assault Gun 3 (7%)
Engineer 2 (4%)
Artillery 1 (2%)

Knight's Cross with Oakleaves:

Infantry 5 (71%)
Tank 2 (29%)

Knight's Cross with Oakleaves and Swords:

Infantry 3 (100%)

Knight's Cross with Oakleaves, Swords and Diamonds:

Infantry 1 (100%)

1940 – 1944 (until the end of May)

Knight's Crosses:

Infantry 100 (50%)
Tank 31 (16%)
Anti-Tank 11 (6%)
Assault Gun 11 (6%)
Reconnaissance 10 (5%)
Cavalry 10 (5%)
Engineer 9 (4%)
Artillery 6 (3%)
Motorcycle Battalion / Company 5 (3%)
Mountain 3 (2%)
Anti-Aircraft 2 (1%)
Special Commando 1 (1%)

Knight's Cross with Oakleaves:

Infantry 21 (73%)
Tank 5 (18%)
Cavalry 1 (3%)
Reconnaissance 1 (3%)
Motorcycle Battalion 1 (3%)

Knight's Cross with Oakleaves and Swords

Infantry 5 (100%)

Knight's Cross with Oakleaves, Swords and Diamonds

Infantry 1 (100%)

The infantry continue to lead the way with 50% of the totals. The tank crews continue to add further awards and close the gap, now sitting at 16%. The other tracked vehicles, such as the majority of the anti-tank and all of the assault guns add nearly another twenty awards to the "armored wing" of the *Waffen-SS.* A great insight into the utilization of those types of vehicles by the Germans, the level of demand placed upon the crews, and also the effectiveness of those crew members. The impact of that effectiveness was felt upon the enemies of Germany, and the huge quantities of destroyed enemy tanks and other war materiel were testament to that. It was this aspect of the war that helped to establish the "legend" of the *Waffen-SS*, a legend that would only increase in status during the remaining year of WWII.

Another notable increase is the volume of higher-level awards given to existing Knight's Cross holders. At this stage of the war, 35 (15%) of the total awards to date were for "additions" to the Knight's Cross. Two of the soldiers (Wittmann and Gille) were recognized twice within this short time; another indication of what they had to endure in the early part of 1944.

Appendix 5: List of Deceased *Waffen-SS* Knight's Cross Holders up to May 1944

Arnold Stoffers.......... February 25, 1944 (Became RK awardee March 1944)
Alfred Lex.......... March 11, 1944
Wilhelm Dietrich.......... March 12, 1944
Hinrich Schuldt.......... March 15, 1944
Voldemars Veiss.......... April 17, 1944
Walter Kniep.......... April 22, 1944
Max Schachner.......... October 19, 1943 (Became RK awardee May 1944)

List of deceased *Waffen-SS* Knight's Cross Holders 1940–1944 (Until the end of May)

Erich Rossner.......... July 30, 1941
Hans-Christian Schulze.......... September 13, 1941
Gert Pleiss.......... November 17, 1941
Ludwig Kochle.......... June 9, 1942
Harry Polewacz.......... January 12, 1943
Theodore Eicke.......... February 26, 1943
Helmut Pfortner.......... February 28, 1943
Erwin Reichel.......... February 28, 1943
Hans Reimling.......... March 7, 1943
Hermann Dahlke.......... July 5, 1943
Karl-Heinz Worthmann.......... July 6–7, 1943
Georg Eberhardt.......... July 21, 1943 (Became RK awardee August 1943)
Simon Grascher.......... July 14, 1943 (Became RK awardee August 1943)
Hans Juchem.......... August 13, 1943
August Dieckmann.......... August 18, 1943
Alfred Nowak.......... September 13, 1943
Emil Wiesemann.......... November 14, 1943
Georg Schonberger.......... November 20, 1943
Arnold Stoffers.......... February 25, 1944 (Became RK awardee March 1944)
Alfred Lex.......... March 11, 1944
Wilhelm Dietrich.......... March 12, 1944
Hinrich Schuldt.......... March 15, 1944

Voldemars Veiss .... April 17, 1944
Walter Kniep .... April 22, 1944
Max Schachner.......... October 19, 1943 (Became RK awardee May 1944)

At that stage of the war (end of May 1944), the list of twenty-five deceased *Waffen-SS* holders of the Knight's Cross (or higher grades) stood at 10% of total awardees. This figure would increase steadily as the war drew to its climax in early 1945.

In addition, seven of the deceased soldiers listed were recommended for the awards after they had been killed. Therefore, these seven posthumous awards accounted for 3% of the total awards issued since the start of the war.

Appendix 6: *Waffen-SS* Knight's Cross Holders' Country of Birth up to May 1944

(Each country is "defined" at the time of the recipient's birth, as there was a lot of movement in the late 1800s and after WWI.)

Knight's Crosses:

German.......... 174
Austrian.......... 17
French 1
Belgian 1
Dutch.......... 1
Czechoslovakian 1
Hungarian.......... 1
Latvian 3
Estonian.......... 1

Knight's Cross with Oakleaves:

German.......... 28
Austrian.......... 1

Knight's Cross with Oakleaves and Swords:

German.......... 5

Knight's Cross with Oakleaves, Swords and Diamonds:

German.......... 1

BIBLIOGRAPHY

Agte, Patrick. *Michael Wittmann and the Tiger Commanders of the Leibstandarte.* J.J. Fedorowicz Ltd., 1996.

Agte, Patrick. *Jochen Peiper. Commander Panzerregiment Leibstandarte.* J.J. Fedorowicz Ltd., 1999.

Brandt, Allen. *The Last Knight of Flanders. Remy Schrijnen and his SS-Legion "Flandern"/Sturmbrigade "Langemarck" Comrades on the eastern front 1941-1945.* Schiffer Publishing Ltd., 1998.

De Bruyne, Eddy and Rikmenspoel, Marc. *For Rex and for Belgium. Leon Degrelle and Walloon Political & Military Collaboration 1940-45.* Helion & Company, 2004.

Corbatti, Sergio, and Nava, Marco. *Sentire – Pensare – Volere: Storia della Legione* SS *italiana.* Ritter s.a.s, 2001.

Corbatti, Sergio, and Nava, Marco. *Karstjaeger. Du SS-Karstwehr-Bataillon a la 24. Waffen-Gebirgs-Division der* SS. Editions Heimdal, 2009.

Forbes, Robert. *Pour l'Europe. The French Volunteers of the Waffen-SS.* Redwood Books, 2000.

Husemann, Friedrich. *In Good Faith, The History of the 4. SS-Polizei-Panzer-Grenadier-Division, Volume 2: 1943-1945.* J.J. Fedorowicz Publishing Ltd., 2009.

Kumm, Otto. *Prinz Eugen, The History of the 7. SS-Mountain Division "Prinz Eugen".* J.J. Fedorowicz Publishing Ltd., 1995.

Laar, Mart, and Suurmaa, Lauri. *The Estonian Legion in Words and Pictures.* Grenader Publishing Ltd., 2008.

Lehmann, Rudolf, and Tiemann, Ralf. *Die Leibstandarte IV/1.* J.J. Fedorowicz Publishing Ltd., 1993.

Lepre, George. *Himmler's Bosnian Division. The Waffen-SS Handschar Division 1943-1945.* Schiffer Publishing Ltd., 1997.

Logusz, Michael. O. *Galicia Division. The Waffen-SS 14th Grenadier Division 1943-1945.* Schiffer Publishing Ltd., 2000.

MacLean, French. *The Cruel Hunters. SS-Sonder-Kommando Dirlewanger. Hitler's Most Notorious Anti-Partisan Unit.* Schiffer Publishing Ltd., 1998.

Meyer, Hubert. *The History of the 12. SS-Panzerdivision Hitlerjugend.* J.J. Fedorowicz Ltd., 1994.

Michaelis, Rolf. *SS-Fallschirmjaeger Bataillon 500/600.* Schiffer Publishing Ltd., 2008.

Michaelis, Rolf. *Estonians in the Waffen-SS. 20. Waffen-Grenadier-Division der* SS *(Estnische Nr. 1).* Schiffer Publishing Ltd., 2009.

Michaelis, Rolf. *Panzergrenadier Divisions of the Waffen-SS.* Schiffer Publishing Ltd., 2010.

Moore, J.P. *Führerliste Der Waffen-SS, Parts 1 to 4.* J.P.Moore Publishing, 2003.

Munoz, Antonio. J. *Forgotten Legions. Obscure Combat Formations of the Waffen-SS.* Paladin Press, 1991.

Nash, Douglas. E. *Hell's Gate. The Battle of the Cherkassy Pocket, January-February 1944.* RZM Publishing, 2005.

Perrigault, Jean-Claude, and Meister, Ralf. *Gotz von Berlichingen, Volume 1.* Editions Heimdal, 2004.

Silgailis, Arthur. *Latvian Legion.* R. James Bender Publishing, 1986.

Skorzeny, Otto. *Skorzeny's Special Missions. The Memoirs of "The Most Dangerous Man In Europe".* Greenhill Books, 1997.

Strassner, Peter. *European Volunteers, 5* SS *Panzer Division Wiking.* J.J. Fedorowicz Publishing Ltd., 1998.

Tieke, Wilhelm. *In the Firestorm of the Last Years of the War, II. SS-Panzerkorps with the 9. And 10. SS-Divisions "Hohenstaufen" and "Frundsberg".* J.J. Fedorowicz Ltd., 1999.

Tieke, Wilhelm, and Rebstock, Friedrich. *Im Letzten Aufgebot: Die 18. SS-Freiwilligen Panzergrenadier Division Horst Wessel.* Nation Europa Verlag, 2000.

Tieke, Wilhelm. *Tragedy of the Faithful, A History of the III. (Germanisches) SS-Panzer-Korps.* J.J. Fedorowicz Ltd., 2001.

Trang, Charles. *The "Florian Geyer" Division.* Editions Heimdal, 2000.

Truppenkameradschaft (Hrsg.). *"Im gleichen Schritt und Tritt". Dokumentation der 16. SS-Panzergrenadierdivision "Reichsführer-SS".* Schild-Verlag GmbH, 1998.

Ullrich, Karl. *Like a Cliff in the Ocean, The History of the 3. SS-Panzer-Division "Totenkopf".* J.J. Fedorowicz Publishing Ltd., 2002.

Weidinger, Otto. *Das Reich V, 1943-1945, 2. SS-Panzer Division Das Reich.* J.J. Fedorowicz Publishing Ltd., 2012.

Westwood, David. *The Waffen-SS An Organisational and Operational History 1933-1945.* MLRS Books

Ltd., 2004.
Yerger, Mark. C. *Waffen-SS Commanders, Volume 1, Augsberger to Kreutz.* Schiffer Publishing Ltd., 1997.
Yerger, Mark. C. *Waffen-SS Commanders, Volume 2, Kruger to Zimmermann.* Schiffer Publishing Ltd., 1999.
Yerger, Mark. C. *German Cross in Gold – Holders of the* SS *and Police – Volume 3: Regiment and Division Nordland.* R. James Bender Publishing, 2008.
Yerger, Mark. C. *German Cross in Gold – Holders of the* SS *and Police – Volume 4: Cavalry Brigade and Divisions.* R. James Bender Publishing, 2009.
Yerger, Mark. C. *German Cross in Gold – Holders of the* SS *and Police – Volume 6: Polizei Division and Police Units.* R. James Bender Publishing, 2012.
Zoepf, Wolf. T. *Seven Days in January with the 6th* SS *Mountain Division in Operation Nordwind.* The Aberjona Press, 2001.

Also various letters and face-to-face interviews with surviving kameraden of the divisions and other units of the *Waffen-SS* from 1998 to 2014.